Empire of **Scrounge**

Scrounge

NEW YORK UNIVERSITY PRESS

New York and London

Inside the
Urban Underground
of Dumpster Diving,
Trash Picking, and
Street Scavenging

Jeff Ferrell

NEW YORK UNIVERSITY PRESS
New York and London
www.nyupress.org

© 2006 by New York University
All rights reserved

Library of Congress Cataloging-in-Publication Data
Ferrell, Jeff. Empire of scrounge : inside the urban
underground of dumpster diving, trash picking, and
street scavenging / Jeff Ferrell.
p. cm. — (Alternative criminology series)
Includes bibliographical references and index.
ISBN–13: 978–0–8147–2737–9 (cloth : alk. paper)
ISBN–10: 0–8147–2737–9 (cloth : alk. paper)
ISBN–13: 978–0–8147–2738–6 (pbk. : alk. paper)
ISBN–10: 0–8147–2738–7 (pbk. : alk. paper)
1. Ragpickers—United States.
2. Salvage (Waste, etc.)—United States.
3. Marginality, Social—United States.
4. United States—Social conditions—1980 –
I. Title.   II. Series.
HD9975.U52F47   2005 2006
305.5'68'0973–dc22   2005016303

New York University Press books are printed on acid-free
paper, and their binding materials are chosen for strength
and durability.

Manufactured in the United States of America

c 10 9 8 7 6 5 4 3 2 1
p 10 9 8 7 6 5 4 3 2 1

All photos in this book, with the exception of those referenced
below, are reprinted with permission of Cécile Van de Voorde,
© 2005 Cécile Van de Voorde.

Photos on pages 7, 123, 140, 146, 153, 154 are reprinted
by permission of the author.

Photo on page 118 by Roger Mallison, is courtesy of the
Fort Worth Star-Telegram.

Photos on pages 4, 202–203, are reprinted by permission
of Gary Logan, © 2004 Gary Logan.

Book design by Charles B. Hames

Never did I try to make of it something other than what it was, I did not try to adorn it, to mask it, but, on the contrary, I wanted to affirm it in its exact sordidness, and the most sordid signs became for me signs of grandeur.

— Jean Genet, **The Thief's Journal**

Contents

Acknowledgments

For ideas, information, and support, my sincere thanks to Marilyn McShane, Trey Williams, Meda Chesney-Lind, Bob Young, Bayless Camp, Dan Phillips, Jeff Ross, Sara Chetin, Peter Leuner, Jimmy Silcox, Sara Lowry, Gene Lowry, Dick Hawkins, and Fran Hawkins. Thanks also to my colleagues in the Department of Sociology, Criminal Justice, and Anthropology, Texas Christian University, and especially to Carol Thompson, for creating an environment as engaging and humane as it is intellectually invigorating—and in a trailer yet.

Certainly *Empire of Scrounge* is but one of many works presently circulating in the intellectual underground—or maybe intellectual back alley— that is cultural criminology, and so I acknowledge with great affection those friends and colleagues who likewise hang out there: Keith Hayward, Mike Presdee, Jock Young, Wayne Morrison, Yvonne Jewkes, Chris Greer, Mark Hamm, Ken Tunnell, Steve Lyng, Stephanie Kane, Michelle Brown, and many others. New York University Press, and its Alternative Criminology series, embrace this same sort of scholarly edge; my thanks to executive editor Ilene Kalish for her ideas and understandings in that regard, and for her gracious support of the book and the series. Finally, my thanks to Cécile Van de Voorde, whose photographs illuminate the pages of *Empire of Scrounge*. Emerging out of the great photodocumentary and photojournalistic traditions, her images are not simply illustrative; they are each in their own right significant moments, decisive moments, in the empire of scrounge.

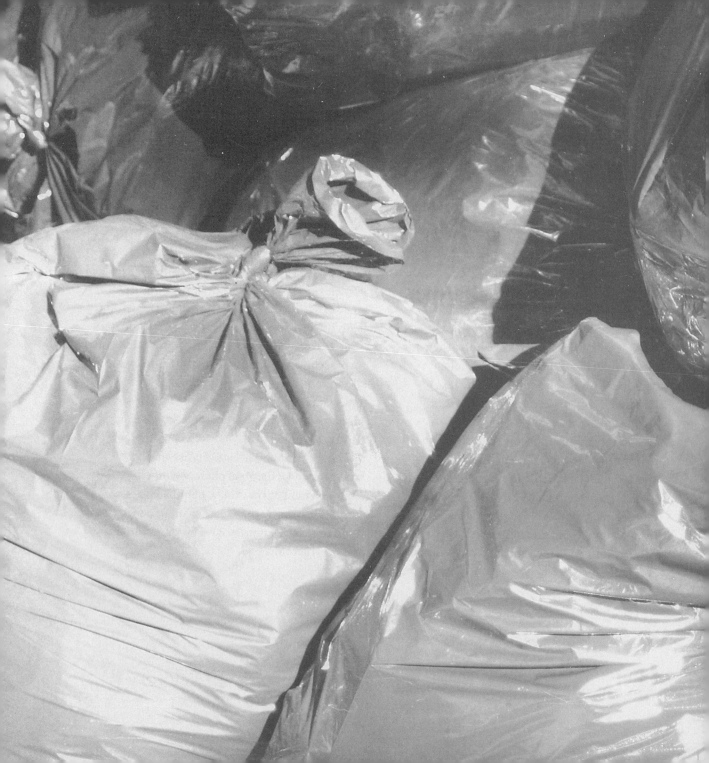

sordid signs

1

I guess it all started the day I quit.

In December 2001, I resigned from a position as a tenured professor at a large Arizona university, and settled back in to my old stomping grounds of Fort Worth, Texas. I knew that, at best, this move would leave me a gap of eight months or so until I might or might not locate the next academic position in the fall of 2002. This gap in turn meant that, in the meantime, my only guaranteed income would be whatever few—and I do mean few—royalties might trickle in from my books. But it also meant that I had an eight-month period for unfettered field research—if only I could figure out a way to survive economically while doing it. Given my long-standing personal and scholarly interest in the often illicit worlds of scrounging, recycling, and secondhand living, the answer seemed obvious, if risky: I'd try to survive as a Dumpster diver and trash picker.[1] I'd try to adopt a way of life that was at the same time field research and free-form survival.

So early in 2002 I rigged an old fifteen-dollar black-and-white Schwinn bicycle with a secondhand front basket and some extra bungee cords for the back deck, and set out mostly on this bike, other times on foot, to see what I could find. With very few exceptions, all my subsequent scrounging was undertaken in these two-wheel or two-footed modes; as an avid bicyclist, I'm not much for the destructive ecological politics of the automobile in the first place, and besides, my guess was that the value of whatever materials I could scrounge would hardly balance against the unrelenting cost of running a car.[2] In fact, as the months of scrounging rolled on, and this old bicycle gradually fell apart, I replaced it not with an automobile but with another bicycle, an old one-speed BMX model I scrounged from behind a Dumpster and repaired with scrounged bicycle parts. This approach to personal transportation seemed appropriate to the worlds of both scrounging and bicycles, by the way. After all, the first modern mountain bike emerged from the do-it-yourself scrounging of legendary bicycle designer Gary Fisher, who in 1974 "blacksmithed the now famous klunker from scavenged objects."[3]

I'm not much for shopping, either, and so, taking my natural proclivities up a notch, I all but boycotted retail establishments during these months, instead relying as much as possible on what I could scrounge for my daily needs. As I found, and as I'll explain in subsequent chapters, urban scrounging did in fact provide me all that I needed for daily survival, with the exception of some food items—and these could likely have been scrounged as well, had I cared to make that

my focus. In fact, my scrounging yielded so much material wealth that I sent much of it on to friends, homeless shelters, food banks, and charitable organizations. Patrolling the neighborhoods of central Fort Worth, sorting through trash piles, exploring Dumpsters, scanning the streets and the gutters for items lost or discarded, I gathered the city's degraded bounty, then returned home to sort and catalog the take. These urban neighborhoods in turn provided a wonderfully varied setting for my work and my research; within an easy bike ride of my house are old industrial areas, rail yards, million-dollar mansions, working-class neighborhoods, middle-class suburbs, little commercial clusters, and the large downtown business district. The scrounger's world, I found, offers many a spatial permutation.

Mention of "my house" suggests an important qualification that shaped this undertaking. During these months I did indeed have a very modest home, and a partner working some thirty-five hours a week at the generous corporate wage of $9.50 an hour—and while neither of these factors would exactly qualify either of us for middle-class approval, both certainly disqualify me from any claim of somehow and suddenly becoming for these eight months a destitute soul dependent entirely on my own scrounging. The point of the endeavor was neither to pretend nor imagine that I was a homeless Dumpster diver, anyway, but rather to explore and embrace the rhythms of urban scrounging as best I could. And besides, as I soon discovered, and as the following chapters document, not every urban scrounger is without a home; many have a little house, maybe even a partner toiling away for a small hourly wage.

Scrounging the city each day, learning to live off what I scavenged, I drifted into a world that I came to call the *empire of scrounge*—a far-flung, mostly urban underground populated by just such people: illicit Dumpster divers, homeless trash pickers, independent scrap metal haulers, activist recyclers, alternative home builders, and outsider artists. By choice or necessity, I realized, their role within the larger social ecology is to sort among the daily accumulations of trash, to imagine ways in which objects discarded as valueless might gain some new value, and always to stay one stealthy step ahead of those official agencies of collection, sanitation, and disposal that would haul away such possibilities. By definition and by practice, the work of these illicit trash scroungers remains marginal. While the director of the city's waste disposal department may earn a handsome living from trash, do-it-yourself urban scroungers do not; they operate at the lower economic margins, finding in the city's trash possibilities of street survival, or other times supplements to minimum wage work. For many who spot a scrounger working a trash pile or emerging from a full Dumpster, the morality of this work is also marginal; to pick through the city's trash is to engage all manner of unpleasant questions about cleanliness, propriety, danger, and deviant career.

This marginality is spatial as well; the spaces and situations that make up the urban scrounger's scattered empire quite literally form the margins, define the borderlands, between the city's social and cultural worlds. In a shared apartment house Dumpster, the leftovers of private lives coalesce into a dirty public collectivity—and if a scrounger later retrieves some of these leftovers, they may in turn become the foundation for someone else's little home or apartment, or for another's temporary shelter under bridge or overpass. In the back alley trash bins of commerce, the item that was yesterday a valuable and marketable commodity today transmogrifies into devalued trash, and often a free-for-the-taking treasure; in the commercial alley, the bright front stage of the shop or shopping mall gives way to a backstage of cigarette breaks, trash piles, and uncertain access. At residential curbside trash piles, the homeowner's property line borders and invites the life of the street, the homeowner's discards turning from private trash to public disposal problem, or for others a public resource.[4] And at all of these social and spatial margins, legal boundaries are likewise negotiated, with Dumpsters and trash piles offering daily situations for deciding between private property and public access, for distinguishing scavenging from theft, if only provisionally.

Day after day in the empire of scrounge, I discovered, yours becomes mine and mine yours —but haltingly, imperfectly, ambiguously, as part of the city's complex everyday rhythms. In this

Jeff Ferrell in his scrap-filled shed, Fort Worth, Texas, October 2004.

cast-off material empire the immediacy of individual consumption becomes an ongoing urban aftermath, a collective dynamic interwoven with the city's daily life. A half-century ago, Donald Cressey wrote of the illicit ambiguities inherent in the process of acquiring "other people's money."[5] In the empire of scrounge, I realized, the issue isn't so much other people's money; it's other people's stuff, and what to do with it when they throw it away.

Standing in the Shadows

Along with learning what to do with other people's discarded possessions, and how to survive from them, I looked to make some particular discoveries. As a start, I wanted to record with some precision the content of the empire's trash piles and Dumpsters, or at least those of them that I happened upon. As one person aboard an old bicycle, I made no effort to "survey" the trash of my Fort Worth neighborhoods, much less the city as a whole. Instead, I attempted to create a close ethnography of objects lost and found by carefully recording and describing the items that I scrounged and hauled home. This detailed accounting of my take as a scrounger became the basis for a second focus as well: exploring the personal and political economy of scrounging as a means of survival. In everyday debates over homelessness or unemployment, in larger debates over an economy that increasingly produces impoverishment for most of its participants, many an assumption is made about the resources available to the homeless person, to the destitute trash picker or itinerate Dumpster diver. But what exactly is out there to be dived into or picked up? What is its value, and to whom? And just how do you cash it in?

The social situations that define the empire interested me as well. Riding an old bicycle, dressed in scrounged clothes often made filthy by the nature of my work, I sought to put myself as best I could into the situations encountered by the everyday urban scrounger, and there to observe and record the interactions that emerged. As the months and the miles rolled by, these situations and interactions began to accumulate; countless encounters with homeowners, apartment residents, police officers, homeless folks, and other scroungers of all sorts begin to suggest something of the values, perceptions, and identities circulating in the empire of scrounge. As the following chapters document, the situations and interactions that emerge inside the empire certainly reflect larger fault lines of social inequality, embody everyday dramas of life and death, offer even moments of poignant irony and good humor—but often do so in ways one outside these situations wouldn't predict.

The steady accumulation of objects and interactions also began to address what was perhaps the broadest agenda I brought to the research. It's long been my sense that, more than any other engine, corporate hyperconsumption drives contemporary U.S. society, along the way constructing a seductive if sad sort of store-bought commonality among many of its members. As disturbing, the profligate waste produced by this endless hyperconsumptive panic seems less an unfortunate by-product than a component essential to its continuation. Worse yet, this wasteful dynamic appears to be picking up pace, both within the United States and across the borders of world culture and economy. The Worldwatch Institute has calculated that, by 2004, the world's "consumer class" had grown to 1.7 billion people—more than a quarter of the world's population—with almost half of this consumer class now emerging in the "developing" world. Seeing in these numbers "a world being transformed by a consumption revolution," the institute documented a parallel intensification of general wastefulness and specific material waste, and with it increasing environmental degradation in terms of natural resource extraction, waste disposal, and shrinking natural habitats.[6] While "Americans remain the world's waste champions," their spreading habits of hyperconsumptive waste now seem to herald material accumulation and environmental destruction on a scale as yet unimagined.[7]

This critique of a proliferating consumer culture —a critique at once political, economic, and environmental—has of course been made eloquently by others, not to mention put into vivid practice by many in the antiglobalization movement.[8] Yet here in these months of scrounging, it seemed to me, was a chance to frame the critique differently, not in terms of comparative political economy, but intimately, sensually, filthily, from the bottom up, from inside the guts of engorged Dumpsters and from atop the towering trash piles of the world's champion consumer society. Here, it seemed, was an opportunity to develop a critical, grounded understanding of contemporary consumption and its relation to collective wastefulness—since damn near every urban alley, every urban Dumpster, offered evidence of one as well as the other. And it was just this material evidence, I hoped, that would focus and define my general sense that contemporary consumer society was, with each new trash heap it spawned, broadcasting the seeds of its own environmental and cultural destruction. Talking broadly of an economically and environmentally unsustainable social order; demonstrating through comparative data that Western societies have perpetually wasted what others could only want, and that these others are now themselves coming to want and waste more; confronting this destructive world dynamic with carnivals of resistance outside the grand hotels of World Trade Organization (WTO) delegates and World Bank members—all constitute critically important efforts at undoing the damage. Looking for this same damage in the Dumpsters of retail stores and the trash cans of the affluent, carefully accumulating evidence of it item by discarded item, I hoped to do my part as well.[9]

In this I also hoped to do my job as a criminologist. By studying the dynamics of crime and law—that is, the dynamic by which certain activities come to be outlawed and legally suppressed on the basis of their supposed social harm, while other activities come to be protected, even encouraged, by the law—criminologists put themselves, inevitably, in the middle of larger debates over morality, decency, justice, and the social good. In this light, a certain irony emerges: despite their academic designation, criminologists cannot do their job well if they confine themselves to the study of "crime," since the crimes of one historical moment are often not the crimes of the next. Instead, they must study ongoing processes of criminalization and legalization, exploring in their research the slippery boundaries between law and morality, crime and victimization, legal regulation and political repression—and presenting in their analysis of these processes their own critical judgments about social benefit and social harm. My own intellectual agenda and preexisting if provisional judgment—that consumption and waste present one of contemporary society's most destructive dynamics—pushed me to investigate this dynamic as a matter of social and criminological concern, and to explore within it the shifting, ambiguous legalities of waste and waste pickers. In turn, my investigation raised a troubling question to which I'll return more than once in the following chapters: Is the criminologist's job to resolve legal and cultural ambiguities, simply to acknowledge them—or sometimes even to celebrate them?

The trash heap of a River Crest McMansion, Fort Worth, Texas, April 2004.

Within the empire of scrounge, I discovered, the boundaries of law and crime have indeed shifted more than once, and are shifting again today; even the word that others and I use as shorthand for this world embodies long-standing historical uncertainty, and ongoing ambiguities of marginality and illegality. The verb "to scrounge" evolved over the past century or so as a variant on the dialectal formation "to scrunge," meaning "to steal," or more vaguely "to search stealthily, rummage, pilfer."[10] Interestingly, the term—and the practice—have taken on special currency during the moral and legal disruptions of wartime, when soldiers and others have been forced to negotiate the ambiguities of an anomic world. In this context, the *Oxford English Dictionary* offers a variety of legally blurry definitions for scrounging —"To sponge on or live at the expense of others. To seek to obtain by irregular means, as by stealth or begging; to hunt about or rummage. . . . To appropriate. . . . To 'pinch' or 'cadge'"—and includes some equally ambiguous examples of popular usage. "Scrounging for wire is legitimized by the War Office," reads one missive from World War I, dated 1918—yet a year later another notes "complaints about 'scrounging,' which are nothing but outbreaks of loss of moral judgment."

By the next world war—during which U.S. citizens were encouraged to scrounge scrap metal and other discards as part of government-organized reclamation campaigns—the situation was nonetheless no more certain. According to one 1939 report, "the Southern Railway gave a staggering figure for the specially dimmed bulbs which had been stolen (I beg pardon, scrounged) from their carriages in the first weeks of the war"; at war's end, another report pointedly noted "that 'pilfering' by a native is indistinguishable from 'scrounging' by an American soldier, and that 'chiseling' and resale of Post Exchange supplies is not an act peculiar to Filipinos."[11] In 1956, during the Israel-Egypt war, *Time* magazine correspondent Frank White likewise described a colleague as "a professional freebooter first; a photographer second," noting that "he'd liberated two jeeps and a truck, procuring gas by signing chits over the name 'Petain, Marechal de France.'"[12] Today, wartime or not, dictionaries continue to define scrounging in terms of salvaging or foraging, but also wheedling, cadging, and more generally "forag[ing] about in an effort to acquire something at no cost."[13]

This long history of legal ambiguity has emerged out of more than wartime necessity and residual etymology. By 1817, for example, New York had enacted a law that forbade junk and scrap dealers from purchasing scrap materials from juveniles.[14] In 1872, Charles Loring Brace explained something of such a law's logic, as he included among the "dangerous classes of New York" those "exceedingly poor people, who live by gathering rags and bones," their "dirty yards piled with bones and flaunting with rags," their little shanties overburdened with "all the odds and ends of a great city . . . heaped up nearly to the ceiling." Their sons and daughters, he added ominously, are themselves "mainly employed in collecting swill and picking coals," a way of life that at least for their daughters "soon wears off a girl's modesty and prepares her for worse occupation."[15] During this same period, itinerant peddlers, who had become a "major institution of nineteenth century economy and . . . recycling" with their bartering of manufactured goods for local rags and scrap metal, nonetheless were "stereotyped as tricksters and confidence men." And a half-century later, when "scavenging and junking were nearly universal for working-class children" in the United States, the Chicago Juvenile Protection Association once again argued in its book *Junk Dealing and Juvenile Delinquency* that "by providing a market, [junk] dealers encouraged children to steal and that boys went junking mainly to get spending money, not to help their families."[16]

In this sense, scrounging has long existed as a central component of what Stuart Henry calls "the hidden economy"—and has long shared with other components of this hidden economy an essential moral and legal ambiguity. Tracing the English hidden economy to the thirteenth century, Henry characterizes it as a place of "borderline crimes" and "part-time property crimes"—that is, activities occupying a shadowy, shifting legal status for participants and legal authorities alike. Endeavors like "pilfering, pinching, poaching, purloining, filching, finagling, flanking, dodging, diddling, dealing, stealing, smuggling, sneaking, gouging, scrounging, and screwing," Henry argues, are "not the province of 'criminals,' but an everyday feature of ordinary people's lives" that blur "the artificial distinction between 'honest' and 'dishonest.'"[17] If in their range these activities read like some plot summary from *Oliver Twist*, they also suggest a long-standing world of shadows that exists around and behind the front stage of everyday life. They sketch a subterranean urban empire of which scrounging is a part, a hidden economy suffused with shifting boundaries between personal property, discarded trash, and lawful public resource.

This uncertain contextualization—this suspension of scrounging somewhere between economic necessity, cultural practice, and petty criminality—continues today. With landfills overflowing and the cost of their upkeep accelerating, even the most mainstream of economic and legal authorities today generally embrace some ethic of recycling and reuse, if only to rescue city budgets and economic vitality. All but the most coldhearted of conservatives would likewise acknowledge a person's need to somehow scrounge clothing, food, and other necessities while being "weaned" from welfare roles or cast out from a job now transferred overseas. In this sense, scrounging remains an integral component of the economy's lower realms, perhaps even an increasingly necessary option for many of its occupants.

Interestingly, many Web sites and magazines dedicated to "frugal" or "thrifty" living have even begun including Dumpster diving guidelines among their tips on coupon clipping, bargain shopping, and other conventional money-saving strategies. Criticized by some of their readers for advocating Dumpster diving, the operators of one such Web site "decided to do some research," and subsequently offered readers their findings in an attempt to calm their concerns. Most Dumpster divers "don't actually get in the bins," they reported, instead relying on "some sort of long pole which allows them to just lean over the Dumpster and pull the items up to them." Of course, based on my many down-in-the-Dumpster experiences, this "finding" offered more in the way of reassurance to thrifty shoppers than it did in the way of experiential accuracy. So did the Web site's absurdly antiseptic guidelines:

carry "wet wipes to clean up with, and anti-bacterial lotion for afterwards. . . . Make sure that there are no ordinances that make this activity illegal in your area."[18]

Perhaps as importantly in the image-driven cultural universe of late modernity, particular images of scrounging—the lone aluminum can recycler working the edges of a highway with a big plastic bag in hand, the urban hobo pushing an old shopping cart from one Dumpster to another—have become near-iconic components in the contemporary cultural stockpile. Moreover, scrounging has found its way into the twin canons of literature and popular culture. In her beloved 1942 children's book, *The Boxcar Children*, Gertrude Chandler Warner drew on her own childhood, growing up near railroad tracks and dreaming "about what it would be like to set up housekeeping in a caboose or freight car," to create a story of the Alden kids. Driven by their "independence and resourcefulness and their solid New England devotion to using up and making do," the four orphans find an abandoned boxcar, but then must set about outfitting it as a home:

> "What are we going to do now, Jessie?" Benny asked his sister.
> "Well, Benny," answered Jessie, "we'll go exploring for treasures. We'll begin here at the car and look and look until we find a dump."
> "What's a dump?" asked Benny.
> "Oh, Benny!" said Violet. "You know what a dump is. Old tin cans and old dishes and bottles."

> "Are old tin cans and dishes treasures?" Benny wanted to know.
> "They will be treasures for us," answered Jessie, laughing.[19]

At the other end of scrounging's literary age spectrum are the elderly scavenger's of Franz Lidz's popular book *Ghosty Men*—scavengers every bit as certain as the Alden kids that they can turn scrounged tin cans into treasure. With *Ghosty Men* Lidz creates a sort of comparative literature of scrounging by interweaving two true-life stories. The more famous of the two is that of the Collyer brothers, wealthy recluses and the stuff of New York City legend, who for decades scrounged the city's trash piles, ultimately packing their old home solid with junk. The second is Lidz's Uncle Arthur, an eccentric "urban prospector" who "never passed a Dumpster without lifting the lid."[20] Like the Collyers, Uncle Arthur was peripatetic in the extreme, walking miles in pursuit of urban discards. And like the Collyers, Uncle Arthur eventually accumulated from his urban prospecting so much material that it all but overwhelmed him, his apartment retaining only little paths through walls of scrounged material. No such luxuries of accumulative indulgence were possible, though, for another writer who turned Dumpster diving into award-winning literature. In *Travels with Lizbeth*, Lars Eighner elegantly documents his life of homeless Dumpster diving— Dumpster diving designed not for material acquisition but for day-to-day survival.[21]

The empire of scrounge—or at least an idealized image of it—also circulates amid the somewhat less literary swirl of contemporary popular culture. The Learning Channel for example features its popular *Junkyard Wars* program, where teams of contestants compete to build machinery from scrap metal. The network also promotes the show through local competitions, one of which was recently staged in a Fort Worth—area shopping mall. Billed as "a way to get Dad to the mall, where you can see what kind of tie he'd like for Father's Day," the event featured competitors who built junk cars and raced them along a "Junkyard Gravity Crash Course." The race was also broadcast on a large plasma screen in the mall itself, and in turn billed as offering contestants "a slim chance of getting their faces on an episode" of the show.[22] Allegedly aspiring to higher levels of popular culture, French photojournalists Pascal Rostain and Bruno Mouron recently mounted an exhibit of "star trash" photographs. Collecting and photographing the discards of Madonna, Tom Cruise, and others, the two claim to "document and illuminate the capitalist-driven consumer culture of the 21st century and its connections to the cult of the celebrity." In any case, they argue that "there was actually nothing illegal about going through these celebrities' garbage—the only crime . . . would have been to photograph any sexual or medical-related garbage."[23]

Maybe so—I suspect that will ultimately be for their lawyers and those of Madonna and Tom Cruise to decide. But for all the beloved children's stories and award-winning books, for all the feel-good television shows and high-profile photo exhibits, one trend is clear: more and more of the empire of scrounge is in fact illegal. Many city governments now prohibit homeless folks and other city residents from scrounging in Dumpsters and downtown trash cans, arguing that such activity constitutes "offensive conduct in a public place."[24] In 1988, the U.S. Supreme Court ruled that curbside residential trash sits outside the constitutionally guaranteed privacy of the home, and therefore is subject to police search without a warrant, basing its ruling in part on the notion that curbside trash is already "readily accessible to animals, children, scavengers, snoops, and other member of the public."[25] Now, in an ironic twist on this ruling, more and more cities prohibit curbside trash scrounging on grounds that such trash (and its recyclable content) already belong to the city and its trash-hauling service. Near Fort Worth, for example, the town of Trophy Club fines scroungers up to $2,000 for collecting "recyclable items, reusable items, household trash, garbage and/or debris," or otherwise "opening, removing, picking up and searching through materials within a closed or sealed container left for curbside collection."[26] In Newark, New Jersey, as part of a "crackdown" on urban scrounging, the mayor has gone so far as to cast such "thievery" as "a national problem with enormous significance for local residents."[27] In addition, of course, scroungers continue to risk charges of illegal trespass as they work their way through back alleys, vacant lots, Dumpsters, and front-yard trash piles—a risk that signage of all sorts often reinforces.

Criminalization and legal regulation continue to accumulate at the other end of the scrounging process as well. Arguing that "in this country, every day in every city, far more edible food is *discarded* than is needed to feed those who do not have enough to eat," the direct action group Food Not Bombs collects discarded food in order to cook and serve healthy meals to the homeless and others in need—yet time and again, city governments refuse Food Not Bombs' requests for permits to serve the meals in public places, then send in city police to arrest Food Not Bombs members for illegally serving scrounged food.[28] The yard sales and garage sales through which others commonly redistribute scrounged goods for a little cash also face ever-proliferating local ordinances regulating their frequency, their location, even the means through which they can be advertised. In Fort Worth, for example, city ordinances allow only two garage sales per year; require a city permit for each event; and limit do-it-yourself advertising to a single sign placed in the seller's front yard. In neighboring River Oaks, where permits are also required, a city ordinance requires that any yard sale sign be taken down "by one hour after sundown on the last day of the sale" —and, as a later chapter will show, provides for

large fines and arrest warrants in conjunction with those that aren't.[29]

Legal regulation likewise increasingly confronts the scrap metal scrounger hauling a load of accumulated aluminum or copper in to the scrap yard. Many urban scroungers search for clothes, tools, small appliances, and other consumer items they might put to use or sell at a garage sale or flea market; but many also search for aluminum cans, aluminum, copper, brass, die cast, and other metals to be collected and sold to scrap metal dealers. As the following chapters document, both of these enterprises became part of my own scrounging, and so every so often I loaded up my old (and seldom used) pickup with scrap metal and headed for the yards. On one of these trips I noticed above the little pay window a new, neatly lettered sign, noting that Texas law now required a photo I.D. from those cashing in copper or aluminum loads over forty pounds. It seemed the legal authorities were concerned that copper and aluminum—relatively speaking, two of the most valuable scrap metals—might in fact be of such value that they could be stolen rather than scrounged. But in a little joke on the authorities, their new requirement, and the likelihood of its enforcement, a cashier had hand lettered an additional note across the bottom of the sign, kidding that the cashiers might also request an I.D. on a load under forty pounds, "if you have that look."[30]

So, it seems, scrounging's long-standing legal and cultural ambiguity lingers today. Charming

Signs of scrounging, Tampa, Florida, June 2004.

children's books bump up against thousand-dollar fines and arrest warrants, literary success against shambling poverty. Celebrity trash piles blur into homeless survival strategies, images of eccentric and independent "urban prospecting" into allegations of "thievery" and "offensive conduct." Even the welter of recent laws and regulations designed to resolve scrounging's uncertain status in the direction of illegality seems only to increase the confusion. Urban scroungers not only remain on the margins of the city's social ecology; they still stand in the shadows of morality and law.

Little Theaters of the Absurd

These unresolved contradictions and ambiguities conspire to create within the empire of scrounge little theaters of the uncertain and the absurd, to stage here and there morality plays scripted along the lines of marginality and illegality—and not just in Fort Worth. In Rome, police arrest Robert Cercelletta on charges of theft and resisting arrest after they discover him fishing tourist-tossed coins out of the famous Trevi Fountain; a few days later an unnamed woman, inspired by media coverage of Cercelletta's arrest, is arrested as she wades in after her own free coins in a fountain.[31] Meanwhile, in England, police apprehend John Collinson as he walks across Leicester's Whetstone Golf Course, wearing a rubber diving suit and carrying some 1,100 golf balls, all of which he and a friend have just scrounged from Lily Pond, a notorious water hazard on the course's fifth hole. Arrested and jailed on theft charges, Collinson argues that once in the water, "the balls didn't belong to anyone," and that anyway, unlike some others in the empire of scrounge, "he paid taxes on his earnings" from scrounged golf balls. Unmoved, Judge Richard Bray sentences Collinson to six months in jail. Protests follow from professional golfer Colin Mongomerie, chief executive Gavin Dunnett of the worldwide UK Lakeballs used golf ball company, and other public figures, all of whom argue, like Collinson, that such balls are in reality "finders keepers" and "abandoned property." Some months later, two Court of Appeal judges overturn the six-month sentence, imposing instead a two-year conditional discharge and warning Collinson away from subsequent "clandestine" dives.[32]

Elsewhere in the empire the morality plays come off more as straight tragedy. In Vietnam, Hanoi alone supports some six thousand "scavengers and junk buyers"; elsewhere in the country, scrap metal scroungers looking to recycle the detritus of war are regularly injured by grenades, mines, and other unexploded ordnance. In Kyrgyzstan, nine people perish while scrounging for scrap metal in a city dump when a twenty-three-foot wall of waste collapses onto them. In northern Russia, four unemployed men scavenging lead generator covers from a nuclear-powered lighthouse expose themselves to disfiguring doses of radiation. Two suffering from burns and radiation sickness are hospitalized; the other two are jailed.[33]

In Argentina the tragedy is more a matter of economic decline than immediate death and disfigurement, with the play suggesting its own sort of do-it-yourself third act. There, the railroad runs a special train each day into Buenos Aires from the impoverished suburb of Jose Leon Suarez. Known as the Ghost Train, it carries only one class of passengers: *cartoneros*, or "cardboard people," scavengers who work the trash bins of Buenos Aires for cardboard and also for cans, scrap paper, and discarded food. Assigned their own dilapidated train away from the railroad's more "respectable" passenger trains, charged five bucks a month for the privilege of riding their rolling ghetto, they have appropriately enough stripped it of its remaining aluminum parts and windows. And why not? After all, "this is our job now. This is how we survive," says Lidia Quinteros who, like the majority of the *cartoneros*, is a laid-off worker. And so, they adapt themselves and their tools to this new work, paying welders to "attach car wheels to a steel frame, creating a contraption that allows one person to push 500 pounds of scrap down the street."[34]

But really, I found, there was no need to travel to Rome, Leicester, Hanoi, Buenos Aires, or other far-flung outposts in the empire of scrounge (and no ability to do so, by the way, while living as a scrounger with no job, no research grant, and no book advance); little theaters of everyday marginality abounded closer to home as well. Jack Kerouac caught sight of one a half-century ago, writing in *Lonesome Traveler* of a friend who reported "scrounging around in the garbage cans and barrels of Hollywood, mind you, going behind those very fancy apartment houses and at night, late, very quietly sneaking around, getting bottles for 5 cents deposits and putting them in my little bag, for extra money."[35] Homeless himself in and around Hollywood a few decades later, other times living on the streets of Austin, Lars Eighner wrote his own script for Dumpster diving—or "scavenging" as he prefers to call it—and along the way developed his own grounded theories of scavenger survival. Out of Eighner's Dumpsters emerged typologies of food safety—keep the scavenged canned goods and the raw vegetables, avoid the pork and the poultry, and always ask oneself, "Why was this discarded?"—and codes of "scavenger ethics," including the setting aside of surplus finds for others to use. As Eighner learned which Dumpsters regularly offered the best trash, he even found himself with "proprietary feelings" about them; and as he taught others the practice of Dumpster diving, he watched them move as he had from the first act's "disgust and self-loathing" to a startling denouement: "The diver, after all, has the last laugh. He is finding all manner of good things that are his for the taking. Those who disparage his profession are the fools, not he."[36]

The anonymous author of the book *Evasion*—a political drama in its own right, a document of

The empire of scrounge, Ankara, Turkey, April 2004.

youthful existential wanderings illuminated by petty theft and Dumpster diving—found himself writing the same absurd script. As he wandered the United States, diving from one Dumpster to the next, moving among a "renegade faction of society living and prospering on what we throw away," he realized that "throwing edible food in a Dumpster was as inseparable an American cultural practice as roping cattle," and he came to understand a certain "guarded secret": "You know what is referred to as the wealthy's 'purchasing power' on CNN? It 'purchased' commodities brought home, unloaded, and *thrown in Dumpsters*! I swear I'm not making this up."[37]

I'm not making it up, either. Like Lars Eighner, *Evasion*'s author, and their buddies, I too discovered in the empire of scrounge all manner of good things for the taking, an absurd and excessive overflow from the daily accumulations of consumer culture. In fact, this was the discovery that first and most strikingly emerged from the trash piles and Dumpsters I investigated: an overwhelming, inundating surplus of objects and materials, the majority of them not "trash" in any conventional sense, but useful, functional, desirable, many times unused and unmarred. So overwhelming, so magnificent was this eruption of scrounged objects from trash bins, trash piles, and city streets that I'm tempted, in hopes of communicating its magnitude and variety, to report it as one long list, one long stream-of-consciousness epic beat poem of waste and discovery, spanning the next fifty pages or so.

Let's see . . . it would start something like this:

Hammered aluminum serving trays, sterling silver baby cups, clock radios, golf clubs.
Old lamps and new.
Video cameras, video tapes, pornography, piles of CDs and cassette tapes,
baby doll shoes, silver candle holders.
Antique mirrors and antique picture frames, old family photos, old hand tools and new power tools, skateboards.
Watches, jewelry, and ash trays.
Baseballs, softballs, basketballs, tennis balls, plastic Easter eggs.
Waterford crystal clocks and big black coffeemakers.
And the money—mostly coins, and no need to wade a fountain.
Coins, coins and dollar bills and five-dollar bills in the streets, in the gutters.
Pennies mangled by traffic still spend.

Liberian five-dollar bills and a Bank of Ghana note in an old
suitcase, pennies and dimes and quarters in the intersections, settled to the bottom of garbage bags, in discarded purses, in the drawers of old dressers on the curb.
Cameras: the Olympus at the bottom of a garbage bag, the old mid-century
Fotron III still in its curved leatherette case.
Telephoto lenses, film canisters.
Clothes to clothe me and my friends and folks at the shelter.
Neiman-Marcus sweaters, little silk scarves,
Polo suits and Henry Grethel, dress shirts, jeans, shoes.
Oshkosh for the kids.
File cabinets, turquoise chairs, Vermont Maple Syrup and bottles of booze.
Cut glass doorknobs and Mardi Gras beads and boxes of bullets.
Books—trashy paperbacks, clothbound first editions.
A bejeweled book on Italy, circa 1907.
License plates, Texas 1949, Mississippi 1969.
Fishing rods, fishing reels, fishing lures, and a little blue Tiffany & Co. box.
More toys than I can haul home. . . .

At the insistence of my editor, I'll omit the next forty-nine pages, though I'll gladly recite them for you sometime over a couple of cold beers; and anyway, many more moments from this poem emerge in the following chapters' descriptions of scrounging situations and discoveries. As even these few lines of scavenger poetry suggest, though, the jumbled juxtapositions in which discarded items are discovered are absurd in their own right; in the trash pile, discrete dimensions of people's lives collapse into one another, the long sweep of cultural history compresses into the present, and fine distinctions between old silver cups and aluminum cans, office supplies and sports gear, get lost. But if the jumbled confluence of objects undermines easy categorization, the situations in which these discarded objects are discovered do lend themselves to a certain typology of urban scrounging. In fact, like Eighner, I soon enough developed my own grounded theory of my efforts, a fairly clear typology of situations and circumstances within the larger practice of day-to-day scrounging.[38] I realized I was operating in more than one theater of the absurd—each one marginal, certainly, but each with its own actors, plots, and dramatic devices.

As I discovered, a first theater of scrounging emerged not at the Dumpster or trash pile, but on the road to it—so long as that road was traversed on foot or by bicycle, that is. Beyond the minimal cost, one of the great advantages of foot or bicycle travel is the proximity in which it puts the scrounger to the street. City streets may not be paved in gold, but if one looks carefully while biking or walking, it becomes clear that they're paved in something else: pennies, quarters, lead wheel weights, small auto parts, lost tools, music CDs, aluminum cans, bits of copper pipe and wire, and other assorted detritus of urban movement. Learning to search for such items requires a different and sometimes difficult sort of bicycle riding, a concentrated focus on proximities of street and gutter, at times to the point of dangerous disregard of traffic or parked cars. Learning to pick up such items, on the other hand, I found to be among the more ethereal and pleasurable of scrounging moments. Spotting a coin or tool or lead weight, quickly checking the traffic behind and in front of me, I'd cut a tight circle, swooping back around to brake and pick up the object. Once I moved to my scrounged BMX bicycle, this sort of rhythmic scrounging also moved to a different level. Built small and close to the ground, the bike offered a particularly detailed examination of street objects, and a very short turning radius upon their discovery. But with coaster brakes that regularly malfunctioned, it also offered others an odd sight: my left leg splayed out, my foot dragging, as I circled and attempted to stop, sometimes on a dime. Walking, of course, provided no such swooping excitement, but did offer a level of detailed peripatetic study that even Aristotle might appreciate.

In comparison with other scrounging theaters, streets are distinctive for their dispersion of lost or discarded items along a trajectory of movement, and in this sense can be classified with another scrounging resource: the outer boundaries of golf courses. As it happens, a number of public and private golf courses sit within a bicycle ride of my house, and so, like John Collinson, I mined their borders for lost golf balls. Unlike Collinson, though, I was able to escape legal entanglement while scrounging (and later selling) hundreds of lost golf balls, a fact that I attribute both to my focus on golf course boundaries rather than water hazards, and to the ecology of North Texas. Along one stretch of the Colonial Country Club golf course—in fact, along "Hogan's Alley," the series of demanding holes made famous by the great Ben Hogan—the boundary is formed by dense underbrush sloping down to the Trinity River. So, crossing the river on a low-water dam from the bike path on the other side, I would hug the river's edge, then slither up the embankment, plucking lost golf balls from the tangle of undergrowth as I worked my way along the length of the border. Once, employing the same strategy in an overgrown creek bed bordering Pecan Valley Golf Course, I scrounged a backpack full of golf balls—but emerged from the tangle of prickly vines with my shorts so badly ripped that the long ride home was, to say the least, breezy. At a third course, the Trinity served me again. Rockwood Golf Course features a series of holes laid out along a long curve in the river, such that a seemingly straight shot toward the green in fact takes the ball out over the river. The stretch of the river is too deep and too dirty for golf ball diving—but on a little-used spit of public land across its long curve from the course, lost golf balls nestle in the tall grass like so many little white Easter eggs.

As must already be obvious, this is absurd: skidding to a stop for a penny, belly crawling for golf balls while having my scrounged shorts damn near torn off, wealthy golfers hooking and slicing me a living of sorts. Obvious also, I would guess, is the absurd fun, the pleasure, the adventure of it all, especially in comparison to minimum-wage work at McDonalds, or the assistant manager's gig at Circuit City. Might this tell us something about the seductions of marginality, the ambiguous line between the legal and the illegal, even the meaning of existence?

More on that later, but for now the second scrounging theater: the curbside trash pile. Curbside trash piles tend to emerge out of two temporal dynamics, one regular, the other not. During my months as a scrounger, Fort Worth's trash collection system allowed residents of each neighborhood to put boxed, bagged, or stacked refuse on the street on two designated days each week. This schedule of course organized residents' disposal habits and the city's collection practices, and it organized my own scrounging rhythms, too, as I and other scroungers took to the streets of each neighborhood to work the curbside piles on the evening before, or early on the day of, scheduled trash pickup.

A second sort of curbside trash pile reflects not regularity but disruption. These piles are the residues of significant life changes, many of them sudden: divorces, breakups, deaths, kids sent off to college, renters running out on the rent. As such, these trash piles often offer, in comparison to the twice-a-week trash piles, magnificent accumulations of discarded goods; sudden tragedies, breaks in social continuity, can leave much of a person's material history piled up on itself, curbside. Because of this, these curbside piles often incorporate also the material residues of shared meaning, fragments of emotion lost and found: bronzed baby shoes, diplomas, wedding photos, ticket stubs, old newspaper clippings. In fact, telling a friend more than once about the nice men's clothes, men's shoes, electronics equipment, and sports paraphernalia I regularly found in big curbside trash piles, she always offered the same enthusiastic, imagined explanation: "Well, I guess she finally threw the bastard out!"

As I'll document in following chapters, these curbside piles at their extreme become material postmortems, life histories of relationships, accomplishments, and accumulations left at the edge of the street or alley. But trash piles can emerge from the other end of the life course as well—and with them new enactments of the absurd. One weekend afternoon, bicycling through a neighborhood whose mansions front an exclusive private golf course, I came upon a pile of cardboard boxes, black plastic garbage bags, and assorted discards at the edge of the little street running behind the houses. Working my way through the bags and boxes, I discovered that they were full of pretty party favors, decorations, gift wrap, used paper plates and paper cups, and expensive baby gifts. Many of the gifts, in fact, were still sealed new in their gift boxes—the absurd aftermath of a baby shower meant mostly for show.

At this trash pile, as at others, I worked as quickly as possible. Supreme Court decisions notwithstanding, curbside trash piles occupy ambiguous legal and personal territory, sitting as they do at the edge of a residential yard, at the street but not in it, and open to various interpretations regarding ownership and availability. For this reason I'd rather not be noticed when scrounging a trash pile—and if upon investigation the pile begins to suggest residues of a domestic breakup or some other interpersonal emergency, my desire to avoid emotional proximity or interpersonal entanglement increases. My preferred and often-practiced approach therefore is the trash pile drive-by: a quick rolling stop, a quick look through the pile, an item or two plucked, and then off again; if possible, I also bicycle a block or two away before stopping to stow the scrounged items. Often, though, this approach isn't possible due to the size of the pile, and the range and value of the items in it. In these cases a longer inspection is required; sometimes a number of return trips by bicycle to load out all the valuables discovered; and less often, a trip in the old truck to haul home the take.

Despite the use of its name as a shorthand for urban scrounging, only now do we arrive at the third theater of scrounging: the Dumpster. Dumpsters denote a degree of permanence in the empire of scrounge, a relatively fixed point in the worlds of consumers and scavengers alike, a receptacle into which trash can be tossed and from which it can be extracted. Lined up behind a strip shopping mall, sitting in the corners of apartment house parking lots, tucked away near grocery store loading docks, Dumpsters carry a set of proprietary claims and financial obligations—but depending on locks, sight lines, and local ordinances, others than their rightful owners may also employ them as so many big, square garbage cans. In some cases, the cumulative residues of residential relocation, or divorce, or a remodeling project may also end up here rather than in a curbside pile. Because of this, Dumpsters offer an ever-changing, oddball assortment of items—items available for perusal, depending on the Dumpster's design, through either large hinged lids on top or sliding side doors. Despite the reassuring claims of consumer Web sites, I have found myself more often climbing in through these openings than simply looking through them; after all, the contents of the Dumpster must often be sorted, and large objects hoisted out. Yet to climb inside a Dumpster is to do more than force oneself inside a big trash can. It is to enter a hidden world, an alternative universe of trash, a big box of surprises sitting in the middle of the city—and, believe it or not, surprises more often exciting, even pleasant, than repugnant. My local Victoria's Secret's Dumpster, I might add, is but one example.

This hidden world holds especially for the biggest surprise box of the empire, a sort of mutation on the Dumpster. This is the "rollaway," by comparison to the common Dumpster a giant of a waste container that is rolled to (and later

The Dumpster's hidden world, Tampa, Florida, February 2005.

rolled away from) construction sites, remodeling jobs, and similar semipermanent settings where waste is produced. A big rectangular metal box, welded and girded but without a lid, a rollaway generally ranges from eight to twelve feet in height—and of course once you climb in, as you will if you're a scrounger, eight to twelve feet in depth. Climbing in by way of a metal ladder usually welded to one end, and usually badly bent, or by grabbing a support rod welded down the sides of the rollaway—climbing also past the sign that warns against climbing on or entering the container—one enters an alternative world so large that it offers its own ecology. In the Texas summer, with the sun angling down into its depths, a rollaway makes for a brutally efficient oven; on a brisk winter day, those depths provide a much-appreciated wind break and shelter.

Once in, clambering amid honeybees buzzing discarded soda cans for their corn syrup, the accidental accretion of tossed-in materials makes for some relatively risky exploration, with false bottoms, angled piles of debris that give way under foot, and accumulations of rain water underneath. Rollaways' contents, though, make them well worth the effort, and worth the consequent cuts, bruises, and bee stings. Especially good resources for copper wiring and copper pipe, aluminum scrap, lumber, tools, and antique fixtures, their size is such that they also become home for everything from discarded doors and windows to riding mowers and bicycles. And the fun of scaling the sides, climbing in and out, engaging this informal archeology of urban trash? It rivals the swooping, leg-dragging bicycle switchbacks of street scrounging.

Like Eighner, I even came to have "proprietary feelings," not to mention affection and appreciation, for some of these Dumpsters and rollaways. These favorites offered a sort of life-sustaining magic, a seemingly endless supply of resources each time I visited them. Often ongoing remodeling or house-cleaning projects produced this effect, filling a rollaway with wave after wave of lumber, nails, screws, tools, clothes, and vintage plumbing and lighting fixtures. Especially fecund were those Dumpsters that rode the boundaries of two worlds, and so regularly received the castoffs from both. One sat behind a nearby row of antique shops and faced a neighborhood with a good bit of home remodeling and real estate activity; this Dumpster I came to consider my personal treasure chest. Another, farther away, was the property of the office building behind which it sat, but was illicitly used by those moving in or out of adjoining, upscale town homes. Its unending bounty led to many a toddling bicycle ride home while overburdened with vases, dishes, food, kitchen utensils, clay pots, office supplies, letterhead stationery, designer sunglasses, power tools—once even a working video camera, snug in its case and strapped to my bicycle's rear deck.

In this way the empire of scrounge organized itself for me as much as I organized it. While almost every ride over those eight months mixed street scrounging with the perusal of curbside trash piles, Dumpsters, and rollaways, I soon learned which situations offered which sorts of needed resources, and which little theaters might offer particular absurdities and adventures. To paraphrase Frank Johnson, a freelance scrounger and junk man whose troubles with the law I'll recount in Chapter Four: my scrounging was my school.

Signs of Grandeur

And in that regard, before we go any further, a confession: truth be told, I'd been going to scrounger school a long time before those eight months of survival scrounging began in early 2002 —and school didn't let out when I returned to academia in the fall of 2002, either.

As a kid, my friend Brett and I would hike along the edge of the highway, looking for returnable bottles, auto parts, and lost tools. During summers spent with my mother's folks in central Texas, my Uncle A.J. would indulge my childhood passion by driving slowly along rural roads, allowing me to jump out of the pickup bed, grab bottles and cans, and jump back in. By graduate school in Austin, I was riding a Harley-Davidson around town, but for weekend scrounging I rode something else: an old bicycle that I had customized with multiple baskets for better scrounging. In fact, it was my fantasy in those days to add a little sign, "Aftermath Enterprises," to my bike, given how much of my best scrounging

occurred in the aftermath of concerts, football games, and other public events.

As my academic career subsequently took me from place to place, my scrounging followed. In Denver I bicycled the bounteous alleys of the densely populated Capitol Hill neighborhood; scrounged Northwest Denver as gentrification was beginning to move the neighborhood's material history from the insides of its old houses to the alleys behind them; and, as a member of the hip hop graffiti underground, learned to use found objects as de facto stencils during late-night wall painting. In London, I scrounged the streets as I moved about by foot and bus, finding jewelry, coins, even old posters to decorate my flat. In Flagstaff, with less of a city to scrounge, I rode forest roads to pick up aluminum cans, dug old bottles out of abandoned high-country homesites, and searched out old parts and tools left behind by early logging crews.

While none of these adventures approached the experiential intensity of those eight months of daily survival scrounging in Fort Worth, they did in many ways prepare me for it—and they did lead me to various odd, early outposts in the empire of scrounge. The empire of insulators, for example, unfolds along rural railroad tracks. Hiking the tracks while looking for thick glass insulators that have fallen or been discarded from the adjoining telephone poles teaches an exquisite lesson in patience and the process of discovery. On a good day, you find perhaps one unbroken insulator for every hundred broken ones, at a rate of maybe one good find for every two or three miles of track walked—and so when you do find an intact insulator, the pleasure is immense, as is the walk back.[39] The empire of hubcaps—of which I've long been a devotee—likewise accumulates along roads and highways. To me, any road trip has always been also a rolling hunt for hubcaps—but when I moved to Flagstaff, along old Route 66, the hunt really began. Stretching east and west from Flagstaff are old, abandoned alignments of Route 66, to be hiked for hubcaps and other automotive detritus. And when one day I found a shiny 1940s Chevrolet hubcap alongside an old lost alignment as it crested a hill overlooking Seligman, Arizona —well, the empire smiled.[40] And those golf balls scrounged from the borders of Fort Worth golf courses? Let's just say I've had some experience in that area also, wading Sycamore Creek for golf balls as a kid, later on scrounging golf balls from the rocky edges of swank courses in Colorado resort towns.

I'm still at it, too, and so later chapters will include accounts of situations that emerged after the end of my eight-month adventure. (I recently found twelve discarded mannequins in that Victoria's Secret Dumpster.) But whether during my eight months of daily scrounging for survival, or before and beyond them, the marginality of the empire has been made clear to me time and again. It seems always to exist somewhere along the boundaries that separate the private domain of the home from the public spaces of social life, the private property of the individual or business from the shared resources of the community. For hobos and homeowners alike, circumstances within the empire often emerge also out of the tension between staying and going, out of the contradictory rhythms of settling in and moving out. For many scroungers, such circumstances likewise define the thin margins of their own peripatetic survival, offering up a personal economy pieced together from the haphazard availability of food, clothes, and other materials to be used, traded, or sold. And in such situations, I've many times seen the margins of respectable identity crowded, if not crossed, by a beggar's banquet of hobos, drunks, homeless couples, and scrap haulers, their shopping carts and busted-out old pickups bulging with the debris of the social order.

These situations crisscross the lines of legality and illegality as well—and, as the following chapters show, in ways political authorities and respectable citizens might not anticipate. In and among the curbside trash piles and Dumpsters lie possibilities of theft, trespass, drunkenness, drug use, illegal disposal, identity theft, forgery, and more, some of it attributable to those who scrounge such trash piles, some of it attributable to those who create them. And amid the trash piles and Dumpsters, the confusion of legality and illegality not only ensnares the respectable and the disrespectable, but hides in the interactions among them. The thin margin between stealing and scrounging, between "what belong[s] to nobody and what belong[s] to somebody," is less defined than it is, always, negotiated—negotiated with the passage of each new city law regarding Dumpster diving or trash collection, with each curbside interaction between homeowner and homeless couple, with each scrounger's on-the-spot decision to take or leave behind some object left sitting at the edge of availability.[41]

Hanging out in such situations, sorting among the scraps of profligate consumption, I've discovered some scraps of hope, too. Hobos, homeless couples, can collectors, small-time scrap haulers—all are busy piecing together survival from the discards of their betters, from the detritus steadily accumulating at the bottom of an unjust social order. And while such marginal work might certainly be thought of as resistance—as the alchemy of inverting the everyday, of inventing possibility where none is offered, of turning trash into treasure—it seems to be a resistance to everyday domination defined less by anger and defiance than by dignity and humor. Over and over I've found inhabitants of the empire operating on their own terms, laughing and enjoying their work, not because they can afford to, but maybe because they can't.

Rolling out to the scrap yards one day, I pulled up behind a thirty-year-old beat-to-hell crew-cab pickup, an old man at the wheel, the bed full of scrap metal—and on the rear bumper a sticker, itself torn and faded, but readable: "I love my job. I love my boss. Self-employed." And this is not to mention the homeless guy I came to know, his old bicycle rewelded, contorted, customized, not in the interest of style but of bigger scrap loads. Or the young guy who drives his electric wheelchair up and down the streets of Fort Worth's West Side, plucking aluminum cans out of the gutter, dropping them into the containers he's lashed to each side of his chair. Or, as a later chapter documents, the countless "outsider" artists who convert found scrap into grand sculptures, ornamental chess sets, and fields of flying whirligigs.

I think I know why they're laughing amid all that trash and deprivation. It's the pleasure of self-determination, the dignity that comes from creating something useful out of a world that others can only confront with scorn and indignation. It's the absurd grin that emerges out of self-made adventure, the sense of purpose and passion that keeps me scrounging as well, through one life change and another. It's the sort of thing that can even get you laughing down in Huntsville, Texas, in the dark shadow of the big Texas prison killing machine.

There, Dan Phillips stays busy building hand-crafted homes, homes of such remarkable architectural quality and innovation that they get featured in glossy magazines like *Fine Homebuilding.*[42] More remarkably, he builds these homes out of cast-off lumber and industrial scrap. With a background in antiques restoration, dance, and academic teaching, Dan brings to his homes a craft worker's blend of technical skill and artistry, and plenty of humor; his homes feature bathtubs built from 2 x 4 cutoffs, hand-carved hickory nut drawer pulls, and beer tap sink faucets. But Dan's not building these homes for wealthy buyers, and he has more in mind than architectural amusement. He means his houses to be material demonstrations, and rebuttals, of pervasive waste —and in building them he intends to provide work and on-site training for unskilled workers, and to create high-quality, low-cost housing for folks who otherwise couldn't afford it.

Folks like Jim Tullos. Dan hired Jim to help him build the first house, then sold Jim the house when it was completed; along the way Jim learned the skills of being a carpenter, and more.

"Dan's contagious," Jim tells me one day while I'm down in Huntsville, taking a break from my Fort Worth scrounging to check on Dan's own remarkable empire of scrounge. Jim, Dan, and I are standing in the half-built living room of Dan's latest house project—a beautiful scrounged-wood structure on which Jim is foreman.

> "I started workin' up there," Jim says, "and [Dan] started [asking], 'You recycle cans, Jim?'"
> "Uh, no, not really."
> "You need to recycle cans."
> "OK, Dan, I'll start recycling cans." He just kinda wears off on you little by little you know.

Jim also tells me how Dan taught him to scrounge the city dump, and how as a result he ended up with, among other items, a chain saw— "I made hundreds of dollars with it 'til someone stole it from me"—and "three VCRs in my house."

"It's all the excitement of stealing but none of the prison time," I tell him, laughing, commenting on my scrounging experiences as much as his. And now we're all laughing. "That's true," chuckles Jim Tullos. "That's true."

Standing there laughing in that half-built house, amid the piles of salvaged lumber soon to be somebody's little home, I think about Jim's on-the-job education, about the kindness of the urban scroungers I've come to know, about the hard-earned autonomy of independent scrap haulers, about bicycles and wheelchairs shaped for scrounging. I consider the splendor of an empire that exists only at the margins of law and society, and built from trash at that. And I remember Jean Genet, writing years ago about his life as an itinerant thief and sexual outlaw, reporting from inside his own proud empire of existential marginality.

"Never did I try to make of it something other than what it was," said Genet. "I did not try to adorn it, to mask it, but, on the contrary, I wanted to affirm it in its exact sordidness, and the most sordid signs became for me signs of grandeur."[43]

Cultural Criminology and Trajectories of Reconstruction

And so one final confession before we move deeper into the empire of scrounge: In the same way that I had some prior experience with scrounging before all this started, I had a certain history with marginal worlds and sordid signs.

Some fifteen years ago now, I wandered into the hip hop graffiti underground, taking with me a background in critical criminology and cultural studies, and a healthy suspicion of all things orchestrated and official. The result was five years of art and adventure, and a book, *Crimes of Style: Urban Graffiti and the Politics of Criminality*. Writing this book, running the streets with illicit artists whose public displays brought forth a strange brew of hyperbolic media coverage and aggressive law enforcement, I began to wonder about this potent mix of cultural forces. Where else was this mélange of symbolism, style, conflict, and crime surfacing? Who else was investigating it? So I began to write more broadly about these issues, to move outside the boundaries of conventional criminology, drawing especially on the work of labeling theorists like Howard Becker and British scholars like Dick Hebdige, Stan Cohen, and Stuart Hall. And with the help of Clint Sanders and other colleagues, I put together an edited book about it, and gave the book a title that I thought caught something of the issue at hand: *Cultural Criminology*.[44]

Through the remainder of the 1990s this criminological reconstruction continued. Mark Hamm and I developed a book that both documented and argued for criminologists' deep immersion in the situated meanings and emotions of crime. While the book mostly explored the politics of field research, *Ethnography at the Edge* also offered, I thought, a corrective of sorts to the tendency to conceptualize the "cultural" in this emerging cultural criminology exclusively as a matter of mass media dynamics. In the same way, Neil Websdale and I edited the book *Making Trouble*, whose content integrated media analysis with scholarship on storytelling, subcultures, and policing. During this time I also made my way into the worlds of freight train graffiti writers, Critical Mass bicyclists, skate punks, BASE jumpers, underground radio operators, and street musicians—illicit worlds linked by their intertwining of culture, crime, and politics. The book *Tearing Down the Streets* chronicled my adventures within and between these alternative universes.[45]

All of which, I suppose, led in some way to the empire of scrounge. In truth, cultural criminology didn't compel me to resign a tenured professorship and immerse myself in the life of an urban trash scrounger—but it didn't do much to stop me, either. After all, cultural criminology has from the first incorporated issues of risk, edgework, and existential autonomy in its commitment to exploring the cultural and phenomenological margins of the contemporary order.[46] And the empire of scrounge, I found, was made up of just such a margin—the margin between profligate consumption and material abundance on the one side, and scrapped together, self-made survival on the other.

As the following chapters document, America's engorged Dumpsters confirm what many already suspect: the culture and economy of consumption runs on waste. It promotes not only endless acquisition, but the steady disposal of yesterday's purchases by consumers who, awash in their own impatient insatiability, must make room for tomorrow's next round of consumption. As a result, it spawns closed communities of privileged consumers who waste each day what might sustain others for a lifetime, and landfills that clog and overflow with barely used goods, growing as big as the shopping malls from which their content not so long ago came.

And yet from atop the trash heaps, from inside the Dumpsters lined up behind the shopping mall, a vast ragtag army of reconstruction emerges. Working with little more than abandoned shopping carts and their own ingenuity, urban scroungers create a complex culture of scavenging, interrupting the inexorable material flow from shopping mall to landfill, and undertaking to redeem contemporary U.S. society from the wreckage of its own failed arrangements. For their trouble, they regularly confront cultural and social stigmatization, and a host of legal strategies that regulate or criminalize most every moment in their redemptive dynamic, from sorting through curbside trash to distributing salvaged food to the needy. It's surely not so simple a question of law and political economy, but living the life of an urban scrounger, I began to wonder whether each statute I encountered, each city code, each emerging community standard regarding waste and its reuse wasn't in reality designed to eliminate any form of material acquisition and exchange except, well, shopping at the mall.

As I trust *Empire of Scrounge* demonstrates, answering such a question, understanding such a world, requires something more than statistical aggregation or theoretical abstraction. The empire of scrounge is a world constructed day-to-day out of human innovation and situational particularity, a world saturated with subtle displays of identity and emotion, a world in this way intricately interwoven with the everyday contradictions of culture and economy. It requires a criminology that can attend to nuances of meaning constructed and displayed within the lives of trash pickers, while at the same time pinpointing these particularities within larger patterns of law and crime. Embracing this sort of cultural criminology, I hoped first to survive as an independent urban scrounger—but I also hoped to challenge taken-for-granted understandings of crime and control, the politics of crime and justice, and maybe even the practice of criminology itself.

With *Empire of Scrounge,* I attempt to demonstrate, by way of form and content, something of cultural criminology's potential. The book documents my experiences as an urban scrounger, and records many of the situations and moments I shared with the denizens of this world, along the way revealing something of our ongoing construction of symbolism, meaning, and emotion. Often the mode of representation is the vignette, a literary form that seems best able to capture the discrete, situational dynamics that animate this world. In addition, *Empire of Scrounge* documents in some detail individual and collective attempts to convert the material trash of consumer society into alternative community, individual survival, social change, even outsider art. In the end, all of this is considered in light of some contemporary trends in law and economy, and in terms of a form of subversion that perhaps moves past law and economy and into the realm of the existential. Throughout, the book incorporates photographs and artistic representations not simply as illustrations, but as visual vignettes, even moments of visual analysis—moments that converse with the text, and illuminate it. In total, *Empire of Scrounge* might be thought of as open-ended experiment in cultural criminology's possibilities.

By design, then, *Empire of Scrounge* is meant to swing with a certain rhythm, to wrap its documentary analysis inside a particular pace and style. Chapter structures, subtitles, and specifics of language may or may not have been chosen wisely, but they were chosen intentionally—that is, chosen with the intention of creating a medium of cultural communication that can indeed become part of the message. These stylistic choices reflect my hope that cultural criminology at its best is now offering criminology not simply a shift in substantive focus, but a cultural reconstruction of the criminological enterprise.[47] That hope of reconstruction, that tension between wasted potential and redemptive possibility, runs through *Empire of Scrounge*.

Street Life

2

As suggested in the previous chapter, the situations and experiences recorded in this chapter emerged out of something closer to survival than to traditional social research. Resigned from a tenured professorship, floating day to day without job, book contract, or professorial prospects, I was outside the academic orbit— and moreover not at all certain that I planned to return to it. In part because of this, I was also not at all sure that my life as an urban scrounger would lead to some future project of writing about that life; mostly I recorded field notes on the chance that it might, and out of habit as a longtime field researcher. In this ambiguous context I also made a conscious decision, and one unusual for someone trained in field research: I would not seek out nor stage interviews with those I met in the streets, instead allowing interactions and conversations to emerge as they might or might not. In fact, since my existence was as much that of scrounger as researcher, I often actively *avoided* interactions with others. Sometimes this seemed necessary for physical survival, as I ducked what I perceived to be dangerous situations or threatening individuals in back alleys or behind Dumpsters. More often this was a matter of practical survival. Living off what I scrounged, I couldn't afford to be run off by an angry shopkeeper whom I had alerted to my presence, or ticketed by a vigilant police officer. In this sense, efficient scrounging often made for inefficient social research—and so what follows is as much autoethnography as a conventional ethnography of others.

The following accounts also take shape more often than not as vignettes, as a series of moments and situations. This, it seems to me, is a matter of homology, an attempt to write in a way that keeps faith with the subject matter and my experiences of it. Riding the city's streets and alleys alone day after day, intersecting on occasion with other scroungers and scrap haulers, the empire of scrounge unfolded for me as an itinerancy of unexpected arrivals at alley Dumpsters, chance encounters with homeowners, and ephemeral situations of one sort or another. To the extent that the empire was organized at all, this was how it was organized—as a meandering series of scattered situations. There were, it's true, ongoing institutions and organizations: the scrap yards, for example, or a city-sponsored bottles-for-cash campaign. But for me and other urban scroungers, I found, even these were made up mostly of comings and goings—a pickup truck load of scrap traded for cash, a shopping cart unloaded and left behind.

In all of this, the archaeology of everyday life became something more than metaphor. Certainly I intended in my urban wanderings to unearth the meaning of waste and reclamation, to expose and reassemble the epistemic frameworks and buried assumptions that constituted the empire of scrounge. Yet doing so required the traditional on-the-ground methods of archaeology: careful and intentional digging amid the detritus of the existing order. As suggested in the previous chapter, and as explicated in this and following chapters, the two were not unrelated. Grounded theories of urban scrounging emerged out of the practical necessity of sorting among the city's trash, and in more than one case, specificities of usable information—books and magazines and manuals that offered insights into material culture and its contradictions—were pulled from the trash piles as well.

Each day for eight months, and most every day in the two years that followed, I scoured the city in this way with a vigor born both of practical necessity and intellectual interest. As a result I uncovered, hauled home, and cataloged an astounding amount of cast-off material—and as a result, many of the following accounts are themselves saturated with an astounding, though I hope not annoying, amount of detail in their description of objects lost and found. Rest assured that I have omitted far more than I've included; yet I've included as much as I have because, again, this inclusion keeps faith with the subject at hand. The amount of the city's daily material waste, I discovered, was overwhelming—and therefore profoundly revealing—in its sheer size and scope. For every object I hauled home each day, I left behind hundreds, thousands more that I discovered but didn't need or couldn't carry by bicycle. And so, I began to understand the scope of the larger problem, and question: For every object that I and every other scrounger can manage to scrounge, every day in Fort Worth or any other city, how many more make their way each day to the landfill, untouched and unclaimed? In my own experience there was the occasional barren scrounging ride, a two-hour tour of the city with only a few aluminum cans and lead weights to show for it. But far more often a ride or walk led me into an alternative universe awash in cast-off goods and commodities, a veritable shopping mall of scrounge strung out along streets and alleys, a cavalcade of consumerism now on its way to material oblivion.

One March day, for example, relegated by steady rain to a short scrounging stroll rather than a long ride, I neared the end of my wet walk with a laughably minimal result: one aluminum can, one lead weight, four little plastic wheels, and a small metal brace. Then, in the last block before my house, I saw through the rain a curbside pile of discarded goods—and ended up struggling home that last block, loaded down with three beautiful old pressure gauges, numerous brass fittings, timer boxes, switch boxes, two band clamps, six porcelain drawer pulls, a doorknob and lock set, a wooden brush, three leather tool belts, two

packages of swag hooks, three caulk guns, a package of insulated stripping, an oil lamp wick and burner plate, a door stop new in its package, two packages of drape hanger assemblies, a shop light, copper wire, a switch plate, an old Riverside State Bank deposit pouch, a utility hook—and a dish pan, in which I carried most of it.

See what I mean? If you're not careful, even a short walk in the empire of scrounge can generate a long list.

Street Situations

For the urban scrounger, street life unfolds as a series of practical opportunities, yet also as a constellation of residual signs. In fact, by learning to pay attention to such signs, I soon realized I could read opportunities found and lost, watch the empire of scrounge operate, even when no one was around. Walking the neighborhood one Saturday in December, for example, I found in a trash pile at the end of an alley two large, high-quality black picture frames—certainly of higher quality than the gauzy soft-porn "art" they framed, at least. I could only manage to get one home by foot, and when I walked back on Sunday to pick up the second, it was gone. Later Sunday, I noticed while out bicycling a discarded fiberglass and aluminum ladder, and when I swung back by in my old truck on Monday to get it, it was gone as well. Driving home in a bit of a hurry, I spotted a large outdoor "hose caddy" atop another trash pile

—and, yes, when I walked back later, it had disappeared also. In fact, the longer I scrounged, the more I learned the importance of remembering a useful Dumpster or making a mental note of a productive trash pile—and in the same way I came to realize that I could gauge the vitality of the empire, the pace of its opportunities and acquisitions, by noticing which objects disappeared, and when. On occasion, this rhythm even operated in the other direction. Once, putting a load of scrounged items that I no longer needed on the curb in front of my house, I walked back down the driveway for a second load, and arriving back at the curb with this load a minute or two later discovered that the first one was already gone. A rapid pace indeed.

Perhaps more than they realize, consumers leave at the edge of the street little signs about themselves by what discards they pile there. But scroungers leave little signs about themselves, too, by what they take from the pile, and how quickly they take it. In this way both consumers and scroungers reveal a constellation of values and preferences, negotiated quite literally by the give-and-take of the streets; together, they orchestrate the empire of scrounge, setting the rhythm and pace by which it operates. In fact, if we were able to build a panopticon above the city's streets and alleys, or gaze down like de Certeau day after day from the city's tallest skyscraper, we could well map the city by the emergence of its trash piles, by their comings and goings, and by the ebb and flow of goods to and from them.[1]

Of course, the street signs that mark the empire of scrounge aren't always residual. That same Monday, walking my dogs through a light rain, I noticed a few houses ahead an older woman wearing a little rain hat and getting out of an early 1990s midsize American car that she had pulled to a stop two or three feet from the curb. Arriving at the trash pile on the curb, she picked out a cylindrical orange water cooler, walked back to her car, opened the driver's side back door, put the cooler in, and drove away. But even before she had gotten out of the car, I was already sure that she was a drive-by scrounger. It was that parking technique, the one I'd seen many times before—the automotive scrounger's tentative pull-over, the same old cruise and the curbside crawl. And as soon as she pulled away, I walked over and investigated the trash pile myself—but this time didn't find anything that I could use.

Day after day, the streets of the empire of scrounge offer signs and opportunities that are sometimes residual, and sometimes observational. At other times, though, they can be directly conversational. In fact, just a week later, a street conversation taught me something about urban scrounging, and the role of sugar bees and wheelchairs in the life of a scrounger.

Not Honeybees, Sugar Bees

Out on a scrounging ride, I roll up on something other than the usual trash pile or Dumpster. It's an electric wheelchair parked up against the curb, a plastic grocery bag of dirty aluminum cans hanging from its left arm, a five-gallon white plastic bucket of cans sitting next to it. Looking around I spot a guy I presume to be its owner at the back of a vacant lot bordering a big town-home construction site, and I remember that I had seen an empty wheelchair at this location once before, but had discovered no one nearby. Getting off my bike, I walk to the back of the lot, where I find the man using a mechanical claw on the end of a metal rod to pluck aluminum cans from the rough ground, all while supporting himself with a rubber-tipped wooden cane clutched in the other hand and carrying over his arm a plastic grocery sack half-full of cans. A plastic bucket like the one on the curb sits nearby.

Introducing myself, I tell him that I'm something of an aluminum can collector myself, but that I've never before seen anyone doing it from a wheelchair. As he starts to answer, he turns away, gasping for breath. Putting his right arm across his forehead, the first thing he's able to say is, "I gotta start eating before I do this."

He recovers and we start to talk. He tells me that this is mostly what he does, that if he comes across some scrap copper or something similar he'll take it, but that he mostly concentrates on aluminum cans "'cause you don't find much copper." Actually, you do, or at least I do—but then again I'm not rolling around the city in a wheelchair. One of these days, he says, he's going to get this friend of his to take him out to the city dump in his big pickup, so that they can scrounge cans out

there. "Can you imagine how many cans are out there?" he asks me. "I've filled up two five gallon buckets and these bags just from this lot."

If that's his future scrounging fantasy, there's also his past. He tells me that when he first started scrounging aluminum cans he was worried about the police, "you know, the open container law and all." Now, this is a permutation of legal control I've never considered—that a scrounger who's just picked up an aluminum beer can still wet inside with stale beer could be busted for being in public possession of an open alcohol container. But, he tells me, not to worry; he called the police about this, and they told him he'd be all right, "first, because you ain't drivin' around drunk," and second because he was performing "a public service, an environmental service."

As we're walking around picking up cans, he talks fondly of this vacant lot, telling me that he hits this place often—so often that the construction workers next door now know him, and greet him with "Oh, you're here for the cans." I tell him, yeah, I get mostly friendly responses, too—"I don't get yelled at that much"—and he says, "Yeah, same here."

The bigger problem, or so he initially thought, is the "sugar bees . . . not honeybees, sugar bees" that often end up inside soda-pop cans in search of sweet residue; in fact, we come upon some bees a few minutes later while sorting through a trash pile that has soda pop cans and plastic bottles mixed in among construction scrap. Highly allergic to bee stings, he was very worried when he first began scrounging cans and came across the bees; but as with the police, they've turned out not to be a problem. "They don't sting me."

I can't help but notice that when he grabs a can with his mechanical claw and then attempts to crush it with his foot, he doesn't crush it much; the same leg weakness that necessitates a wheelchair and a cane leaves little power for crushing cans. He has a mechanical can crusher at home, he tells me, but he at least has to try to crush cans as he finds them in order to get them all home on his wheelchair. Stomping some cans for him, I assure him that I know what he means. Whether your scrounging vehicle is a two-wheeled chair or two-wheeled bike, field dressing your finds is essential.

I also can't help but notice that, like many scroungers—hell, like myself—his approach to his work wanders somewhere between thoroughgoing dedication and existential seduction. Even with his halting mobility, he scours every corner of the vacant lot, working in and around piles of lumber, walking a circuit more than once between the half-completed town homes, determined to get every can—even the sort of wet, muddy cans that I would typically take the luxury of leaving behind.

Now back at the curb, he hangs the second bucket off the wheelchair's right arm, attaches the plastic bags, and gets himself ready to go. This done, he lights a Marlboro Red that he's pulled from a mostly empty pack, and swigs from a one-liter Dr. Pepper bottle that's been sitting on the wheelchair's footrest. His shirt, I notice, has the "No Fear" logo on front and back, and on the back also a slogan that says, "When You Get To The Edge, Jump." Waiting there while he smokes his Marlboro and drinks his Dr. Pepper, this slogan makes me smile. A while back I spent some time with the young, athletic daredevils that make up the BASE jumping underground—those who illegally parachute from bridges and buildings. Quite literally putting their lives in their own hands time after time, they joked about the "No Fear" clothing line, and wore instead shirts that read "Know Fear." My friend here, on the other hand, looks to be about sixty years old, a small, skinny white guy whose "No Fear" shirt and jeans bag off of him, a guy whose orbit is proscribed by a slow electric wheelchair and a wooden cane. Still, maybe there's more than one way to know fear, and to travel to a place where you can confront it.

In fact, before he leaves, he tells me a little more about that place. His wife is bedridden at home, and so he doesn't get out to scrounge cans as often as he'd like. In fact, he tells me, between her circumstances and all the rain we've had lately, everything has "gotten a little ahead of me." He's fallen behind on his regular route and his regular schedule for scrounging.

Earlier in my ride today, I've pulled two boxes of little give-away mirrored compacts from a Dumpster—some sort of now-discarded pharmaceutical promotion, with each mirror imprinted "Valtrex, Valacyclovir HCI 500mg 1000mg Caplets." So now I give him a couple, telling him maybe his wife could use them, and he thanks me for my help, saying "I sure can use all of it." I try to exchange phone numbers, so that I might help some more, but he declines.

So off he goes, a slow, smooth electric wheelchair cruise down the gutter heading west, as I turn back on my bicycle to the east. Looking back as I ride away, I see him hang a slow turn in the middle of the street, so I dawdle a bit, thinking that perhaps he has something else he wants to say. But instead he stops on the opposite side of the street, bending over the chair to pick up an aluminum can he's spotted, and then resumes his route west.

I know that can. It's a Red Bull energy drink can, crushed flat by traffic. I saw it myself as I was making my own U-turn an hour or so ago, circling back to check on a wheelchair parked in the gutter.

16 December 2002

And Go Scrounging in the Streets

All my storage bins for scrap aluminum, copper, brass, die cast, and lead are full, so I'm busy getting a big load ready to take in to the scrap metal yard. In addition, I found fifteen or twenty big, busted aluminum window screens, an aluminum screen door, and an aluminum pole and awning set in various curbside piles yesterday. It's time to turn all this big scrap into a smaller and more manageable form—money— before it overwhelms my storage bins and shed.

While I'm at the job of sorting and processing scrounged materials, I decide I'll also get a load ready to take to the ReStore, a salvage store that Habitat for Humanity runs to generate money for its home building projects. In the past few days I've found a big, bifold louvered door set that I'll donate to the ReStore, along with other scrounged items that I've saved and stored, including a large porcelain sink, three boxes of floor tiles, eight wooden window shutters, and four glass door inserts.

Arriving at ReStore after a dawdling drive through the funky old neighborhoods of south Fort Worth, I unload the materials and have a pleasant talk with the store manager; he and I have worked together before on Habitat's "decon-struction" projects, where an old house is broken down for salvaged materials that can be sold at ReStore. I ask him if there's anything in particular ReStore needs these days; he tells me they can always use doors, and I promise to be on the lookout for good-quality doors discarded in trash piles or Dumpsters. Just last week, in fact, I found four abandoned doors that weren't of good quality —cheap, hollow Home Depot–type doors—and so used them to build a little more storage space into my attic.

Heading home in my empty pickup, taking the back streets through a neighborhood that mixes modest homes with light industry, I'm listening to a compilation tape that my buddy Mark Hamm sent me. As Townes van Zandt is singing his cover of Springsteen's "Racing in the Streets"—a tribute to down-and-out folks who don't give up, who somehow manage to avoid dying a little, piece by piece, and instead come home and go racing in the street—I spot a big trash pile on the curb in front of a little home. Atop the pile is a painted interior door. Slowing down, I can tell it's not in good enough shape to be of any use to ReStore, but I also see that it appears to retain some old lock plates and other door hardware. Stopping, getting out of the truck to check it out, I soon notice something else: the blond pit bull mix, chained in the yard, that's noticed me. So as quickly as I can I heave the old door into the truck bed, figuring I'll remove the hardware when I get home—and when I later get the door home, by the way, I do indeed find some beautiful old brass hardware hidden under all those years of paint.

Pulling away from the pile, I see up ahead of me an old full-sized Chevy truck easing to a stop, and an elderly African American guy getting out. Hobbling over to another curbside trash pile, he begins loading metal scrap from the pile into his truck. One of these days I'll probably see him at the scrap yards—maybe in a couple of days, when I get around to taking in my own scrap load.

Or maybe I'll just run into him the next time we both decide to go scrounging in the streets.

06 January 2003

Elaine

Out walking with my partner Karen, walking our dogs and scrounging, I spot a residential curbside pile I want to investigate, but then see that a woman is standing on the house's front porch, about to carry another load of discards to the pile. Not much in the mood for an encounter, and with three dogs in tow, I decide to just walk on by, though I do smile and nod hello as I pass, and she smiles back. I've noticed this house before, by the way. About four blocks from my own house, it's the one with the mannequin on the front porch, and sometimes a good bit of other junk scattered around the grounds.

Back from our walk, Karen and I jump in the truck to pick up a very large box of clean bedding that I had found earlier in the day beside another curbside trash pile; we plan to take some to the local homeless shelter, some to the local animal shelter. Arriving at the trash pile, there's already a woman there, systematically working her way through it, her little Honda Civic parked in the usual scrounger manner, a couple of feet from the curb, passenger side door open.

Getting out of the truck, abiding by the scroungers' code of deferring to someone who is already mining a trash pile or Dumpster, I ask her if she minds if we grab the box of bedding. "Fine," she says, a bit cautiously. "I'm just doing what you're doing, digging in the trash." Then Karen realizes something. "Hey, aren't you the woman we just walked by, on her front porch?" She is; her name is Elaine.[2] And as we begin to talk, and share scrounging stories, we all get more comfortable with each other and the situation.

"I'm psycho," she tells us, laughing, "addicted to digging through trash pile." Having grown up in one of Fort Worth's nicer neighborhoods, she tells us, her old friends tell her that they hope they don't have to catch her digging through their trash piles. But a Fort Worth code enforcement officer has caught her; he recently came by and made her clean up her yard, she tells us. In fact, over the next year or so I'll get to know Elaine, running into her more than once as we both follow our addiction to the next trash pile, and hearing from her more than once about subsequent problems with the city over her yard clutter. Best of all, though, Karen and I will learn to look forward to Elaine's elegant touch in decorating with scrounged objects. For each holiday or occasion— Halloween, Christmas, the Fort Worth Stock Show and Rodeo in January—she dresses her mannequin in the appropriate found costume, and decorates the big tree in her front yard with appropriate found objects. And oh yeah, one more thing: during the next year, Elaine's addiction will lead her to trade her little Honda for a used truck, the better for hauling costumes, decorations, and damn near everything else.

Pulling back into our driveway with the big box of bedding after running some errands, I notice that a little, outdated portable television I'd put out on the curb is gone. I'd scrounged it from a trash pile a few weeks back, but discovering that I couldn't get it to function properly, I'd cut off the power cord in order to recycle it, and pulled off all the knobs to add to my stores of supplies. So I say to Karen, "Now who the hell would take a little old television that didn't work in the first place, and now has no power cord and no knobs?"

"Elaine," she says.

03 February 2003

Seventeen Cents

I'm out on my bicycle, just underway, checking the Dumpsters strung out behind one of those Gap/Victoria's Secret/Harold's/Pottery Barn/Starbucks shopping strips, this one situated along University Boulevard. Two years later, as I noted in the previous chapter, I'll find and haul home twelve Victoria's Secret mannequins from these Dumpsters; but today I find a hobo. He's hanging out behind the Dumpsters, killing time while waiting for a freight train to hop. The sprawling Union Pacific rail yards run not 500 yards from where we now stand, an accident of urban ecology that regularly forces train-hopping hobos up against the affluence of Fort Worth's West Side—and forces them to lay very low lest they be perceived, and prosecuted, as threats to the economic order of things. But back here behind the strip stores, between the big Dumpsters, we figure it's safe enough to kick back and talk. He tells me he's heading home to the East Coast, by way of the East Texas piney woods, then Little Rock, Arkansas, where he'll catch a mainline back east. After we talk awhile, he asks me if I might have change for a cup of coffee—there's a Jack in the Box a short walk away—and I tell him honestly that I haven't. I don't carry money or identification when I'm out scrounging; my job, I figure, is to find valuables, not chance losing them. Then I remember. Along with an eyeglasses case, a bike reflector, some lead weights, and a license plate, I've also scooped up seventeen street cents in just my first mile or so of riding. So I give him the seventeen cents, wish him well, and watch him disappear back behind a Dumpster as I head off to continue my scrounging. From the streets, to the streets; in the empire of scrounge, what goes around comes around.

12 February 2002

Afghans and Mohawks

I'm on a run to the scrap yard, my truck bed loaded with scrounged aluminum, copper, brass, die cast, cast iron, auto batteries, and tin, but my bed and cab also loaded with scrounged blankets, mats, and rugs; the animal shelter needs bedding for the strays, and I plan to drop the found bedding there after I unload the metal at the scrap yard. On the way to the scrap yard, though, rolling down a parkway through the affluent Monticello neighborhood on Fort Worth's West Side, I spot a large curbside trash pile in front of a Monticello McMansion and stop.

In the pile are the discreet charms of the bourgeoisie.[3] Among the many items I pull from it are new picture frames, RayBan sunglasses, earrings (including one pair that appear to be either very large earrings or standard Christmas tree ornaments), lockets, broaches, a shiny black Braun eight-cup coffeemaker, bottles of liqueur, a new Lancôme compact, a new-in-the-package telescoping window cleaning tool (a must for the two-story McMansion), a new-in-the-bag "Giant Suction Cup Wreath Holder," two new life preservers (Coast Guard approved), and a fancy wine corkscrew, apparently stolen from the "Renaissance Hotels and Resorts." My favorite discoveries are the high-quality area rugs and tightly woven Afghans, which I add to my truck load of found bedding—from the homes of the rich to the cages of the oppressed, I suppose, or is that from each according to ability to each according to need?

At any rate off I go, the bed of my truck full of scrap metal, the little cab now piled even fuller of newly minted dog blankets, booze, picture frames, and jewelry—off to a world of poverty, scrap yards, and *panaderias* that couldn't be any farther from this Monticello McMansion, even if it is just over on Fort Worth's North Side.

Out at the American Recycling scrap yard on North Main, leaning on the dirty oversized scale next to the office, watching as they weigh in my load of assorted metal, I almost have a conversation with a big white guy, maybe thirty-five, sweating heavily in the Texas heat, hair hacked into a disheveled mohawk. "How ya doin?" I say. "Gettin' by . . . somehow," he smiles, and then proceeds to tell me something I can't hear over the cacophonous din of the scrap yard. A few minutes later, inside the little room where you get paid, I get in a conversation with another customer—nice guy, white, filthy from hauling scrap, 300 pounds or so—while we're both waiting for the clerk to cash out our scrap. Overhearing me tell the clerk not to forget the buck she owes me for a salvaged auto battery, he offers some friendly advice: "I take mine to Steve's Battery over on 28th. They pay $1.50; it's close enough to my [scrounging] route." As I thank him and we talk a bit, he nods toward the owner, who's sitting behind the cash-out counter, and adds *sotto voce*, "That guy in the hat, you know, he's a millionaire."

Cash payment in hand, I walk back out to my truck to drive my remaining load of tin and short iron to the drive-over scale out in the yards, but notice that the Latino yard workers have decided just to load it all into a forklift and weigh it on the office scale—so I walk back to the office. Now I notice a third guy, also white, also big, maybe 250 pounds, no shirt, huge beer gut hanging low over filthy jeans, farmer's tan, disheveled hair, the sort of dangerous redneck son-of-a-bitch you learn to respect in Texas. Shit, I figure, today anyway, I'm Fort Worth's skinniest scrap hauler by a good 100 pounds. Stealing a glance at him a moment later, I catch him checking out the I.W.W. tattoo that my own dirty, sleeveless cowboy shirt leaves exposed; I decide against pursuing a discussion of radical history. Among independent scrap haulers, as should be obvious by now, clothes and tattoos and truck models don't really matter, anyway; it all comes down to the sweat, the metal, and the money.

Walking back to my truck with my second payment, rolling out of the yards, I pull in across the street to get my cash and receipts stowed away —at, no kidding, the "Jeff Stop," a little run-down convenience store with two old gas pumps. I'm double-checking today's scrap payment against my receipts—at $38.60, I'm just short of being a millionaire—when I notice an old white guy, skinny, full gray beard, gimme hat, T-shirt, dirty jeans, limping along behind an empty shopping cart on his way out of the yards, holding onto it as much as pushing it, his right leg stiff and splayed out to the side. Rolling back down North Main, I spot another scrounger, an old black guy resting in the shade of a building, his shopping cart full of scrap, bags of aluminum cans hanging over both sides. And as I pass him in my truck, so does a younger black guy on foot, who gives him an elbow down, wrist up, shoulder forward handshake and a smile, all while barely breaking stride. Like R.E.M. says: "Automatic for the people, baby."[4]

Twenty minutes later, pulling into an old South Side industrial area where the animal shelter sits, I spot a large rollaway, maybe ten feet deep by forty feet long, sitting for some reason out by itself away from the factory buildings. Parking the truck next to it, climbing the side, jumping in, I see that one end of the rollaway is full of various items, the other end clean and empty. Needing badly to take a piss (the empire of scrounge

Save-A-Lot—scrounging aluminum cans, Tampa, Florida, June 2004.

doesn't offer many bathroom facilities), I utilize the empty end first, then turn my attention to the materials at the other end. They appear to be the remains of a yard sale, various household objects and personal possessions, most tagged with little homemade price stickers, and all dumped in here together. Sorting through, I extract various books, a Johnson Century fishing reel, and eleven toy cars. One of the toy cars, and again I'm not kidding, is a green windup toy pickup truck with a load of scrap—Beverly Hillbillies–style barrels and crates—that bounces up and down as the pickup moves forward. (My initial excitement over this scrounger's totem cools considerably when I later find on its side, in small print, "Mfg. For McD Corp, China TCW Chine, Disney.") I plan to give these toy cars to one kid or another later on; but still, the majority of the many discarded toy cars and other toys in the rollaway I leave behind, happily imagining some South Side kid, out on the sort of wandering adventure I undertook as a kid, finding—"Hey, look at this!"—a Dumpster full of free toys.

On the way home, after dropping the bedding off at the shelter, I'm completing my tour of Fort Worth's points of the compass, now cutting back through the impoverished East Side, when I see an older black man at the side of the road, walking along, trash sack in hand. Pulling to a stop at a red light, looking over, I know what's coming. Yep—he stops, stoops, picks up an aluminum can, stomps it flat, and drops it in the sack.

Automatic for the people, baby.

17 July 2002

Matching Curtains

After spending the first part of the afternoon sorting and cataloging yesterday's finds, I'm off on a long looping scrounge ride, down behind that same University Boulevard strip mall, up the big hill past the posh homes above Colonial Country Club, then northeast through Forest Park to Mistletoe Heights—an aging beauty of a neighborhood that often offers some very nice trash. Circling back west on Mistletoe Drive as it arches out over the bluffs above the Trinity River, I see ahead on the right one of those big clean-out-the-house trash piles, and two people already digging

in it, their half-full grocery cart sitting in the middle of the street.

Cycling up, I offer greetings. The man—white guy, ruddy complexion, older, heavy, maybe a little drunk—responds with a grunt, though not a threatening or unfriendly one, as he keeps busy plowing through the pile. But the woman—older, white, gray hair parted in the middle—strikes up a conversation. "The man said we could look around in here, as long as we put it back and don't leave a mess," she tells me. Guessing she means the homeowner, I answer, "That seems like a fair enough trade," and she says, "Yeah." But the old guy says, again gruff but not unfriendly, "Yeah, but who's gonna put it back?" "Well, I'll pile it back up before I leave," I tell him—and I do, later on.

Meanwhile, the woman's already pulling clothes and coats out of the pile and handing them to me. She hands me a couple of vintage U.S. Navy wool pullover uniforms, and thanking her I tell her, "Well, sure, I'll take these if you don't want them—but you were here first." She assures me I should have them, and continues to pull clothes out of the pile for me. "Is there anything in particular you're looking for that I could help you find?" I ask her, looking to return the courtesy. "I'm trying to find a curtain to match the first one I found," she tells me. "I found the one, but can't find the other—it's sure to be in here." I ask the color—it's brown stripes—and we look for it, but without success.

About this time we notice a big, tinted-window Chevy Yukon SUV rolling up on us, a large, middle-aged white guy at the wheel, looking us over. "Honey, you gotta get your cart out of the middle of the street," the old lady tells her partner. "It's in that guy's way." But he doesn't, and the SUV eases past the cart and moves away down the street.

A few minutes later, the old guy is ready to take off. "Goddamit, honey, we're gonna be late for the hothouse," he tells her—at least I think he said hothouse. Is this maybe a term for the homeless shelter, or the evening meal there? Damned if I know, and I'm not going to ask him for clarification. "All right, I'm coming," she tells him, but she hangs back, still poking around in the big pile, showing me finds, talking, looking for the lost curtain. This little gendered couple's dance, I think to myself, could just as well be taking place at the mall—except this time she's shopping curbside, where everything's always on sale.

By now he's reclaimed his cart and headed off down the street, still admonishing her. She gives up her scrounging, begins to walk to catch up to him, and I stand up from my scrounging and tell her, "Good luck to you." "And to you, too," she says. A minute later, they've disappeared around the corner, though I can still hear him hurrying her.

I'm back to working the pile, and the Yukon rolls up on me again, the driver easing down the power window. "Anything good in there?" he asks me, friendly enough. "Well, I don't know, most of it seems to be broken," I tell him, looking to put off any well-heeled interlopers—but in fact I get the clear sense that he's less interested in checking on the trash than in checking on me.

A while later an older white woman in a nice jogging suit and running shoes strides up, seemingly out for her afternoon constitutional. I brace again for possible trouble—or momentary unpleasantness, anyway—but instead she smiles as she gets to me and says, "Just a beautiful day, isn't it?" Indeed it is—sunny, in the 70s, a great day for walking or scrounging—so I agree. "Just spectacular," I tell her.

Spectacular also, at least in my estimation, are the items I've scrounged from this big curbside trash pile. Loading my bicycle to go, my big backpack pulls heavily against my shoulders, and the bike's rear deck is stacked to well above seat level. Included in this load are the Navy uniforms my friend found for me, and some other old uniforms as well; a signed silver-plate bowl; a Cadillac insignia; old eight-track tapes and single "45" records; Camus's *The Stranger* and Hesse's *Siddhartha*; Cool Ray Polaroid clip-on sunglasses; a vintage 1970s woman's leather jacket; a Neiman Marcus black and white striped woman's sweater; fourteen colored plastic liquor bottle stoppers; and thirty-two shiny silver bullets, unspent.

Laboring the five miles or so home under this load, my aching legs remind me of a passage from Susan Strasser's book on the social history of trash and scrounging, a passage I've thought about more than once while hauling storm windows, window shutters, cast iron sash pulley weights, lead weights, ceiling fans, pole lamps, old manual typewriters, books, and big brass and copper fittings home by bicycle. "While peddlers and street scavengers occasionally collected iron," Strasser wrote of nineteenth-century scroungers, "they had to carry their recyclables on their own backs or those of their horses, so they tended to concentrate on more valuable metals: copper, brass, especially lead."[5]

Mostly, though, I'm thinking about the old lady who helped me scrounge that big trash pile, taking the trouble to find clothes for me when she had few enough for herself. I'm thinking about doting grandmothers, sorting through the sale racks at Macy's or the strip mall, pulling out clothes for the grandkids—grandmothers that might or might not be sympathetic to the plight of an old homeless woman, digging in the trash. I'm thinking about my own grandmother, a central Texas farm woman known on occasion to haul home cast-off clothes or stray animals herself, an old woman that's a long time gone and sometimes still around.

12 March 2002

Material Culture

Curtains, Camus, Cadillac insignia, Cool Ray clip-ons—pick a letter of the alphabet, and the empire of scrounge provides enough material for endless alliteration. The empire features discarded accumulations that cut across an astounding range of consumer choices and disposable lifestyle options, and trash piles into which collapse decades, even centuries, of cultural history—from books and antiques of the 1800s to, quite literally, yesterday's purchases. As a result, the empire offers, one trash pile and Dumpster at a time, a cornucopia of material culture. It's as though a thousand shopping malls, antique dealers, and hardware stores have all disgorged their contents at once, their collective spew settling here and there into little piles and pockets of lost material. If, as Jim Tullos and I were saying in the previous chapter, the empire offers all the fun of stealing with none of the jail time, it offers all the benefits of shopping with none of the bills. Of course, you may have to dig a bit to get the goods; sorting through trash piles, squeezing and pinching plastic garbage bags, climbing down amid a rollaway's rubble are part of the process. Then again, as I found time and again, this archeology of investigation makes each material discovery all the more appreciated. Once, for example, I was pleased to scrounge two new stainless steel bowls, two Phillips-head screwdrivers, a pair of locking pliers, a pair of wire cutters, an adjustable wrench, and a Nokia cell phone—all from underneath a full black plastic garbage bag stuffed inside a Styrofoam cooler buried at the bottom of a big curbside trash pile.

Many times this process unearthed goods that actually did seem like so much buried treasure. Those seventeen cents I passed on to the hobo I met, for example, were but a bit of the lost cash I recovered. Many days produced a similarly small accumulation of nickels, dimes, and pennies—eleven cents one day, twenty-three cents the next —but many days produced more. Once, working my way through a curbside pile of boxes, I had already found copper, aluminum, a silver chafing dish, a children's book, a candy jar lid, doorknobs, screws, tools, and other items when I discovered, in the bottom-most box, thirteen U.S. pennies, nine five-dollar Liberian bills, and two thousand Cedis in Ghanaian currency. On one ride I found in the gutter a ten-dollar bill, neatly folded in half, and later, in monetary counterpoint, a penny. Another afternoon of scrounging produced, in sequence down one street and then the next, $6.02, with a first penny in the gutter followed by a dollar bill next to a trash pile, a five-dollar bill in another gutter, and, later, one last penny in the middle of the street. And one time, busting up an old scrounged Kirby vacuum cleaner for its salvageable die cast metal, 1977 and 1986 nickels fell out on the floor of my shed, swept up long ago and forgotten.

Then there's the loot. The many cheap plastic watches found while scrounging I keep out in my shed, in a scrounged metal box; the better watches I wear, or some—an old Elgin, a Benrus, many Timexes, a Wadsworth, even an antique child's silver Snow White watch—I keep in my office, in a round black Barney's New York box that I, of course, also scrounged. Much of the found jewelry I've given away—but still, gold chains and Mardi Gras beads hang from my bookshelves; various scrounged containers hold broaches, pins, and bracelets; and I wear one particularly nice silver bracelet that I found buried deep in a trash pile. A little Waterford cut glass clock, perfect save for one tiny chip, I found and passed on to my father. Along with countless pieces of funky old stainless steel flatware, I've scrounged various old silver and silver-plated knives, forks, spoons, and serving utensils, which I keep in a scrounged hardwood silver service box. An antique silver baby's cup, an antique silver-plated serving dish, silver saddle buckles, a solid silver candleholder— all these and more have emerged from trash piles and Dumpsters.

One sweltering August day I found an old, beautifully stylized, chromed brass showerhead, perhaps three times the size and weight of the showerhead then in my bathroom. Taking this as an omen of a cleaner and cooler future, I brought it home, replaced my existing showerhead with it, and enjoyed a fire-hose shower of fresh water at the end of a long day's scrounging. (Soon enough my environmental conscience got the better of me, and I replaced this old showerhead with a newer, European-style controlled-flow showerhead I had also scrounged.) Common castoffs from home remodeling jobs, brass, copper, and chrome plumbing parts are everywhere in the empire, a shiny loot that I enjoy salvaging as much as silverware and candlesticks. Most I break down and sell for scrap, given brass and copper's relative value as scrap metal. A few I've used in home repairs or passed on to friends. But many, I must admit, I've kept—especially those heavy brass and chrome faucets from the 1930s and 1940s, and single-spout faucets that date from even earlier times. On yet another hot

Texas summer day, for example, I salvaged a heavy old chromed faucet with four-prong handles, and an old chromed built-in soap dispenser, from the Dumpster of a school that was being remodeled. Another time the rollaway outside a downtown office building yielded a lovely 1940s faucet made of hammered brass. As a result of all this, old faucets, handles, showerheads, and spigots dangle from the walls and rafters of my shed like so much plumber's jewelry.

An especially touching aspect of the empire's material culture are the innumerable discarded toys. Marking, if not childhood lost, at least the rapid maturation and changing tastes of children, toys by the hundreds and thousands appear in trash piles and Dumpsters—boxes full of toys, garbage bags full, time and again. The military action figures and toy guns I sort out, and leave behind in the trash; the remainder I generally try to haul home as room allows. Along with giving them to friends' kids, I enjoy giving away these toys at garage sales—a gentle subversion, perhaps, of the consumer culture that produces both the toys and kids' desires to buy each new iteration of them.

Sometimes, though, discarded toys suggest a story of longer duration. Sorting through a big curbside trash pile one February afternoon, digging amid old canning jars and bedding, pulling out books and tools and an antique DyanShine shoe polish bottle shaped like an elongated bee hive, I found also a trove of old toys. I would say they took me back to my childhood— but they were so old they predated even that. Here were antique marbles, little wooden checkers in an old child's sock, little metal ships and airplanes, an antique toy watch, wooden ink stamps, faded wooden building blocks, a cast iron squirrel perched on its hind legs, a single old "Red Ryder" black and red child's Western-style riding glove, a little wooden bowling pin, a wooden school ruler, a plastic Warren Spahn coin, and an old pencil, sharpened half the way down, with the lettering on its side now reading "oy's milk . . . It's Sure-Good."

At times I found the empire to be so saturated with material culture that I could hardly make my way through it. Gearing up for a long scrounging ride one December day, I couldn't help but stop after getting only four or five blocks from my house. Here was a nice home, a new Range Rover SUV in the driveway—and on the curb an expensive set of golf irons, a high-end stereo receiver and CD changer with name-brand speakers, and a big box of very plush bath towels, each freshly laundered and neatly folded. So, back to my house for the truck to haul all this home, and now out again on the bike. This time I go eight blocks. Stopping to investigate a huge curbside trash pile, I find various tools and parts —and an astounding collection of old promotional items. Still held neatly in their original boxes and plastic sleeves are hundreds of pens, pencils, plastic cup coasters, collapsible cups, pocket screwdrivers, key chains, emery boards, oversized plastic paper clips, golf tees, tape measures, and rulers, each featuring a promotional slogan. There's a little giveaway plastic cheese grater with "For 'Grater' Savings, 1st United Bank and Trust, Sales Builder Sample L-75" printed on it, crooked pens with "We Bend To Please" and "Get Me To My Chiropractor Quick," a can and bottle opener with an "Opening the Way Since 1901" slogan. And there's a stack of old business cards collected from small-scale retailers and manufacturers, many with personal names penciled on the back—contacts for selling these "sales builders." Like the boxes full of discarded toys, here is yet another collection of clues into the historical dynamics of marketing and consumption.

Back to my house once again to get the truck. When I return a few minutes later, a guy is pulling up in his own pickup truck, there to do some remodeling work on the house. As he sees me walking to my truck with a box of scrounged items, he's apparently afraid that this is all I intend to take. Encouraging me to reconsider, he says, "Hey, there's plenty more here."

Indeed there is.

Ginny's Shoes and Socks

Cycling west through Arlington Heights, scanning the side streets for garbage piles as usual, I spot a big one—and a promising one, too, since it appears from a distance to consist of boxes and loose items in among the black garbage bags. Gliding up, I jump off the bike quickly—it looks even better up close. In no time I pull from the pile an old adding machine in pristine condition, a 1930s or 1940s record player, and an old wood-framed wind-up clock. Soon enough a middle-aged fellow eases up on foot. He's dressed in disheveled clothes and holds an unlit pipe between his teeth. "I saw the pile from over on Camp Bowie," he tells me, referring to a major thoroughfare a block away, and so he decided to come over to investigate. While he rummages around and we talk sporadically, I keep at my scrounging. He's welcome, of course—but as per the scrounger's code, I don't intend to be run off the pile by a late arrival.

I can't fit the old record player on my bike, and so I leave it behind. It's gone when I return a while later—maybe the guy with the pipe walked it away. I do manage to strap the old adding machine and the clock onto my bike's rear deck, and utilizing my front basket and my backpack, manage to carry away a few more items as well. Among these are a lovely chrysanthemum-pattern hammered aluminum tray; a pair of heavy-duty scissors ("Made in Germany") in a leather case; an antique salt and pepper set; a bag of antique buttons; some ornate switch-plate covers; a little scrolled brass ashtray in the shape of a shoe ("Made in India"); old wooden shoe trees; old ink pens; a little red metal tray; an old silver-plate spoon from The Wooten Hotel; an old chromed flashlight ("Marbo Lite British C.C.Hongkong") containing two Ray-O-Vac batteries, their price, "20 c [cents]" still marked on their ends; lengths of copper tubing and wire; and an old brass frame holding a hand-

Scrounging's material culture, complete with wind chimes, New York City, October 2004.

colored photo of a young woman, signed "To my one and only, With all my love, Carolyn."

In my left hand I carry what I suspect is the most valuable find of all, dug out from the depths of the trash pile: a cardboard box the size of a squared shoe box, full of little unopened pink and white boxes, each labeled "Ginny's Shoes & Socks, Vogue Dolls, Inc.," and each, indeed, holding a pair of doll shoes and socks. I know enough about design history to know that the color and printing on these little boxes dates them to the mid-twentieth century; I don't know a thing about doll collecting, except that its enthusiasts are known to be . . . enthusiastic. Besides, there are some fifty little boxes in this bigger box, each with a different color combination of shoes and socks. And there's a bonus: a few little jewelry boxes each containing "Ginny's Locket," a delicate gold heart imprinted with "Ginny" on the end of a tiny gold chain.

When the next day I bicycle with my find over to a local doll shop—maybe a mile or two from the trash pile—I walk out with, well, enough cash to keep me going for a while. In fact, on return trips to the trash pile, finding newly discarded items added to it over the next few days, I figure it's well worth it to look *very* carefully for any more of Ginny's little shoes and socks. I never find any, but I do haul home bundles of yellow and brown bathroom tiles from the 1950s, a matted watercolor in a painted frame, a decorative bell on a satin rope, a couple of funky, looping stainless steel towel racks (now installed in my kitchen),

and a 1950s pillbox fur hat that I sell to a local antique dealer for ten dollars—not doll-shoe money, mind you, but not bad.

26 January 2002

Empire of Shoes

Other shoes extant in the empire of scrounge, I found, are a good bit smaller in monetary value than Ginny's, but a good bit bigger in size—and so a good deal more directly functional.

Biking one day along a little road that parallels the Trinity River and its levee system, near a spot where a riverside hike-and-bike path swings over to intersect the road, I spot a single athletic shoe off in the weeds. I'll admit, I think about stopping to snag it—but then I think about the long-term accumulative consequences of starting to collect single shoes in hopes of someday finding their mates, and I ride on. A hundred yards later, though, around a little bend in the road, there sits the mate. Circling back, gathering up both shoes, pulling over into the shade of a big tree, I discover that the shoes are fairly new men's multipurpose outdoor "cross trekkers," and about my size, so I try them on. Great fit; very comfortable. Into my scrounge bag go my holy Chuck Taylors, onto my feet go the cross trekkers, and away I ride. Baby's got new shoes.

If not already offended to the point of abandoning the narrative, the delicate reader may now wish to turn away, for as an ethnographer I must also report with some precision the stink that accompanies these shoes. I don't notice it while still out and about; but arriving back home I realize that the shoes, having been warmed on my feet by a few hours of riding and walking, now, well, stink. More precisely, it's the right shoe that stinks; the left is fine. And joking similes aside, it's not that this guy's right foot stunk like a skunk; it's that his right shoe really has been "skunked." I'm sure of this; I recognize the smell from spending summers as a kid in the Texas countryside, and from more than once experiencing the sort of middle-of-the-road olfactory carnage put to music by Loudon Wainwright.[6]

For some reason this stink bothers me less than whatever residual foot odor might linger in a pair of found shoes; it seems somehow a less pathological, more natural source of shoe stink. I mean, hell, I've had my dogs skunked before while out hiking—and after six weeks or so, the odor sort of grows on you. Besides, a little deodorizing baking soda, a night outside hanging from the screen door, and the shoe's better; the next day better still.

While waiting out this cleansing process, I can't help but imagine the one that preceded it. Having found the shoes near a section of the path that skirts a long stretch of fairly wild river bank, with gullies and undergrowth and big trees, I imagine that a jogger or walker comes upon a skunk, or maybe the skunk comes upon him. He kicks at it with his right foot to shoo (or is that shoe?) it away, and gets his right Cross Trekker skunked for the trouble. Sickened, disgusted, he takes it off,

throws it away, all while hobbling away from the skunk as quickly as he can. And then he realizes, as I did upon finding the first shoe, that in the long run the left shoe isn't much good without the right, and discards it too. A few weeks of scorching Texas summer sun, maybe a purifying rain storm or two later, and I find a nice pair of shoes that, if not pristine, are by now certainly less painfully revolting—and certainly more functional for scrounging than what I was wearing when I found them.

To the delicate reader still abiding my indiscriminate scrounging, I must make one final admission: these aren't the only shoes I've found and then worn during these months of scrounging. There were the running shoes rescued from an alley trash can, the black suede loafers pulled from a trash bag, the fancy bicycling shoes sitting atop a curbside trash pile—though in none of these cases, I'm happy to report, did my subsequent wearing of these shoes resurrect any foul odors. No, really.

On the remainder of the ride during which I acquired the skunk shoes, and on a later walk in my new cross-stinkers, I also scrounge aluminum cans, copper wire, seven feet of aluminum carpet tack stripping, lead weights, a steel bolt, pieces of tin scrap, a large brass-coated bolt, some old wooden fan blades, a pair of needle-nosed pliers, a large trowel, and a quarter-inch socket. I find two beach towels, a pottery vase, and a small plastic dinosaur stencil. I pick up six pennies where a commercial driveway intersects a busy street. I spot a hemostat, its burned, burnished tips suggesting . . . well, we all know what they suggest, and so when I get home I scrub off the burnish just in case some badly misguided multijurisdictional drug interdiction task force ever launches a raid against my junk shed.

And in a curbside trash pile I find a pair of Justin lace-up Western boots, women's 8D, lightly worn, now carefully resituated in the boot box from which they came . . . and thrown away.

27 July 2002

You Know, Like the Ones in My Kitchen?

Out on a long lovely unplanned urban loop, I ride for an hour and a half through the summer heat, past the Cultural District museums, down through a little pocket of light manufacturing, across the 7th Street viaduct and the Trinity River, and up the long hill into the western edge of downtown—then south out of downtown to the hospital district, and on through the grand old Fairmount, Ryan Place, and Berkeley neighborhoods that follow. I'm digging this shambling tour of the city, but not finding much: only an extra-large nut (for an extra-large bolt, that is), a locking screw assembly, a dime, a penny, a heavy aluminum canister, and two lengths of copper wire.

Cutting down through the beautiful old Berkeley homes and onto a manicured ridge-top street above Forest Park and the Trinity River, I spot a pile of scrap and appliances. Out of place in this aesthetically precise neighborhood, dumped no doubt illicitly on a plot of open park land across the street from the upscale homes, it immediately draws my attention. Pulling up, it looks to be the illegal last stage of some high-end home remodeling job—after all, a remodeler's costs are lower if they're not inflated by a long drive to the landfill and a dumping fee upon arrival.

Dismounting my bike, I first pull a large knob from an upmarket dishwasher, a KitchenAid—the knob's shape and black-and-silver, circle-on-circle design suggest a miniature 1950s spaceship when I set it flat on the ground. Next I extricate from the pile a small piece of aluminum window screen frame; surprised that I don't find the remainder of the screen, I guess that maybe another scrounger has already been by for the aluminum and missed this one bit.

Then, flipping over a pile of wood, I see the knobs. The wood pile, I now realize, is made up of cabinet doors and broken cabinet sides—further confirmation of a remodeling job dumpsite. Attached to doors stamped "Made in West Germany" on their inside panels are heavy, deep-chromed door pulls, a wavy design surrounding a little hole in the middle, a real pleasure to see and hold, and all of them secured to the doors by a sturdy double-screw arrangement. Damn, these pulls are beautiful, remarkably pleasing to the touch, and so I take the time to remove all twelve—that is, to back out twenty-four long screws with the screwdriver blade on my old Swiss Army knife while dripping sweat in the sun and the heat and the humidity, blissed out on all this found beauty and sensual intensity.

Bicycling away, my fanny pack is heavy with the pulls—I most always put items of small size and large value in my fanny pack, or in a buttoned pants or shirt pocket, while everything else goes in the front handlebar basket or the big scrounge bag strapped to the rear deck. A block or two away I notice a house for sale. The fliers, the ones rolled in a clear plastic tube attached to the for-sale sign, note that the home sits on "the most exclusive street" in the area, and that at $450,000, the home is "priced for quick sale . . . ($75,000 under appraised value)." Indeed, for that kind of money, the house does feature 3,752 square feet, a greenhouse, Jacuzzi, courtyard with fifteen-foot cascading waterfall and nine-foot stone fence, and a kitchen with stainless steel appliances and granite countertops.

Yeah, but does the kitchen have those cool, wavy, chromed West German pulls on the cabinets? You know, like the ones now in my kitchen?

30 July 2002

And I Do Mean Elected

Rolling west through the Arlington Heights neighborhood, I come across a site I've noticed a couple of times before, and even stopped to check out once. It's a large lot on its way to being cleared by the political economy of the growing class divide. It's not just affordable housing that's being torn down; in this case it's largely unaffordable high-end housing that's being razed, to make way for the even less affordable housing of the nouveaux riches. I didn't find much when I stopped to check the site earlier, but today I can see that more housing has been razed. There's a big, new pile of broken wood, pipes, old photos, and other unsaved human detritus, all pushed together by the bulldozer which now sits off to the side of the lot. I walk my bike up over the broken, bulldozed ground, set it against a large chunk of broken concrete, and get to work.

I'm beginning to find a nice range of copper pipe and brass fittings; in fact, I'm at work twisting and cutting away some copper pipe from what appears to be a very old, now mangled central-water-heating unit, when I see a guy, white, maybe fifty-five, gray hair, baseball cap, tape measure on belt, walking up to the pile a few feet from me.

"Finding anything valuable?" he says, friendly enough.

"Nah, not really," I say, employing my usual mode of downplaying my presence and my finds— you don't want to provide too much of an answer until you figure out more about the question. "Just looking for brass and copper, really. Finding just a little copper."

And I figure it is indeed best to find out more about the question, since I'm after all on a private lot, though I haven't seen any "No Trespassing" signs. "You tearing this down?" I say, guessing that he's the worksite foreman come to check on me.

"Nah, I'm working on this house across the street. Thought I'd see if I could find a board to use in this pile." For what he doesn't say.

"Well, there might be a few not broken," I tell him, friendly but not hopeful, given the bulldozer's indiscriminate destruction.

So, he circles the pile looking for a board, and I keep at my work—and then he says, from the other side of the pile, "Here you go, here's some," and tosses me a length of copper pipe.

"So, you're building a house in the neighborhood?" I ask, after thanking him.

"Nah, my youngest son just bought this house. I'm a contractor, I build houses, so I got elected to do some work on it." This, I'm thinking to myself, explains his facility at spotting copper pipe in the pile of debris—he works with it all the time, and understands functional relationships and likely metallic juxtapositions as well.

"And I do mean elected," he adds, after just the right pause.

"Didn't have much choice in the matter, huh?"
"Right."

I tell him about working construction myself a long time ago, and the way my pickup truck keeps getting elected—and I do mean elected—for friends' moving jobs; he keeps finding chunks of copper and brass and tossing them my way. I appreciate his skill, his help, and his friendly sense of material community. He also tells me that during this past week two different guys were out working the bulldozed ground with metal detectors, covering every foot, he ways. "One of

'em was out there all afternoon. And he told me he found just one penny, and it wasn't even wheatstraw."

Probably so, I figure, and I tell him I generally trust my eyes to find stuff more than I do machines. Then again, that metal detector guy could've been in downplay mode, too.

After a while, he finds the board he needs—about five good feet, I'd guess, before it splinters into bulldozed disutility. And as he's walking away, almost to the edge of the lot, after I've thanked him again and wished him good luck, he turns back, says "here you go," and tosses me, in a soft underhanded arch, just the motion of a slow pitch softball pitcher, a nice brass sprinkler fixture.

25 August 2002

Gettin' Rid of That Old Bike?

I'm walking on a cold, windy, unpleasant March day when I see a couple of guys busily adding material to an already large pile of curbside discards. Easing over, I ask one of them, "Mind if I look through this to see what I might want?" "Sure, God bless you, go right ahead," he tells me, adding that he's here cleaning out the house that his girlfriend has just sold. I quickly realize that this trash pile merits some serious scrounging attention; in fact, before the afternoon is over, I will have taken a first load of scrounged items home by foot, then four more by bicycle, with items lashed to my rear deck, stuffed in my

Scrounger's cart with bedding and bicycles, New York City, October 2004.

backpack, and held in one hand while I ride with the other.

Others notice the potential of the pile as well. Returning from walking the first load home, I lean my bicycle up against the pile and get to work digging and sorting. After a little while a guy crosses over from the other side of the street.

"Gettin' rid of that old bike?" he asks me, assuming both I and the bike belong to the trash pile.

"Hell no, that's my ride!" I answer, laughing.

"Well, I broke the sprocket on mine, so I was looking to replace it."

Later, a rugged-looking guy with a scraggly beard slows to a stop in an old pickup.

"Anything good?" he asks out his driver's side window.

"Depends on what you're lookin' for," I tell him.

Getting out, he begins to sort through the other end of the pile. And when I get back from my next bicycle trip ferrying items home, he's still there—and the bed of his pickup is almost filled with scrounged materials.

Still, there's enough for everyone, and for everyone's material needs—including, for example, the need to stay warm. Along with finding women's sweaters, old buttons, and a new portable electric heater in the pile, I discover a Samsonite suitcase stuffed with six pairs of wool and wool/polyester military pants, all freshly dry-cleaned, and a large military coat. A blue pair with a red stripe fit me perfectly, and so I wear them when I go out that cold evening; the rest of the clothes I give to the homeless shelter. Any gardening needs I may develop with spring's arrival are met by a pair of antique pruning shears, a large pruning tool, a large pair of hedge clippers, a pair of grass clippers, a box of plastic lawn edging, and a pole-style garden sprinkler. A package of sheet metal screws, various bolts, numerous hook-and-eye assemblies, various anchor screws, assorted boxes of nails and wood screws, new hinges, a dimmer switch, shelf mounts, six door knobs, a doorbell, four light fixtures and globes, three utility knives, two faucet/spout sets, a lavatory stopper, a paint brush, a steel brush, a caulk gun, chain-link fence hardware, various handles and knobs (some new in their boxes), plastic and metal switch plates, new electrical outlets, door and door mounting hardware, two cans of spray paint, a paint scraper, two rolls of joint tape, a half roll of masking tape, and two boxes of fuses certainly go a long way toward addressing any home repair needs I may have. For my kitchen, there are the two metal "Delta Air Lines" spoons, the vegetable steamer, the five glass plates, the silver-plated serving tray, and of course the old "Speedo Super Juicer," circa 1940 or so, a heavy wall-mounted model with its own juice receptacle and pour spout. For reading and writing there are various books, ten copies of *Mother Earth News*, pens and pencils—and an eyeglasses repair kit; for recreation, a Sears plastic tackle box full of fishing lures and fishing gear, some of it new in the box. Should I wish to abandon my walking and bicycling, the pile offers a car windshield-wiper blade (new in its box, $3.99 retail price) and a windshield ice scraper and brush combo. And should I need to buy anything beyond all this, the pile provides more than the nickel I find there. It provides a way to earn some cash: aluminum window-screen frames and extruded aluminum parts, copper wire and copper scrap, and brass fixtures and parts; a storage bin in which to keep such scrap until it can be cashed in; and a screwdriver, a nine-millimeter wrench, and an insulated hacksaw for breaking it all down.

Amid all this, I discover also a half-empty box of bullets, and a couple of old beer bottle openers, one stamped "Falstaff." I'm not sure I want to consider what material need these serve, especially in combination—but I've certainly found and considered such things before.

02 March 2002

The Drinking Life

One might say that the empire of scrounge is awash in booze. Time and again I've pulled from Dumpsters, trash piles, and garbage bags bottles of liquor and liqueur, some full, some half-full; bottles of champagne, generally of the cheaper sort; and countless little "shooters" (50 ml bottles) of liquor and liqueur. For whatever reason—drunken forgetfulness, tanked-up satiation, police intervention—unopened cans and bottles of beer also appear regularly in and around city Dumpsters. Applying some sort of drinker's street logic I haven't quite figured out, I generally haul the liquor and liqueur home, but leave the beer behind for others. In fact, I often line up a found beer or two on the edge of the Dumpster, bartender style, a little offering of conviviality to the city's other scroungers.

So, as I say, the empire is awash in booze—but more to the point, it's awash in the culture of booze, and its aftermath. Here I don't refer to puke-filled Dumpsters or back-alley puddles of piss, though I've found some of both. Instead, I mean the day-to-day material culture of drinking, and the way that it accumulates. Unsurprisingly, Dumpsters behind the city's bars overflow with beer and wine bottles, sometimes placed back in their cardboard cases and stacked in the Dumpster, more often emptied into the Dumpster helter-skelter from some smaller in-house receptacle. Perhaps more surprising—and certainly more worrisome—is the phenomenal ac-cumulation of beer cans and beer bottles along major streets and highways. In fact, I'd been productively scrounging aluminum cans for a while when my success began to worry me: How can there be *this many* beer cans along this short stretch of road? How is it that, if all else fails, I know I can always pick up plenty of crushed beer cans in the street, and empties along the roadside? This, it seemed to me, was an uncanny, unobtrusive measure of alcohol consumption *in transit,* well beyond the indicators offered by drunk-driving arrests or convictions. On occasional trips out of the city, I even turned this into a sort of test, or maybe contest, seeking out the smallest, isolated dirt back road to see if . . . yep, beer cans all along the bar ditch, the high grass lousy with them too. Back in the city, as I'll describe in Chapter Five, a program that paid scroungers a few cents for each discarded beer bottle or malt liquor bottle they picked up from the streets resulted in such a steady stream of bottle-filled shopping carts rolling into the reclamation center that funding for the program was quickly exhausted.

The residues of private boozing also find their way out into the empire. As already seen, my scrounging uncovered liquor bottle stoppers, stolen hotel corkscrews, and old beer bottle openers. Scrounged wine and champagne I stored at home in a scrounged black metal and wicker wine rack. And in less than a week in July 2002, I hauled home a whole history of drinking. Out riding north of my neighborhood on the 21st, I discovered a pile of full black garbage bags on a homeowner's curb. Massaging the side of one bag to get a sense of its contents, I felt what seemed to be some sort of curved textured metal and, pulling a small whole in it, discovered a tall, hammered silver flask, "Tin-Lined, 12 oz, Made in West Germany" stamped on the bottom. On the 23rd I pulled from another big curbside trash pile an old silver-capped glass flask, its gray rubberized cover featuring a Scotty dog wearing an apron and serving a drink, with the logo "One Scotch After Another." A ride on the 26th produced curtain rods and hardware, lead weights, copper and brass scrap, a metal hairclip, five shelf brackets, wood molding, an aluminum window, five aluminum window-screen frames, numerous aluminum cans (almost all of them beer cans), and a brightly painted metal "OE800" sign—an advertisement for Olde English 800 malt liquor.

The following February, I found, among a big pile of old toys, old magazines, fishing gear, and tools, eight old promotional bottle openers. One reminded me of the Falstaff opener I'd found a year before, with its logo of "Falstaff—America's Premium Quality Beer." Another featured "Coors—America's Fine Light Beer"; a third urged its recipient to "make the *most* of nature's *best*" by drinking Lone Star Beer. In fact, as a result of my scrounging, there today hangs from a hook in my shed a length of recycled wire, on which are strung some forty-five old bottle and can openers, bottle stoppers, stirring spoons, wine corkscrews, and the like. A few are the generic sort that might have been bought at a grocery or discount store; but the majority are promotions for America's long-standing culture of booze. Hanging from that wire are Beam and Four Roses bottle openers/bottle stoppers, a Lord Calvert Blended Whiskey bottle opener, a Gordon's Gin bottle opener, two combination stirring spoons/bottle openers courtesy of Majestic Liquor Stores, a Keglined bottle and can opener, four Falstaff openers, three "Drink Jax Beer" openers and a Jax Beer cigar cutter, three Coors openers, two from Grand Prize beer, three from Country Club Malt Liquor, and others from beers like Lone Star, Hamms, and Pearl.

These openers' straightforward injunctions to join the drinking life—"make the most of nature's best" with Lone Star, "Drink Jax Beer"—seemed distinctly old-fashioned, though, in light of a later find and its ambiguous call to booze. The more recently manufactured "Bar Master Electronic Drink Calculator/Index" was still new in its box when I pulled it from yet another curbside trash pile. Its package offered all sorts of fun in learning to mix over five hundred drinks for "most major holidays and party occasions," and in mastering "mixing terms and bartender slang"; it even boasted that the Drink Calculator could "calculate blood/alcohol level based on the weight of the drinker, number of drinks consumed and time since last drink." But then, in smaller print, the package got serious: "If you have been drinking, please use a designated driver. Be safe. Blood/Alcohol calculations are for entertainment purposes only and are not to be used to determine fitness to drive or to conduct any other functions or activities." And at the bottom, in large print—all capitals, in fact—it got downright injunctive.

"DON'T DRINK AND DRIVE!" said the Bar Master. "DO NOT DRINK UNLESS YOU ARE OF LEGAL AGE!"

Law and Crime, Curbside

Roadside beer cans and Bar Masters aren't the only residues of likely illegal intoxication left behind in the empire of scrounge, though the detritus of drinking is certainly the most common. As we've already seen, hemostats burnished by their use as marijuana joint holders are also to be found. So are the sorts of improvised beer can marijuana pipes—the can's side bent concave and perforated with little holes so as to hold and light the dope, the smoke drawn through the can's opened top—that I found more than once while scrounging roadside aluminum cans. Roadside gutters, I discovered, also occasionally offer up the used plastic hypodermic needle, as does the occasional Dumpster—certainly a reason for some caution in digging through a darkened Dumpster full of unsorted trash. Less threateningly, a garbage bag full of various old discards once yielded two small boxes of antique hypodermic needles. Each elegantly decorated red box contained "One Dozen Firth-Brearley Stainless Steel Hypodermic Needles," trademarked "VIM," and manufactured by "MacGregor Instrument, Needham, Mass, USA."

Each box also held a small paper envelope containing "Non-Corrosive Needle Wires" for use with the needles. So beautiful are the little red boxes, so lovely their antique black and gold lettering, so precisely crafted the stainless steel needles and wires, that I keep them on a shelf near my desk. For some reason the used plastic needles in the gutter don't hold quite the same aesthetic appeal, and so I leave them, untouched but not unnoticed.

Discarded bullets, on the other hand, I take out of circulation by bringing home and storing in my shed. The bullets noted above—the thirty-two bullets in one trash pile, the half box in another—are but a few among many. Confirming a bad stereotype about the United States, maybe a worse stereotype about Texas, I find bullets everywhere as I scrounge—in the streets, in the gutters, in parking lots, in Dumpsters and rollaways. I have jars in my shed filled with various bullets found one at a time on rides and walks. Stored away there also are full boxes of bullets scavenged from trash piles, boxes of self-load bullets pulled from a rollaway in front of a house under renovation, and various scrounged gun accoutrement like shotgun carrying cases, gun barrel cleaning rods, and bore brushes. And that's not to mention the bullet holes—like the one cleanly penetrating a classic 1930s hood ornament that I pried off an abandoned car in rural Wyoming a few years back.

More recently—on a scrounging ride in September 2004—I was exploring a Dumpster in the parking lot of a neighborhood elementary school, where a couple of days before I had found expensive socket wrenches, socket sets, and other tools, tossed in among yard trimmings and other trash. This time I found only one new addition: a 12 x 12 inch square white cardboard box. Pulling it from the Dumpster, opening it, I found hundreds of collectible sports trading cards, most in protective plastic cases, and each assigned a value by a little affixed price tag. Prices ranged from ten cents to 125 dollars, and the cards themselves ranged across the history and variety of U.S. professional sports, from the 1962 Mets to Michael Jordan. The box also held a sports-style man's watch, apparently needing only a battery to run. And the white box held a smaller box as well—a box of fifty new .45 caliber steel-case bullets, manufactured in Russia and imported to the United States by Wolf Performance Ammunition, the brand name made manifest by the image of a red-eyed wolf glowering from the front of the box.[7]

Across the street from the school, I noticed, was a sign featuring a different sort of eye—a large, wide-open, watchful human eye—proclaiming "Crime Watch in Progress, To Report Crime or Suspicious Activity Call 817 335 4222." On the chain-link gate granting access to the school grounds, a larger sign warned "Tarrant County Crime Stoppers, 469-TIPS, Report Crime 871-6010, FWISD Safe Campus Program." On the school's front door, and on either side of it, paper signs noted that "All persons entering the building including FWISD personnel must sign in at office."

Plenty of warnings, I thought, and plenty of telephone numbers. But who's watching the Dumpster?

Just Junk, Paper Junk

A productive day of scrounging by bicycle and foot has yielded a large haul of scrap metal: aluminum cans, aluminum, brass, and copper wire and fittings. I've also picked up ten cents, three knobs, a cup hook, a wall mounting brace, a circular towel hanger, switch plates, a small electric motor—and a Gloria Vanderbilt button. I've hauled home wooden stakes that held campaign signs in last week's primary elections, and that will now help hold up my garden. And I've salvaged eleven discarded books, including *Texas: The Lone Star State*, *The American Heritage Cookbook* (1964), *The Horizon Cookbook* (1968), Gladys Taber's *Stillmeadow Cook Book* (1965), *The New Lexicon Dictionary of Basic Words* ($59.95 retail when published in 1989), a *Holy Bible, Family Heritage Edition*, and a *Webster's Seventh New Collegiate Dictionary*, published in 1963, and inscribed "Congratulations on your graduation from high school. We hope this book will be useful to you in the years to come. Our best wishes are with you. Ann & Bill, July 1964."

The day's first stop, though, hadn't suggested such a good haul. Rolling up on two big cardboard boxes on a homeowner's curb, looking through them, I'd found nothing but the cheap tricks of the corporate hustle. In the boxes were packet after packet of information for "sports drink" promotions, including detailed promotional agreements, advertising fliers, posters, and contest forms. While I was bent over studying these little windows into the service economy's soul, these newer versions of the "sales builder" promotions I'd found in that other trash pile, I heard a voice. It was the guy from inside the house, standing in his half-open front door, a grumpy middle-aged scowl on his face, saying something I couldn't quite make out through the heavy south wind blowing his words back at him. Then I picked up a bit of it. ". . . just junk. There's nothing in those boxes," he yelled, "just junk, paper junk."

I agreed, but not much liking his line of work nor his tone of voice, decided not to respond. Instead I kept on with my bent-over reading, recalling as I did Lars Eighner's account of a similar episode: "I have had only one apartment resident object to my going through the [trash]. In that case it turned out the resident was a university athlete who was taking bets and who was afraid I would turn up his wager slips."[8]

Then the guy in the doorway added, tersely, louder, "I'd appreciate it if you'd get out of there." So I stood up slowly, gave him a big smile, a thumbs-up, and a loudly enthusiastic "OK." He paused, then answered with a half-hearted thumbs-up of his own as he turned to retreat into the house, closing the door behind him, apparently no more sure than I whether mine was a gesture of acquiescence or contempt.

14 March 2002

Illegal Paint

Bicycling through the upscale Forest Park neighborhood—only a few blocks and a few days removed from the illegally dumped materials that yielded those nice kitchen knobs—I notice an oversized, rolling trash can sitting behind yet another house that's for sale. "For Sale" and "For Rent" signs often harbinger useful items discarded in movings in and out, and the black garbage bags stuffed in this big can look by their stretch marks to contain something more than kitchen or yard refuse, so I stop to take a look.

Tearing open the bags I first find can after can of paint, paint thinner, and varnish, many unopened and unused. This, I figure, offers me some protection and buys me some time. Whenever the sheer amount of curbside scrap in any one spot forces me to linger for a while, and especially when that spot rests in an upscale neighborhood, I take time while sorting through the scrap to formulate a line of talk, a bicycle route out, or whatever other strategy might help extricate me from an offended homeowner unaccustomed to uninvited guests. This one is easy: Should anyone come out of the house and threaten to call the authorities, I'll encourage them to do so, since this big, now-exposed collection of curbside chemicals clearly violates widely publicized city ordinances regarding the proper disposal of dangerous waste.

As it turns out, though, no one bothers me, and so over the next thirty minutes or so of careful picking and sorting, I do indeed find some useful items, including screwdrivers, wrenches, paint brushes, shop knives, antique tongs, candles, knobs and handles new in their packages, clamps, braces, and nails. All of this and more I strap to my bike and haul away. The cans of illegal paint and varnish I leave behind, just as I have countless others I've found time and again, surreptitiously buried under trash piles or stuffed into Dumpsters.

06 August 2002

Then the Guy Comes Out of the Old Garage Carrying a Rifle

Scrounging a curbside garage-cleanout pile off 7th Street, I'm finding some useful items—brass knobs, a coat hook, anchor bolts, aluminum scrap, a wallet (empty)—but I'm wary. The yard sports multiple "no trespassing" signs, as well as a hand-lettered sign warning folks away from the leaning, dilapidated garage.

Then the guy comes out of the old garage carrying a rifle.

"How ya doin'?" I ask, turning toward him, throwing him a quick nod. To my relief, he answers with a friendly "Good." Apparently he's just moving the rifle as part of the garage cleanup. "Mind if I look through this stuff?" I ask, resuming my work. "Sure," he says, and then walking toward me, gesturing a closed circle in the air, the rifle tucked under his arm, he adds, "Just

try not to scatter it all around." "No problem," I assure him. "If I'm gonna look through stuff I try to leave it neater than I found it."

This isn't just a line of talk to keep from getting shot, by the way. Over my months of scrounging, an assumed social contract seems to have evolved, a negotiated curbside agreement that I try to follow by cleaning up trash piles as I remove items from them, hoping to leave in their place some sense of informal neighborhood solidarity. Other scroungers seem to share a similar sensibility. When, early in his career as a Dumpster diver, the author of *Evasion* began to let other kids in on his newfound secret—that the Dumpsters of their suburban town offered a bounty of scrounged goods—he soon realized that those new to the endeavor actually understood little about it. They "transgressed every law of Dumpster diving—'leave the area surrounding the Dumpster cleaner than you found it,' etc.," he recalls. "I would find torn bags and trash strewn around my favorite Dumpsters. Bad for community relations. Store managers and shopkeepers grew frustrated, padlocking our spots of choice. What had I created?"[9] Likewise, Zoe Bake-Paterson, writing on "the art of Dumpster diving" and "rules for the down and dirty diver," presents fellow Dumpster divers with Rule #5: "Don't make a mess, keep the garbage in the bin. In fact, leave it cleaner than you found it."[10]

05 August 2002

Homeland Security

My eight months of intensive urban scrounging emerged in the panicky aftermath of the September 11, 2001, attacks on the World Trade Center. As airports clamped down on passengers and their belongings, and the news media trumpeted fears of terrorist infiltration and attack, I mostly went about my business of scrounging—and, with the national economy in freefall and jobs going down with it, I wondered if this might remain my business for the long run. Like most everything else, though, even the city's trash piles and Dumpsters began to suggest some new meanings and possibilities in the days and months after 9/11.

Walking my neighborhood one Sunday in early February 2002, I came across a curbside trash pile that offered the usual variety of usable or recyclable objects: a golf club, a chandelier, brass pipes and fittings, copper wire, an aluminum cleaning wand, two picture frames (one an old oval frame with convex glass), chair leg braces, and a box of twelve new "opal ointment jars." Sorting through the pile, I also found a new carrying case for a Dell laptop computer, containing all the retail documentation for the computer—but not the computer (a case that, three years later, I still use as my everyday briefcase). Digging deeper, I uncovered a cardboard box at the bottom of the pile, and opening it found something that was by turns amusing and disturbing: a complete female Delta flight attendant's uniform, including flight pins and other accoutrement, and a flight attendant's carry-on bag.

H'mmm . . . a complete flight attendant's outfit, available curbside? I had always thought this area was for loading and unloading only. The airports were under surveillance, the country's borders were being watched—but, as with that schoolyard box of bullets, I couldn't help but wonder who was watching the trash piles. Maybe this required further investigation; maybe someone should track down the party responsible for leaving a flight attendant's uniform exposed to illegal acquisition, not five months after 9/11. And as it turns out, that's just what I did.

Eleven days later, on a ride through a somewhat more upscale neighborhood a couple of miles north of the flight attendant's trash pile, I came upon another curbside pile. While digging through and finding, once again, all manner of usable objects—twelve feet of copper pipe with brass fittings, a small tea tin, a box of English tea, a book on Fort Worth's history, a Yale University umbrella—I began to get a sense of déjà vu, a sense that some of these cardboard boxes and discards seemed familiar. At any rate, I kept at it, extracting from the pile dinner and party plates, candles, a bag of decorative marbles, masking tape, more brass scrap, aluminum cans and scrap, a small paint brush, a cracked 13/16-inch spark plug socket, four old TV knobs, three refrigerator magnets, a pants leg clip for bicycling, various hardware, a faux leopard-skin eyeglasses case, and $1.12: a new dollar coin, a dime, and two pennies.

And down at the bottom of the pile, mixed in with the coins that had settled to the bottom of a black garbage bag, I found a "Laura Bush for First Lady" campaign button—and a fancy Delta Airlines lapel pin. And of course then I knew why this stuff seemed familiar. In the space of ten days, I had accidentally tracked this woman from the trash pile that had accumulated as she moved out of her old house to the trash pile that accumulated as she moved in (and moved up) to her new one.

I wondered if the FBI could have done any better job of surreptitious—not to mention unintentional—tracking. And I wondered if Laura Bush would think leaving flight attendant uniforms out on the curb was any way to support her husband's war on terror.

10 February and 21 February 2002

Nor Make Any Provisions for Her Comfort

I'm up early to help out a friend who owns a little bookstore, and to earn a bit of cash to supplement my scrounging, by delivering books to some twenty-five elementary schools scattered around Fort Worth. At one point, driving through an impoverished black neighborhood on the east side, I notice across the road a thin, elderly black man carrying a very large bag of uncrushed aluminum cans—and as I pass, he's balancing the big bag on his back while stooping to pick up another can along the side of the street. With many stops to make before the elementary school offices close at 4 P.M., I limit my scrounging to twenty-three pennies, which I find piled, for some reason, in the parking area across the street from I. M. Terrell Elementary School.

All the books delivered, I'm heading down Forest Park Boulevard to drop off the delivery van and, as always, scanning the side streets for trash piles when I spot a large curbside trash pile just down a street to my left. Circling back a few minutes later after picking up my old truck, I pull up to the pile, which I now see is sitting in front of a very spacious and elegant older home. A middle-aged white guy is adding more boxes and bags to the pile, so I get out and ask him, "Mind if I poke around?" He tells me to go right ahead, take what I want, because "we're moving out in two days."

Bent over, digging through the pile, I straighten up a few minutes later to see a young white kid, tall, lanky, maybe fourteen or fifteen, standing in front of me on the sidewalk.

"You looking for something?" he says, not aggressively, but a little arrogantly, as it strikes me.

"Just scrap metal, that sort of thing," I say with a smile.

This seems to put him at ease, and as I continue to dig and he continues to bring out bags and boxes, he begins to point out items to me in the pile.

Few provisions for comfort, New York City, October 2004.

"There's four or five more ceiling fan motors just under here," he says, pointing to a spot under the middle of the pile.

Soon enough, we're talking for a minute or two each time he returns with more discards, not just about the trash, but about his family and their upcoming move.

"Don't even open that one up," he says of one thick black garbage bag. "It's just clothes that haven't been out in like ten years, and they stink." I don't know if they do, or if he's protecting his family's privacy, but since the advice is friendly, I go along with it.

A few minutes later a woman I would take to be his mother comes down the driveway, and while hurriedly walking across the street waves to me and says, "Take what you like." I appreciate the family's courtesy. Just a couple of days ago, rolling up to a trash pile, I wasn't even off my bike when I heard an older woman's voice from behind the shrubs lining the back yard. "Stay out of there," she yelled—and before I could move or respond, an older man's voice added, "There's nothing in there you'd want." Today the empire is friendlier.

After a while, three Hispanic guys roll up in a big late-model SUV, and jump out in a hurry. On the one hand, they don't seem to acknowledge my prior claim to the pile—an informal code that I've found to be almost always honored in the empire. On the other hand, they're friendly enough, handing me items they don't want, and chatting with me while we all work. Interestingly, they focus almost exclusively on consumer electronics, on items like an automatic golf putting device and an automatic paint stirrer, and on a pile of electrical connections, leaving me to take items that I consider to be of far greater historical and aesthetic appeal, and maybe monetary value as well. Our divergent interests help assuage any concerns caused by their claim-jumping.

But if the three late arrivals don't recognize my stake to the pile, it appears the kid does. Bringing out more boxes and items for the pile, he now begins to hand many of them directly to me, rather than putting them on the pile where the others might get to them first. In twenty minutes, we seem to have moved from mild antagonists to coconspirators—though I hope the conspiracy isn't a racial one. At one point he brings out some metal scrap, and holding it out to me says, "Hey, you want this?" "Sure, all metal is good metal," I

tell him, smiling and taking the scrap from him, hoping that my answer might serve as a mild recycling reminder amid the disposability of his privilege and relocation.

Finally, setting a box down, he tells me, "Just two more boxes to bring down"—from the attic, I assume. When he arrives with the first one I thank him again for all the help—having already thanked his folks—and while he's away getting the next one I decide to take off. There's another code of honor in the empire—"take what you need and leave the rest"—and so I decide to leave the last box for the three guys in the SUV. Besides, it's been a long day, and my little pickup is all but full already—full of items I'll need to sort and process once I get home.

Along with the scrap metal and a variety of practical or resalable items—a catcher's mitt, a new softball, a zippered leather pouch, a faucet attachment—my truck is full of history. Down from this family's attic have come three old boxes of J. C. Bair Company round wire staples, "Bair in Mind" and a bear's image on the metal-edged boxes, and "The Businessman's Office Supply Store," 103 E. 9th St., Austin, Tex., Tel. 8-5688" on the back. Mrs. Butterworth was up there, too— or more precisely an old Mrs. Butterworth's syrup bottle in the shape of, well, Mrs. Butterworth. So were a Singer Dressmaking Guide, copyright 1936–1947, "price 25 cents"; a "Souvenir Good Luck" token from Abilene Town, Kansas; Tom Ivey's 1948 desk diary, an insurance company giveaway now filled with daily entries; and several old sepia-tone photographs of a young woman.

Little leftovers of childhood also fill my truck. I'm taking home a big cylindrical "The Original Tinkertoy/Big Boy, #155," tin, with many of the Tinkertoy pieces still inside, color-coded by length so that "child selects parts by color." I'm packing two old toy guns, one chromed cast metal, stamped with "Daisy" and "Bullseye" and "Made in USA," the other a "Flintlock Jr." featuring a cast metal barrel and dark orange Bakelite body and handle. I've scooped up all sorts of old, tiny toys, perhaps prizes from a gumball machine of the past. Most interesting, a "Savings for Baby" boxed set features a small metal coin bank, fabricated and painted to look like a leather savings account book, and an oversized, white leather "Baby's Wallet," with interior envelopes for "Baby's Birth Certificate," "Snapshots—Baby's First Pictures," "Baby's Bank Book and other Valuables," and "Baby's Life Insurance." Tucked in the back are cards, letters, and telegrams, circa 1936, offering congratulations on the new arrival, and a smoothly handwritten note from George Bagby of George B. Bagby Life Insurance. "To the mother and the new baby are sent best wishes that life's richest blessings may shine upon them as the golden chains of affection draw them ever closer through the years to come. And may the pages of this wallet record events of joy and gladness; the round of happy days that are the sweetest years of life, the years of infancy."

It appears I've salvaged other hints of family and personal history as well: a Memphis, Texas, class of 1926 high school diploma, in its presentation case; an elegant Mother's Day card, mailed from Fort Worth to Memphis, Texas, for Mother's Day 1928; and a 1928 teacher's certificate. For me as a criminologist, though, the most fascinating piece of salvaged history predates these cards and diplomas by two or three decades. It's the law docket of J. M. Elliott, Attorney at Law, Albany, Texas, a leather-bound, handwritten account of local legal cases as they unfolded between 1894 and 1908.

If Fort Worth streets and Dumpsters awash with lost or discarded bullets confirm some bad stereotypes about the United States and Texas, J. M. Elliott's Albany law docket just as surely confirms some common images of nineteenth-century Texas and the American West. Albany sits some 120 miles due west of Fort Worth, out where West Texas today unfolds into a vast landscape of big ranches, little towns, and lots of cattle. Judging by Elliott's law docket, it was much the same a century ago. An 1894 case involved "theft of cattle, changing marks and brands, unlawful branding, [and] receiving stolen property," with various parties testifying that "the hide . . . was not the hide that came off the animal that defendant had killed," and that "B. got a part of the beef if he would let up on this prosecution." The docket for 1902 recorded a case involving "one red cow about 4 years old" killed at a railroad crossing, and many suits against the railroads for damages to livestock during shipping likewise were filed. An 1895 suit involved a "claim for Bal[ance] on wolf scalps. $435.00." In 1896, a verdict of not guilty was returned on charges of "giving away whiskey on election" day. An undated entry from around the turn of the century recorded a dispute over "seven thousand acres of land" that "had gold mine on it at one time." The following entry listed details of a murder case, including a fragment of "told George Wallace that he would whip the Hensons boys before they left town and would . . . ," and a note: "Ben told Charly Parks that Tim Sullivan and John Watts promised that if Ben should get into it with Henson that they would never give him away and would stick to him to the last just a few days after the killing."

These accounts of whiskey and cattle rustling and gold mines, these promises to "whip the Hensons boys," sound like a plot synopsis from a bad B Western—and that's not to mention Elliott's notes on "Indian claims" and town drunks disturbing the peace, or the unsuccessful 1896 prosecution of a train engineer for "failing to blow the whistle," or the 1898 "fight at Riges saloon" that eventually led to murder. Yet among these clichéd cases of Western crime and justice, a less expected sort of case was almost as common: divorce. Time and again, Elliott records the details of marriages gone bad—and with these the welter of assumptions and expectations in which such marriages and their participants were caught. In one case, he writes that "W. E. Adams will say that . . . he heard Mrs. B cursing and swearing and did not go in afterwards saw [her] lying on pallet under shade tree with her clothes up above her knees was

rolling around in a careless manner." In 1906, he details a case in which a wife "refused to accompany . . . and still refuses" to accompany her husband after "it became necessary for plaintiff to remove to Texas." In another he notes that "he renewed the quarrel . . . and acqusation [sic] of Sept 25, 1902 in such a manner that [she] could not stand it."

Of all these, Elliott's last two divorce cases are surely the saddest. In the first, he records that the defendant "on April 4th slapped plaintiff and cursed her. On Sept 17th cursed and abused plaintiff and accused plaintiff of unchastity." The case, seeking divorce and custody of the children, was dismissed. In the second, a woman married only a short while files for divorce because of her husband's "failure to support in September 1906 when plaintiff was sick and not expected to live." "Def would not stay with her," Elliott writes, "nor make any provisions for her comfort."

28 May 2002

Just Checking

As seen throughout this chapter, my day-to-day scrounging elicited a range of reactions, from humor and encouragement to threat and accusation; often it elicited no reaction at all, as homeowners or business owners carefully declined even to make eye contact with someone they perhaps saw as beneath or beyond their own sensibilities. Other times, though, their discomfort drove them into direct action.

Behind a Tuesday Morning store, a store manager with a thick Eastern European accent screamed, "Get out of my Dumpster!" and warned, when I lingered, that she would "hate to have to call the police." As I was scrounging a curbside pile of after-Christmas discards, a woman ran out of the house threatening to call the police, and, having forgotten in her haste to grab her cell phone, sent her friend back inside to do so as I cycled away. Far more often, though, my encounters with homeowners, store owners, and others were pleasant—in part, I suspect, because I almost always made an effort to smile and calmly explain my intent. And my intent, after all, was to survive by scrounging, not to promote interpersonal drama; shouting matches and police calls were something I couldn't afford.

This was especially the case with security guards and police officers. Trying to stay alive day-to-day as a scrounger, I made every effort to avoid visual contact with them, much less interaction. When my strategies of general invisibility and avoidance failed, I tried to diffuse the situation by exiting it. A number of times private security guards rolled up on me while I was digging in commercial Dumpsters, and as they slowed their car or truck to check on me, I always adopted the same strategy: stop what I'm doing, make eye contact, smile, climb on my bicycle, and ease away. In every case this seemed to have the desired effect of avoiding a confrontation by obeying an order I hadn't yet been given.

Given that I took special care to scout streets and alleys for police officers before scrounging, my interactions with the police were less common, though generally followed the same unspoken dynamic: a police car, especially a slowing police car, was already reason enough to cease and desist. In fact, to be sure that I didn't force a confrontation through inattentiveness, I regularly reminded myself to look up from a trash pile, to peer out from a Dumpster, to climb up to the lip of a rollaway, lest I not notice a police car's presence until it was too late. Knowing this safeguard, reminding myself of it, I still found it difficult to follow; a Dumpster found to be full of treasures, a trash pile revealing more of its bounty with each opened trash bag, can be seductive indeed. In fact, many times, despite my best intentions, it was only my aching back that reminded me just how long I'd been bent over a trash pile or leaning deep into a Dumpster, my head buried in all that glorious trash.

Most Dumpsters have sliding plastic or metal doors on either side, along with large flip-up lids on the top, and it was these sliding doors that once framed this very predicament. Leaning in to one of my favorite Dumpsters through a side door, sorting through trash bags and loose items, I caught out of the corner of my eye some sort of movement through the opposite open door. Straightening up, peering through the Dumpster's darkness and out that opposite door, I saw some bad news: a Fort Worth Police Department cruiser rolling to a halt, so close that its front end now completely filled my little square frame of reference. As I pulled my head and upper torso out of the Dumpster and began walking around the Dumpster toward the police car, I thought I saw the white, middle-aged officer inside give me a thumbs-up or some similarly affirmative wave. Not sure—and certainly not wanting to disregard what may have in fact been a gesture to approach the car—I kept stepping toward the car. Then, powering down his window, the officer decided to clarify the situation.

"Just checking," he tells me. "Saw the bike there but didn't see anybody, thought it might be stolen."

"Well, thanks for checking," I say.

"No problem—have a good one," and he powers up the window and rolls away.

08 February 2003

Fuckin' Lan-Côme!

I'm already finding some nice scrap on today's ride—a personal organizer, a baseball, some loose change—but I can't resist cruising back over to that Monticello McMansion trash pile from the other day. After all, I kind of liked the booze and the jewelry, and the coffeemaker is working great. And besides, a woman at the house—the one who wouldn't make eye contact, much less answer my friendly "hello"—was hauling still more big, black, shiny trash bags full of something or other out to the curb when I left.

The return trip turns out to be well worth my while. I haven't been there fifteen minutes, and I'm already assembling a bike load of usable items, including a clock radio; an ornate silver jar; various movie videos, some still sealed new in their shrinkwrap; a glossy *Great American Kitchens* magazine ($13.95 retail); and a variety of expensive hardcover books, including William Safire's *Freedom*, Joseph Heller's *Good as Gold*, and Samuel Beckett's *End-Game*.

Best of all, though, is the company I'm about to keep.

Bending over, sorting through bags with my back to the curb, I'm aware of a car rolling up on me from the north—strange, since this east side of the parkway seems by convention and likely by law to be reserved for travel from the south. As I look up, the car, a ten-year-old American midsize, I'd guess, does indeed roll up—and right into the curb, hard, its front left wheel bouncing off as the driver angles it in, it's butt jutting out in the street, blocking traffic should there be any. Leaning her head out the window is a thin, way-too-tan, middle-aged, working-class Texas white woman, asking me with a slur and a smile, "Shit, are they home?" "Not that I can tell," I answer with a smile of my own, having already checked, as usual, for any signs of occupation or annoyance in and around the house. And so she gets out, as does her daughter, maybe twenty, visibly pregnant in a gauzy white top and shorts, not nearly as tan or thin or drunk as her mom.

And by God we get with it. They both jump right in, opening bags, sorting through, talking to each other and to me. Wanting to be friendly, and with the limited space on my bike already about full, I start handing them stuff as I pull it out of bags; each time the mom offers an earnest "thanks." At one point I dump a bunch of makeup and the like out of a trash bag and into a small container lying on top of the bags; her happy response upon seeing this is "Fuckin' Lan-Côme!" Her daughter adds that she spotted the makeup, too, and was about to go for it herself. I ask if there's anything in particular they're looking for. "Just the good stuff," the mom tells me, though later she asks me if I'm finding any "kid's stuff," and I do indeed find some Disney audiotapes and other children's tapes and hand them to her. A little later, the girl picks something up and asks her mom, "You want this?" "Yeah, yeah, anything new," she tells her.

About this time, the daughter decides that she wants a large, well-made ottoman, having discovered that its top lifts for storage. But her mom's concerned as to whether it'll fit in the car, and so I offer to help. As I carry it over to the car— the car that's still idling, still angled out into the street—the mother instructs her daughter to "pull on the lever, the orange one in the console" inside the car, and tells me "push down hard on the trunk." Putting the ottoman down I do, and after some effort on the daughter's part and mine, the trunk pops open and I load the ottoman. "You was

divin' and we just drove up, and now . . . ," the mom tells me by way of apology and thanks, but I cut her off. "Hey, no problem."

A little later she asks me, "Hey, you live around here?"

"Yeah, down across Camp Bowie, where it's not so nice," I tell her, laughing.

"Well, they throw out some good stuff in *this* neighborhood," she says.

As I'm getting ready to leave, she eases over to me. "Shit, there's some paper hangin' stuff in there—checks and stuff," she says, laughing. I laugh too, and I tell her "Yeah, I found some checks just the other day, some of 'em signed." I did, too—just a few days earlier I found two different sets of checks in two different trash piles, some of them signed and made out to the local Ridglea Country Club. Now that's some *serious* paper hangin' stuff.

Finally, as I'm strapping my scrounging bag onto my bike's rear deck and straightening the pile of books in my front basket, she sees the *Abs of Steel* workout videotape I've pulled out of a garbage bag and left on the pile.

"How to stay healthy," she says, reading from the tape cover. "Shit, how to stay high!"

She laughs, I laugh, and away I roll, high myself on the absurdities of law and crime curbside.

18 July 2002

Street Knowledge

3

Excavated for their possibilities, the city's streets, trash piles, and Dumpsters yielded items in such assortment that scrounged materials seemed simply to wash over my various needs and desires. Shoes and booze, shelving and bolts and buckets were as easily discarded by others as they were available to me, so long as I was willing to wander the city and, sometimes, wait a bit for their appearance. So bounteous was my daily urban harvest, in fact, that it regularly provided not just the material solution to my own needs, but bedding for animals, clothes for homeless shelters, gifts for friends and family as well. Certainly the streets and alleys can't sustain every person who turns to them for survival, nor should they be made to; my experiences in no way write a prescription for general urban sustenance, nor in any way excuse the conditions of inequality and injustice that leave so many with little else than the Dumpster and the street. But for me—privileged as I was to have my health, a bicycle, and a steady place to sleep—the empire of

73

scrounge offered up a daily exercise in free-form self-reliance.

Still, I was after more than this. While my primary task was to survive day-to-day by way of my scrounging, I also set myself the task of examining my own scrounged survival, and more broadly set the goal of understanding the empire from which others and I gleaned daily existence. This search for understanding, it seemed, offered both an opportunity and a test: Could I rely on the empire not only for my material needs, but for the very perspectives by which to make sense of it? Put differently, if the empire could offer a sort of shambling material self-reliance, could it offer some sort of analytic and aesthetic self-reliance, too? Such questions, by the way, did not occur to me at the beginning of my scrounging adventures. Early on, my plan was simply to scrounge the city and record what I found—and if, later on, I did decide to write about it all, I assumed I would bring to bear the usual array of exterior analytic models. But as the days and items accumulated, so did the moments in which I realized the empire offered scraps of knowledge and bits of beauty along with its other accumulations—knowledge, even, of the empire itself, and of those who had discarded something of themselves in becoming part of it.

These moments began to suggest to me that, while I was out there collecting shoes and shirts and silver spoons, I might as well also scrounge the city for . . . some understandings.

Some Understandings

Chapter Four will explore in some detail the practical process by which scrounging over time loops back on itself, with scrounged backpacks, hand tools, storage containers, sturdy clothes, and other items becoming a self-sustaining material support system that facilitates further scrounging. But a different sort of looping reflexivity also emerged from scrounging, one that I found especially enjoyable while attempting both to live from scrounging and to make sense of it. This process built from the regular discovery while scrounging of discarded books, instruction manuals, magazines, and other sources of information—and from the further discovery that many of these resources could in fact help me understand the experience of scrounging itself. It seemed entirely appropriate, really: I learned to scrounge analytic tools as well as hand tools, to scrounge the very ideas and information by which to understand my own scrounging. Years before, during my days in the world of urban graffiti and underground urban art, I had learned this dynamic from street artists who scrounged canvases and paint, and who scavenged discarded objects to use as stencils in their artwork—artists who utilized the city as a resource for creating the very art with which they decorated it. I soon realized that the same dynamic was available in the empire of scrounge. Information of all sorts was lost out there in the city—and finding it meant, in many cases, finding out about the world around me and my place in it as a scrounger.

Scrounging rides so often led to the discovery of books and magazines, in fact, that I soon learned another lesson: my love for scrounged books was not without pain, tending as it did to produce loads so heavy that my legs ached as my bike's rear deck swayed under the weight. This was not from indiscriminate book hauling, by the way; over time I left behind hundreds, perhaps thousands of books, often boxes full of books destined only for the landfill. Mostly I chose books that I considered classics, or that I wanted to read, or that I thought friends or their kids would want to read; less often I chose books based on their anticipated resale value at secondhand bookstores or with antiquarian book dealers. In the process I became a harsh critic indeed, leaving behind masterworks, best-sellers, and whole collections of cheap romance novels. And yet the books and magazines kept coming, burdening my rides home, piling up in my office and shed.

One February ride, for example, produced copper wire, aluminum cans, three pennies, an old high school diploma—and, along with a 1941 copy of *The Aero Engineer's Manual*, two copies of the *Drill and Ceremony* manual, published in 1953 by the Department of the Air Force. One copy showed no evidence of ownership. The other, as it turned out, once belonged to my future employer —it's front page was stamped "Texas Christian University, AFROTC, Govt. Property." In later

months I would scrounge from curbside trash piles and Dumpsters a number of 1950s and 1960s TCU annuals as well—and on one July ride a companion piece to *Drill and Ceremony* emerged. The small, hardbound *Service Mechanics' Handbook, Model PV-1, Restricted* offered a detailed mechanical guide to the Navy's PV-1 airplane— and given the manual's use during World War II, its "restricted" status was reinforced with a reminder on every page. The manual likewise reminded military mechanics who read it that "the ship—and perhaps the pilot's *life*—is in *your* hands." And it in particular warned them of the dangers posed by the gremlinlike "Groundlin."

Sailor beware! **Groundlins** *are the little guys who get in the mechanic's hair. They don't fly and they don't want your ship to fly either. Most of the time these imps are busy trying to keep the airplane grounded; the rest of the time they're figuring angles to keep it there. Keep **your** ship up in the air where the groundlins can't touch it. . . . Don't Listen To Groundlins. Know your job. Do it right. If you're not* **sure**—ask the man who knows.[1]

Perhaps the mechanic who owned this handbook during World War II took seriously this call for attention to detail. In the same pile of discards was Henry B. Fried's 1973 *The Watch Repairer's Manual*, 3rd edition.

Other scrounged books also offered instruction of one sort or another, and along the way glimpses of lost cultural history. Found in a big curbside

Sailor Beware!

GROUNDLINS are the little guys who get in the service mechanic's hair.

They don't fly and they don't want your ship to fly either. Most of the time these imps are busy trying to keep the airplane grounded; the rest of the time they're figuring angles to keep it there.

Keep YOUR ship up in the air where the groundlins can't touch it.

You'll meet some more of the GROUNDLINS as you read on.

"SKIP IT, MATE—
DON'T WORRY
ABOUT THAT
JOB—
IT AIN'T
WORTH IT—"

DON'T LISTEN TO GROUNDLINS

• KNOW YOUR JOB
• DO IT RIGHT
• IF YOU'RE NOT **SURE** —
  ASK THE MAN WHO KNOWS

RESTRICTED

"Sailor Beware!" from *Service Mechanics' Handbook, Model PV-1, Restricted,* a scrounged book.

pile of toys and tools, an undated U.S. Navy recruiting booklet—seemingly from the 1940s or 1950s—asked, "Ever wonder what it's like to see the far places of the world . . . ? Of course you have! You're an American, red-blooded, eager for adventure." Another pile of discards produced a later guidebook to such militaristic adventure: an *F16 Training Manual,* dated 1986. A scrounged 1940 Boy Scout *Handbook* suggested certain cultural ironies, not to mention political contradictions, circulating in the United States in the year before it entered the fight against authoritarian fascism. "A Scout Is Obedient," read the *Handbook.* "Obedience to orders is an essential of winning games. There must be a directing head to everything. There must be some one to give orders or else every human endeavor would be fraught with confusion and a team would become a mob instead of a highly intelligent composite of several men. In unison there is strength. Unison comes from obedience to a central power."[2] In other curbside piles and Dumpsters were a 1933 *Young Citizen Reader,* produced by 10-Cent Books, Inc. University Club Bldg., Columbus, Ohio; a 1934 *Business Speller,* with the names and addresses of a series of owners inside the front cover; an ancient, undated book of *Latin Exercises,* wrapped in the remains of an old paper school book cover, on its back a football play diagrammed in purple fountain pen; and *The Seven Sacraments,* an instructional pamphlet mailed from St. Boniface Parish, Fort Worth, Texas.[3]

Instruction in gender had likewise been taken, and discarded. One June 2002 ride produced *Glamour's Beauty Book, by the Editors of Glamour Magazine,* dated 1957–1966. Other rides found me hauling home 1960s issues of *Bride's* magazine, the *Ladies' Home Journal*—with the June 1968 issue of *Ladies' Home Journal* featuring "Psychiatric Marriage Checkup To Do at Home" and "Color Close-Up: The New White House China"—and a gargantuan, February 1965 issue of *Simplicity,* over 1400 pages of dress patterns and "lively looks for the modern miss." A most instructive find was Arlene Dahl's book *Always Ask a Man,* undated but appearing by its illustrations to have been published around 1960. As the book's owner had made her way through chapters like "Slim Down— Measure Up" and "It's Fun To Be a Redhead!" she had underlined key words and phrases in blue pencil. "Enlist the aid of a trusted male friend," "femininity," "feminine," "All truly feminine women have one basic quality in common. They like men," and "Aggressiveness is a trait men deplore" were among the passages she had highlighted—and in the back of the book she had written a single word: "Femininity."

A later scrounging ride produced related, if not subsequent, documents. In a trash bag of discards I found old, 8 x 10 professional photos of twin babies, and a 1939 edition of *Our Baby's Book,* which recorded the twins' January 1941 births and held various small cards that had accompanied their baby gifts. One of the twins' faded 8 x 10 baby photos—sitting together, leaning on each other, both laughing, one with his head tossed back happily—now hangs in a scrounged frame in my hallway, a little inspiration on the way to and from my office.

A May 2002 ride unearthed an alternative if weighty script for doing gender: Steve Hogan and Lee Hudson's 704-page *Completely Queer: The Gay and Lesbian Encyclopedia.* A late July ride produced a bricolage of books and audio tapes, as Barry Manilow, Reba McEntire, and Neil Diamond shared a trash bag with Bill Cosby's *Fatherhood,* Dale Dye's *Platoon,* and Jean Gould's 1964 *Robert Frost: The Aim Was Song.* Scrounged magazines likewise offered a mélange of discarded meanings and lost historical references. I discovered twelve issues of *Architectural Digest* on the curb in front of an architect's office, hauling them home along with five boxes of commercial vinyl tile samples. In a remodeling rollaway I found hundreds of old British and U.S. automotive magazines, all neatly bound in twine by year—and when the owner of the house arrived to find me in the rollaway, she explained that the magazines had belonged to her ex-husband's father, and urged me to take all I wanted.

From a curbside pile that included wooden shutters, window screens, switch-plate covers, drawer pulls, electric fans, a store-bought "Garage Sale" sign, and a cook's "Splatter Screen" new in its box, I salvaged six copies of *National Geographic,* dating from 1940 to 1966, and offering among other features "Brazil's Big-lipped Indians" and "A Community of Dwarfs." In a nod to Texas culture, I found and brought home copies of *Dave Campbell's Texas Football* magazine from the 1970s and 1980s. But my favorite found magazine—one I carried home by hand, rather than strapping to my bike's rear deck and risking wrinkled defacement—was a June 10, 1966, issue of *Life.* Its cover juxtaposed a photograph of Elizabeth Taylor in the film *Who's Afraid of Virginia Woolf,* and the headline "Liz in a Shocker: Her Movie Shatters the Rules of Censorship," with a second headline: "Plot To Get 'Whitey': Red-hot Young Negroes Plan a Ghetto War."

Certainly the most reflexive moment in my scrounging of books and magazines came with my discovery of three curbside cardboard boxes stacked full of books, many of them paperback copies of "New York Times Best Seller" titles, as they took pains to point out in big lettering above their own titles. Hauling them to a used bookstore, browsing around the store while waiting for my books to be evaluated, I spotted an interesting title on the "cultural studies/sociology" shelf: Susan Strasser's *Waste and Want: A Social History of Trash.* With the ten bucks the store paid me for what were originally, and recently, books worth hundreds of dollars retail, I bought that used copy of *Waste and Want.* In this way I convert trashed books into a book about trash, and as the reader of this book may notice, acquired a book that became an essential reference in my own writings about urban scrounging.

This wasn't the only time that scrounged ideas stimulated my own ideas about scrounging.

Stimulate Your Thinking

Having hauled home two big pickup loads of scrounged materials in the past few days, I'm faced with a backlog of items to be sorted, cataloged, and stored away, or else broken down and sorted for scrap. So, I plan to take a rare break from my daily scrounging rides and walks, and spend most of the day working in and around my shed. This plan is also the result of the day's "Red" air-quality forecast—a colorful euphemism for a sickening stew of auto pollution and industrial gas, cooked with summer heat and humidity, and held in place over the city by an absence of the usual southerly winds. A long, strenuous bike ride through yesterday's red air, along with some hard physical work outside, left me with an ache in my lungs and unusually tired legs.

Heading out to my shed in the early afternoon, though, I notice that the trash up and down my street is yet to be picked up—for whatever reason, the garbage trucks haven't completed their usual early morning rounds. This sight suggests a change in plans—a rare chance for last-minute trash-day curbside scrounging—since my usual scrounging rides the evening before trash day miss whatever might be put out on the curb early the next morning. Grabbing my bike, I hop on for a quick if atmospherically filthy forty-minute cruise through the neighborhood. I can hear the big trash trucks closing in—at one point they catch up to me as I'm working my way down a block near my house—and so I scrounge quickly, haphazardly, down streets that I have already scrounged once, sometimes twice, since the last trash pickup a few days before. Despite this, I manage to scrounge aluminum cans, die-cast fence parts, five CDs (including the two-CD *Encarta 98 Encyclopedia*), a large Revere Ware copper-clad cooking pot, a working Weed-Eater lawn trimmer, the bottom half of a fishing rod (Cosmos, Made in France), and a spinning reel (Mitchell, Made in France). Inspired, I suppose, by the fact that two consecutive days of red air rides haven't yet killed me, I decide to go out again later for a short ride, and later still to walk my dogs, in the process finding more aluminum cans, a lead weight, a paint can opener, a die-cast/alloy casing (with raised "Valmont" lettering), a penny, and an L-shaped metal rod.

A bit of old newspaper that I found a few days ago while unpacking a found trunk helps put this dirty red cloud into some perspective—a cloud that's due back tomorrow if the forecasters are correct. At first I had tossed the newspaper toward the recycling bin, since it was just packing wrapped around an old picture frame in the trunk. Then I noticed what it was, decided to save it—and remembered it yesterday when my lungs began to ache. A supplement to the *St. Louis Post-Dispatch*—apparently from 1965 or 1966, although the date

in the corner has been torn away over the years—it offers "A Positive View of Good Driving Habits . . . with expert tips on developing your personal safety program," courtesy of the Ford Motor Company.[4]

Inside its front page, an introductory letter from Henry Ford II communicates his hope that the supplement will "stimulate your thinking about traffic safety," and includes his encouraging report that "urban traffic congestion is being reduced as new freeways are opened and electronic traffic controls are installed." The supplement provides similarly good news about the new 1966 Fords, noting brightly that "it will take just minutes on the road in a '66 Ford-built car to discover that driving has become easier, smoother, more enjoyable than ever—and this by design." A few pages on Major Robert D. Quick of the New York State Police adds that "good driving is really a matter of being a good citizen," and warns, "above all, obey the laws. They were enacted for your safety and are enforced for your protection." Meanwhile, at the new Ford Automotive Safety Center, "scientists probe to learn more about human factors and the close physical and psychological balance between car and driver." Finally, John Gearhart, "America's best teen-age driver" and winner of the 14th Annual Safe Driving Road-E-O, notes that as an aspiring symphonic musician, the "80-mile drive to Symphony rehearsals gave me plenty of driving practice."

With such a solid foundation laid back in 1966—freeway-induced decongestion, ever more safe and enjoyable driving, stern cops and concerned scientists, eighty-mile drives for eighteen-year-old symphonic safety champs—it's no wonder that our automotive prospects, not to mention our air, are so rosy red today. In fact, were I not such an avid bicyclist, all those advances toward automotive safety and pleasure might seduce me off my scrounger's bicycle and into a Ford-built car.

Well, that and the danger of bicycling through a filthy red-alert automotive cloud day after day, all while dodging cars and hoping not to become one of the 45,000 or so yearly street casualties of automotive progress in the United States.[5]

09 July 2002

Un Momentito de Liberación

Back from a swim with my dogs out at muddy old Lake Benbrook, there's time to get a scrounging ride in before dark—important, since it's the evening before trash pickup. Cutting west through the wealthier section of the Arlington Heights/River Crest neighborhood, I haven't picked up much—two pennies, two packets of bolts (on the curb alongside a complete garage-door opener), an aluminum can, a *Fort Worth Opera* CD—when I roll up on one of the biggest of the old neighborhood mansions. Pulling to a stop I can see past the back of the big house, out over the high bluff on which it sits and north across the West Fork of the Trinity River; I can only imagine

the view that must accompany breakfasts in the mansion's sunroom. From here I can also read the City of Fort Worth Landmark plaque and the Texas Historical Commission Official Historical Medallion that are embedded in the home's eight-foot brick-and-iron front fence. Built in 1910–1913, the Baldrige House was a "showplace of the time," the marker says, what with its "massive limestone columns" and "carved oak woodwork." I'd guess that guests were equally impressed in those days by the elaborate fountain that sits just inside the front gate, its three fat stone cherubs still busily grappling with a big stone eagle.

I didn't stop for the history or the view, though. Rounding the corner, I'd noticed across the street a woman walking a box down a long driveway, adding it to an already large pile of boxes and other scrap on the curb, then walking back down the driveway for more. So now I wait on my bike in front of the Baldrige House until she completes another trip and disappears back down the driveway behind the house. Then I swoop in, thinking maybe I can grab what I want before she returns; given the neighborhood's very tony nature, I fear unpleasantness if I force an interaction. Braking to a quick stop at the pile, though, I realize this won't be a quick drive-by after all, as I now see before me something too good to hurry: box after box of high-quality hardback and paperback books.

Seeing her coming back down the driveway toward me, I change my strategy. Still straddling my bike, I turn, smile, and say, "I love books—do you mind if I look through these?" And in one of those little miscommunicative moments that sometimes emerge as strangers meet, I soon enough begin to understand by her shrugging body language and quizzical expression that she doesn't understand English; as she walks closer I guess that she's Latina. Fishing my brain for my limited Spanish, I smile some more, and gesturing toward the boxes say, appreciatively, "Libros!" She nods, smiles, and continues toward me. Arriving at the pile, she puts down her latest load, then lifts out a row of paperback books from another box to show me the larger hardcover books below. "Sí, muchos libros!" She's smiling, I'm smiling, and I say, "Gracias, muchas gracias!"

She returns a couple of times with more boxes of books—pausing, smiling, telling me "más libros!" as she reaches the curb and puts them down—and I continue to thank her and smile in return. Given the elevated purity of this neighborhood's ethnic and class composition, I'm fairly certain that what we have here is a nice moment of marginal community—and of all places just across the street from the Baldrige mansion's staid eminence. The Latina maid, left the task of lugging heavy boxes of books out of the garage and down to the curb on "trash night," meets the disheveled white boy bicycle scrounger, and together we find a bit of relaxed good humor, maybe even a little moment of liberation from the day's predictability. I'm reminded of the nineteenth-century itinerant tin peddlers and rag collectors described by Strasser in *Waste and Want*, their visits to rural farmhouses welcomed by farm wives as "diversions from the everyday," as moments of "joking and laughing and trading" amid the drudgery of hard domestic labor. A century or so later, and here we are still: hard domestic labor of another sort, interrupted by the unanticipated arrival of a two-wheeled itinerant scrap collector.[6]

So, playing out my part in this historical reenactment, I get to work collecting the books from the curbside. And what books these are: big, nicely bound hardcover editions, classic works some of them, and many apparently never read hard or otherwise damaged, despite their relegation to the trash pile. Except that now there's a problem: thunder's booming, a storm is sweeping in from across the West Fork out past these mansions, and if there's one thing old books don't like it's water. Working as fast as I can, I put some of the books in my scrounge bag as the rain begins and, when the bag's full, pull it tightly closed. Next I hurriedly empty out one of the cardboard book boxes, begin to fill it with the books I want, and put another emptied-out box over the top to block as much rain as I can.

With the rain spattering down on me, but the books I most want stowed away, I quickly turn to some bulging, heavy-duty black garbage bags lying among the book boxes. Massaging them from the outside tells me that they're full of something other than household or yard waste, and so I employ a technique I've refined over the past few months. As I've increasingly come to realize that plastic "trash bags" are regularly used not as containers for the dirtiest or wettest of waste, but simply as holding bags for collections of small discarded items, I've invented a way to investigate such collections discreetly. Using both hands I pull open two small holes in the bag. One, about halfway down the bag, gives me a general sense of the contents. Another at the bottom of the bag is based on another of my emerging street understandings: that the good stuff—coins, jewelry, tools—generally settles.

In the next few minutes this technique yields a heavy extruded aluminum bar of some sort; a leather Calvin Klein purse; an expensive black and reddish-brown leather purse; a large, seemingly new South American–style, multicolored wall hanging/table runner; and a collection of jewelry and earrings, scooped out from the bottom of one of the bags, including a lovely old red Bakelite barrette with small rhinestones, and what appears to be a silver broach.

The rain now stopping for a moment, I load all this and the many books I've chosen onto my bike. It's a terrible load, really, my packed-full scrounge bag bungeed to my broken rear deck, a big box of books balanced across my handlebars as I ride away. Other times I might have left some of the books for later, but not this time; I'm worried that the rain will ruin them by the time I can mount a return trip.

And for what books am I willing to suffer so, pushing down hard against the pedals, feeling the strain in my legs and back as I slowly build up some speed and ride away?

The Subject Was Roses, by Frank D. Gilroy, 1965. A Texas Christian University library book, it's a bit overdue—the due date reads December 22, 1972.

A Brief History of Time, by Stephen W. Hawking, 1988.

The Basic Writings of Sigmund Freud, edited by Dr. A. A. Brill, a 1938 hardcover. A thousand and one pages heavy, the book has a handwritten "Private Library of - Herman Hart, Jr." inside the front cover, and a large woodblock-style "ex libris Herman Hart" stamped on the next page.

Webster's Legal Speller, 1978.

Teach Yourself Spanish Vocabulary, a 1996 paperback with "Elaine Hart" printed on the front page. Perhaps if I put this book to good use, on my next visit I can manage something more than "libros" and "muchas gracias."

Roget's 21st Century Thesaurus, 1992, a large hardcover book, 836 pages heavy.

Texas: A Novel, by James Michener, 1985, another large hardcover, 1,096 pages heavy.

The Bethany Parallel Commentary on the New Testament, 1983, a still larger hardcover book at 1,499 handlebar-bending pages.

Supplement I, The American Language, by H. L. Mencken, first edition, a 1945 hardcover, 739 pages heavy, plus index.

Supplement II, The American Language, by H. L. Mencken, first edition, a 1948 hardcover, 890 pages heavy, plus index.

Lonely Planet Travel Survival Kit, Thailand, 1995.

Brideshead Revisited, by Evelyn Waugh, 1944/1973, inscribed "To Elaine Hart 1983 W. Frank Combs."

Michelen Tourist Guide, Italy, 1981.

Treasures of the Prado, a small 1993 museum-edition paperback with the price sticker still on its back cover: "11.95"

Earl Mindell's Soy Miracle, 1995.

Neil Sperry's Gardening GreenBook, date unknown.

Encyclopedia of Organic Gardening, 1997.

Vegetarian Soup Cookbook, 1992.

Shopper's Guide to Natural Foods, 1987.

Once A Lullaby, a hardcover children's picture book, 1986.

The Age of Faith, by Will Durant, 1950, 1,196 pages heavy. Written inside the front cover: "Return to Mrs. Herman Hart (Borrowed by RT Jan 10, 63)."

Legend, Myth, and Magic in the Image of an Artist, by Ernst Kris and Otto Kurz, 1979, with a price sticker on its back cover: "MMA [Museum of Modern Art], $5.95"

The Eternal Present: The Beginnings of Art, by S. Gideon, a large hardcover, 1962, illustrated, 588 pages heavy.

The Elephant Tree, by Penny Dale, a children's hardcover book from 1991, with a sticker still on the front cover: "Sale Price, Not! $14.95, 81% Off, $2.98." Loaded onto my bike, it's now 100 percent off.

Nicky the Nature Detective, a hardcover children's book from 1983.

Art and Illustration Techniques, by Harry Borgman, a large hardcover book from 1979.

Color: Order and Harmony, by Paul Renner, 1964, a large, elegantly bound hardcover book with color plates.

Some of these books I later give to family, friends, and friends' kids; others I put out for sale at my next yard sale; the art books, travel books, thesaurus, and Mencken volumes I keep. In fact, the thesaurus provides a useful if uncomplimentary perspective on the very process by which I've acquired it. Looking it over later at home, I find under the entry for "scrounge" a definition—"beg, forage for"—and a list of sorry synonyms: "bum, freeload, hunt, sponge, wheedle."[7] As might be expected, Mencken provides greater historical depth—but not much more in the way of etymological encouragement. A "scavenger" he describes as "a longshoreman who eats the sailors' leavings aboard ship." "Scrounging" he cites as a synonym for "liberating," a term utilized by Allied troops in World War II as their own synonym—or maybe ironic euphemism—for "looting."[8] Damn—looting, begging, freeloading, sponging, wheedling, eating leftovers—quite a sorry mix of criminality and bad character indeed. I'm glad I salvaged these books; they remind me that the scrounger's marginality is encoded in language as much as in law.

Of course, the great majority of books I discovered in those boxes that day weren't of any use to me—or, at least, in the few rainy moments I had to decide the matter, I didn't consider them useful enough to load onto an already overburdened bicycle. In this sense the books that I liberated and hauled home were certainly not typical of all those I found in that big curbside pile. In fact, as I soon noticed that day, almost all the books in those boxes fell into one of five categories. Three of them I picked from as I gathered books to carry away: European travel, natural foods, and art. Two of them I didn't: Christianity and the Bible, and Alcoholics Anonymous.

Quickly sorting through these five categories of books in the rain, I began also to imagine a life history, one written by the books themselves— and I began to chuckle a little, realizing that this imaginary life history seemed an almost perfect cultural stereotype of those who would choose to live in the shadow of the Baldrige House. Indulging their class sensibilities, they would dabble in art and aesthetics, travel abroad, seek the sort of "healthy" lifestyle that can prolong their privilege, yet find themselves caught between the twin addictions of booze and religion—or is that between the oscillating salvations of the Almighty and Alcoholics Anonymous? For that matter, maybe they would put that big *Commentary on the New Testament* to good use as regular members—when not in Europe or Thailand, anyway—at All Saints Episcopal Church just down the road on the corner of Pentecost and Dexter Streets, from whose remodeling Dumpster I another time salvaged an oversized Italian marble lamp and discarded candelabra.

But honestly, this isn't much of a life history. After all, which books *weren't* thrown out that day, and what different history would they write? In what sequence did these five dimensions of someone's life unfold, or to what degree did they develop somehow synchronically? And whose life is this, anyway—Elaine's, or Herman's, or a bit of both?

Damned if I know. In this instance, anyway, I was willing to settle for whatever glimpses the curbside afforded me into the lifestyles of the well traveled and well lubricated. But my scrounging did end up offering me one other clue about the Hart family's life course. Remembering that on an earlier occasion I'd scrounged from a trash pile the *Fort Worth Social Directory* for 1981–1983, I pulled it off my shelf and decided to check. Sure enough, there was Mrs. Herman Newton Hart— the former Elaine Stanton, one of eight Assembly Debutantes presented in 1941—and in the next listing, a Mr. Herman Newton Hart III.[9]

What with the rain and my *todo mojado* Spanish, I didn't get their maid's name, so I couldn't check on her. Still, I'm sure I didn't see her name in the directory.

Mine either.

11 July 2002

Hey Cowboy

Out on a scrounging ride I see a pile of material on the curb of a commercial street, and as I'm rolling up to it I'm vaguely aware of a voice, though not sure it's directed at me. As it turns out it's the voice of a weathered, white, middle-aged homeless guy, missing some teeth, sporting long hair and a beard. He's sitting back off the street in a little 10 x 30 foot space between two fenced property lines, in the shade of some scraggly trees. He's also sitting among more of the sort of materials I spotted on the curb—old bedding, magazines, and a broken wooden door. We speak for just a moment—he says something I can't quite understand while he holds up a 40 and points it toward me.

Thirty minutes later, finishing a scrounging loop through the neighborhood, I roll back by and ask him through the fence, "Where did all this stuff come from?" He tells me, "That guy threw it out," gesturing to a now-closed secondhand home design and yard decoration store next door. There's a second guy with him now—or maybe he was there before, and I didn't see him, though I don't think so—also Anglo, heavily tanned, bigger, cleaner cut, in dark shirt and pants. They're both thumbing through and reading glossy magazines. "Fuckin' 1987," the first guy tells me, holding up the photomagazine *Texas Highways*. Scattered around them also are countless copies of interior design magazines, copies of magazines like *Marie Claire*, presumably castoffs from the closed shop. "Go check it out," the first guy tells me, referring to the pile out by the curb, but since I've already checked out the dozens of high-market magazines there, I hang back.

Then the second guy chimes in, speaking to me for the first time, a good bit more menacing than the first guy.

Reading the day's scrounged news, New York City, October 2004.

"Hey cowboy, get the fuck over here."

I don't do that, either, and ride away. Sometimes holding one sort of street knowledge trumps betting on another.

18 July 2004

Scrounging Categories

Rolling through the Mistletoe Heights neighborhood, riding a long scrounging loop through the central city, I'm already carrying a large load of copper wire and extruded aluminum that I've found in the nearby Fairmount and Ryan Place neighborhoods. Now I come upon a pile of six or eight cardboard boxes, sitting on the curb between two expensive homes that look out from the heights over the Clear Fork of the Trinity River. The boxes are mostly full of books, some of them with markings that indicate their purchase and use at Princeton in the 1970s, one listing members of Princeton's class of '71. Given the name and Texas origins of one of those Princeton boys, and some old campaign literature for Fort Worth City Council that I also find in the boxes, I'm fairly sure that these books have been discarded by a well-known Fort Worth political figure.

Whatever their current political ramifications, the books take me back to my own college years as well, and to my introduction to the sorts of sociological research and critical theory that would lead me, years later, not to Fort Worth's City Council but to its Dumpsters and trash piles.

Among the books I select from the boxes—if nothing else, for old time's sake—are Liebow's *Tally's Corner*, Whyte's *Street Corner Society*, Marcuse's *Eros and Civilization*, Dos Passos's *Manhattan Transfer*, Burroughs's *The Ticket That Exploded*, Bonhoeffer's *Letters and Papers from Prison*, Nietzsche's *On the Genealogy of Morals* and *Ecce Homo*, Ibsen's *Hedda Gabler*, Steinbeck's *The Winter of Our Discontent*, Heidegger's *Existence and Being*, García Márquez's *One Hundred Years of Solitude*—and, in an oddly discordant note, Billy James Hargis's 1960 screed to reactionary paranoia, *Communist America . . . Must It Be?*

With my existing carrying capacity about exhausted by the copper and aluminum, I load the books into a nifty little Nokia travel bag that I find among the books in one of the boxes, strap the bag over my shoulder, and head out—but I don't get far. Two blocks down the street, around a long left-hand curve, I spot on the curb two old fifteen-drawer library card catalogue cabinets. Cycling home, then heading back in my old truck, I struggle to load them into my truck bed; sturdily built from oak and oak veneer, they're all I can handle. But I do get them home and, installed in my shed, they make ideal containers for categorizing and storing scrounged items. In fact, a month later, the little labels I've made out of scrounged paper and slipped into the brass holders on the front of each drawer reflect something of the empire of scrounge, and its range of salvageable objects. They read: old gas valves, brass doorknobs, door lock parts, drill bits, files and rasps, springs and spacers, switch plates, sockets and socket wrenches, writing pens, staplers and staples, light bulbs, auto parts, window locks, old handles, bar/rack mounts, gun supplies and bullets, flatware, small glassware, hand tools, baseball cards, and eyeglasses.

Not bad for one afternoon's work. I've reclaimed some of the categories of meaning and morality that set my trajectory toward the empire of scrounge in the first place—the ethnographic attentiveness of Liebow's *Tally's Corner* and Whyte's *Street Corner Society*, and certainly the model of ethical commitment and political urgency offered by Bonhoeffer's *Letters and Papers from Prison*. At the same time, I've scrounged a cabinet that once held library cards on the likes of Liebow and Whyte and Bonhoeffer, and now holds something of the categories by which the empire of scrounge is itself organized.

05 September 2004

Lives Lost

A lot gets lost in the empire of scrounge—people's lives, for instance. In a sense, most everything in the empire has been flushed out from its place inside the lives of its owners, and so suggests something of the pace and patterns by which they live. An outgrown shirt, an old tool, a garbage bag filled with toys, a door discarded as part of a remodeling project—all are residues of decisions made, of lives moved on, of opportunities taken and not taken. Collectively, as gathered and accumulated over months and years of scrounging, these objects sketched for me a sense of social and cultural history, and certainly exposed the contours of contemporary consumption. But discovered one or a few at a time, outside a single residence or in a single apartment house Dumpster, they always reminded me of their previous owners, and of the ways in which the empire resonates with the residues of human life even when no one is around.

While such everyday, practical objects mark moments in the lives of those who have now discarded them, other found objects do so even more directly. With disconcerting regularity my scrounging uncovered high school and college diplomas, marriage certificates, achievement awards, family photos and photo albums, sports trophies, baby keepsakes, college annuals, and other detritus of human endeavor come loose from its place within personal and family history. While my discovery of such life fragments now discarded amid everyday trash carried for me a constant sense of poignancy, if not tragedy, the precise nature of the problem of course remained at issue. Did a discarded family photo album denote a death in the family, a sudden relocation, a family falling apart? Did a discarded high school diploma or college annual suggest an existential breaking point in someone's life, their death—or simply an overcrowded closet?

On one occasion I found out. Digging through a trash bag of discarded books and papers, I was

Portrait of a woman, scrounged photo, Fort Worth, Texas.

Train wreck with tourists, scrounged photos, Fort Worth, Texas.

thrilled to find a 1954 *Bear Cub Scout Book* that had belonged to a friend of mine; his name was neatly lettered into the book, as was the name of his mother, who had also served as his "den mother." Eager to return it to him, anticipating the fond memories it would bring back for him, I called and left a message—and, a few days later, his wife called back to tell me that he had discarded the book while cleaning out the house of his recently deceased mother, and didn't want it returned.

This sort of direct confirmation was the exception, though. Following my general notion of interrogating the empire for its own meanings, I decided not to utilize discarded keepsakes and mementos as entrees into broader investigations of people's lives through, for example, searches of legal documents or information databases. Mostly this resulted from a certain allegiance to the empire of scrounge and a commitment to my immersion in it—that is, from a desire to see if the empire could explain itself on its own terms, through its own ensembles of the lost and the found. But also, it seemed to me, I was by my scrounging already to some degree intruding—if not into people's lives directly, then into the trash bags and Dumpsters where they had perhaps intentionally hidden away their lost secrets. If I wasn't engaged in identity theft, I was certainly engaged in identity scrounging—and so I decided to learn all I could from the discards I happened upon, but not to pursue my investigation further.[10] I settled for curbside biographies, for fragments of people's lives, and for the best I could make of these in reconstructing lives lost, though I'll admit I did once or twice check the obituaries, concerned that I should show the proper respect if I were in fact digging through the discards of the dead.

As a result, my work in salvaging and reassembling lost lives rested at times on the tiniest of fragments, at other times on elaborate constellations of discarded objects and documents. On one February 2002 ride, for example, scrounging golf balls and tees, copper and aluminum scrap, lead weights, wood screws, a circular saw blade, furniture rollers, and five pennies, I discovered also the cast-off shell of a past life: an ancient metal and wood military trunk, "B / Cudeajan 129th Inf" handlettered on its top, its decaying interior now holding only a few loose beads. As already seen, another ride and another discovery—books piled in boxes across from the Baldrige mansion—sketched at least a blurry outline of their owners' lives, as did a scrounged *Social Directory*. And on a May 2002 ride perhaps a bit more was revealed—or perhaps not. Working my way through a big construction site rollaway, pulling out pieces of pipe, mounting brackets, and a nice three-way level, I came upon some distinctly nonconstruction related discards. Here, amid the construction debris, were two silver- and gold-plated wine goblets, three fancy wooden bowls, and a silver-plated, eight-sided jewelry box, all jumbled together with a leatherette wallet (empty), numerous padded bras and slips, Tommy Hilfiger slacks, and other clothes and undergarments. And here also was an expensive wedding photo album, dated 1998—with all of its photos torn out.

I couldn't help myself—I was constructing a story even as I was pulling this stuff from the rollaway, which, by the way, sat in a parking lot near desirable high-end housing and the exclusive River Crest Country Club, and just down the street from many of the city's better restaurants. Mixing the found items with the proximate urban ecology, here's how I wrote the story in my head: A marriage off to a good start, the couple residing in one of the city's better neighborhoods, but it goes bad. Four years after the ceremony, in fact, it falls apart—and so the wedding gifts, the ones they never really wanted anyway, are jettisoned, along with some of the accoutrements of sexual appeal that maybe helped hold things together for awhile. And pulling away from the nice house for the last time, maybe driven by anger as much as remorse, she dumps it all in the rollaway, intending for it never to resurface—but she can't quite part with the wedding photos. True? I'm not sure I would want to find out if I could.

Another day, a few miles to the west, a big curbside trash pile told a different story, this one an awe-inspiring tale of a young man and his compulsion for consumption. Back in Chapter One, I kidded about how scrounging offered "all the excitement of stealing but none of the prison time," but this trash pile was something else again —this was curbside stealing from only the better

Relic of a lost life—a scrounged photo of baby's first birthday, Fort Worth, Texas.

retailers. Even a *small* sample of what I pulled from that pile reads like a no-credit-limit shopping spree: new Nike tennis shoes; Cole Haan shoes and sandals; a leather portfolio; a Neiman Marcus silver/pewter bull's-head bottle stopper new in its black velvet box; an Olympus OM77AF camera with custom lenses; a "Raphael Angel Vase" new in its box; a Pottery Barn flower vase; a Sony Walkman and a carrying case full of audio cassettes; a compact disk case; a Panasonic Auto-Stop electric pencil sharpener; numerous new soaps, candles and candle holders; assorted expensive Christmas decorations, along with eleven new gift bags; a wooden picture frame, new in its box, and embossed with little commodified emotions like "Best friends make good times better. We have so much fun together," "Sharing dreams, all the laughter. Sometimes I think you know me too well," and "Our friendship is like a favorite pair of blue jeans that improves with time"; a fancy backpack (which I use to carry home some of the loot); and my personal favorite: twelve 50 ml "shooters," including Tanqueray, Gran Marnier, J&B, Kahlua, and Bailey's Irish Cream.

So thoroughgoing was this cavalcade of consumption and its disposal, so personal was this pile—which also held hundreds of photos, assorted bits of personal identification and information, and a pair of hemostats—that I later decided to check the local obituaries carefully, afraid that perhaps here were accumulated all the residues of a life recently lost. Finding nothing, I relaxed and enjoyed the spoils of what I considered a curbside party—because, among all the other items, the pile held seven sets of festive mariachis, still wrapped in their retail plastic. And it held a stylishly designed invitation to a party now three weeks past—an invitation which, now discarded, I took to have been meant for me:

Let's Celebrate!
Jon's Summer Soirée
Saturday, August 7, 8:00 P.M.
7471 Elmwood Avenue
Fort Worth
Regrets if you must, 787 2332

During my scrounging days, two other trash piles in particular offered up lives less current and all-consuming, and so perhaps more poignant. The first pile I found while on my way out to Lake Benbrook for yet another summer swim—and so, unconstrained by the usual hauling limitations of my bicycle, I just loaded what I wanted into my truck bed and took it with me. Part of the take was a big, flimsy cardboard box, contents mostly undetermined. After a swim, I sat down in the shade of a shoreline tree to go through it—and the first twenty-five years of Rosie Ward's life came tumbling out, all mixed together in a mélange of letters, keepsakes, and diplomas.

Sitting there in the shade, sorting her hundreds of personal items into little piles organized around year or event, I was able to recalibrate at least something of Rosie's life. Here are two ticket stubs to "The Osmonds in Concert" at Louisville's

Kentucky Fair and Expo Center in 1971, and Rosie's entry form for the "I hope I win Vince's 1st Kiss Contest" at age fourteen. High school is here as well. A red and blue "Connie" brand shoe box holds, along with "Junior Pilot" wings and a Camp Judy Lane patch, a small corsage, a football made of construction paper and black marker, a grade 11 vehicle registration card for a 1975 Pontiac "silver black t-top," and a postcard to Rosie from "Miss." in Hawaii, dated 6 April 1977. I also discover Rosie's high school diploma from Russellville High School in Russellville, Arkansas—and something of what it means to move at that age from Kentucky to Arkansas.

In the shoe box is a letter to Rosie in Russellville from John back in Kentucky, postmarked 27 December 1975.

"Dear Rosie," the letter begins. "It's Christmas Eve and I've been meaning to write this letter and get it there before Christmas, but as you can see, I haven't. (It's really because I get so nervous writing to someone as nice and *good-looking* as you that it's almost impossible to write and I can't keep from drooling on the paper!)."

Three tortured pages later, John closes. "Please send me your phone number, I may call you (if it's all right) while my parents are out so they won't yell at me for the phone bill! (You see, I don't have any money.) Goodbye! *I Miss You!!! I love you always*, John. Write back."

Sadly, as the mementos show, Rosie and John didn't reunite. Instead, she ultimately went off to attend TCU in Fort Worth, taking courses,

according to her large blue binder, in "Urban Studies," "Cooking," "Marketing," and "Advertising." By the time she graduated in 1983 with a Bachelor of Science in Home Economics and a Specialty in Interior Design, her diploma shows, she had become Rosie Atkins, wife of Charles Atkins, himself the recipient of an MBA from TCU in 1982. Apparently a job in office furnishings and design followed, along with some serious home redecorating and a move to St. Louis.

But what particularly interests me is the quality of the education Rosie received along the way. The final semester of her senior year at Russellville High, she earned a 99 on a "Midterm Covering Juvenile Delinquency" in Mr. Eisenmitter's 5th-period class, correctly answering short-answer questions that Mr. Eisenmitter had written so as to include himself in each scenario, and writing *"Welcome Back Eisenmitter!"* on her answer sheet. The following fall, before transferring to TCU, she began at the University of Arkansas, where campus staff helpfully provided her a guide on "How To Ask Intelligent Questions." Above all else, the guide emphasized, "Do not be afraid to ask your instructor what he thinks are the important questions! Most instructors are happy to tell you what they think is important! Give them a chance, and they'll take a mile!"

The second curbside pile, which I discover on my way back from selling those scrounged books and buying Strasser's *Waste and Want* at the secondhand bookstore, reveals a different sort of

Scene from a doctor's life—scrounged photo with handwritten note on the back: "He looks like a big rough football player." Fort Worth, Texas.

education, and different sort of existence. There, to my surprise, sealed away in a pyramid of black plastic trash bags, is the life of a prominent local physician. And indeed the bags do seem to contain much of the course of his life, from his birth in 1889 to his death in 1971. They hold a single antique bronzed baby shoe, an antique silver baby spoon, a little handmade wooden airplane, some twenty lovely old sepia photos and photo postcards, old forged tin snips and wood-handled pipe-cutting tools, and two purple three-cent stamps. They also encapsulate a professional career well spent. Along with his 1917 Doctor of Medicine diploma from the Fort Worth School of Medicine, Medical Department, Texas Christian University, the bags include a framed photo of a group dinner held at The Palmer House in Chicago, a photo of the doctor and his friends labeled "A Southern Gentleman," and various European travel maps. They hold a bow tie, brass plaques and framed certificates from the American Cancer Society and the Radiological Society, and a plasticized newspaper clipping, headlined "Dr. Bob Howard Is Recipient of Gold Cane," and noting that this "Oscar for MDs" has been presented by the Tarrant County Medical society to "modest, well-liked" Bob Howard. The bags even suggest something of the three grandchildren noted in his yellowed obituary, with the Putt-Putt tokens and the little children's book, *How Chicks Are Born.*

But lest this begins to sound like a full life story, there are the mysteries. The first is a sealed square envelope, never opened, a name written across it that would seem to be that of Dr. Howard's son. After wondering why it's never been opened, and wondering if it's my place to do so, I decide to open it—and discover love unrequited still, a big red Valentine's Day card, inscribed "Just always know I will always love you!! Always Your Meg." The second is a handmade book, now eaten away by age and inattention. Pasted inside the front cover is a calendar for September and October 1939, captioned "Clean Clothes Make School Day Happier," and on each page a different collage of poems, religious verses, newspaper and magazine clippings, and photographs of animals, flowers, toys, children, food, and fruit. Bob Howard would have been fifty in 1939—did he help a grandchild construct this little book? If so, which grandchild? And with what in mind? Then there's a final layer of mystery. While many of the collages are now lost, hidden away by pages melded together with age, other pages have torn and bled through, and so continued to create new collages out of collages now sixty-five years old.

Perhaps these accidental collages are the appropriate representation of lives lost within the empire of scrounge—lives fractured, discarded, pasted back together when discovered. But if such an imperfect process couldn't confirm the full truth of Rosie Ward and Bob Howard and the other lives lost, it could teach me another kind of truth. All those lost diplomas and family photo albums, all those discarded award plaques and sports trophies, accumulated for me into a deep deliberation on life's transience, a stark reminder that *sic transit gloria mundi* is more than a phrase you memorize in Latin class. Digging amid the detritus of people's lives, I came away with a disturbing sense of existential rubbish—a sense that we'd best live our lives like they matter, because ultimately, we're all disposable heroes.

Salvage Operations

The empire of scrounge is littered with the residues of change. A homeowner's decision to remodel a kitchen pushes appliances and plumbing fixtures to the curb; a developer's retrofitting of an old building fills a big rollaway with copper wire and aged lumber. As a couple falls apart, the man's suits and shoes end up in a curbside trash pile—and, more than once, find a subsequent home in my closet. Moving out of an apartment, belongings that don't make it into the pickup truck or the moving van wind up in the apartment-house Dumpster, or stacked next to it. And of course, among a certain class of people, the unveiling of this year's fashions forces last year's out of the closet and into a garbage bag bound for the charity shop, or for the curb.

In this sense, the lost and discarded objects that make up the empire of scrounge exist as moments in an ongoing process; their solid materiality is matched, or maybe undermined, by the emphemerality of their status. In fact, this sense of a material world in transition first struck me not during my months in the empire, but many years ago, shopping and studying charity shops and secondhand thrift stores. Trying to understand how it was that a $25 sweater in a high-end resale shop could be had for twenty-five cents at the Goodwill Store across town, how it was that last year's $40 pair of jeans could sell six months later in the thrift store for $1.40, I began to realize something: price tags aside, these sweaters and jeans carried no inherent value. Their value was a shifting process, as much a matter of their context as their content—and even more interesting, the process didn't move in a straight line. The object that was originally of great monetary and emotional worth might later be discarded or given away as "worthless," only to reappear in a charity store with a small fraction of its worth restored—and, discovered there, might well find all its lost grandeur restored, and more, if now reimagined by someone as a "collectible" or "antique." Sweaters, tea sets, toasters—they seem solid enough, but their meaning remains malleable.[1]

As does the legal status of those selling them, by the way. During my time as an urban scrounger, a little Methodist church in my neighborhood started a "mission" in a small portable building next to the church. Operated by Enid Randolph and Nadine Nichols, two elderly churchwomen, the mission—"Jenna's Hope of Grace: A Mission Shop"—opened for four hours each Friday and Saturday to sell donated, secondhand clothes and toys to neighborhood residents whom one sympathetic observer described as "90 percent . . . Mexican immigrants . . . [who] live in over-crowded housing [and] work as servants for minimum wage."[2] Stumbling upon the mission while "out looking for illegal yard signs," a City of Fort Worth code enforcement officer, though, saw the little building not as a mission but as an "illegal secondhand retail store," and had it closed. As a result, "Enid and I [don't] know what to do with ourselves on Fridays anymore," said Nadine Nichols. "It's a shame. We gave the people little pamphlets and invited them to our Easter egg hunt or to the Spanish worship [service]. We got to know so many nice people. It was good for the community."[3]

But that was only the first legal shift for Enid, Nadine, and their secondhand items. A month later, with the help of the neighborhood's city councilperson, the city and the church had reached an agreement. The church would remove the word "shop" from the little sign out front; Enid and Nadine and the other volunteers would remove the price tags from the clothes and toys, and instead rely on a sign reading "We Accept Contributions"; and the mission would reopen. And so the status of all those clothes and toys changed once again. Clothes and toys that had started their careers as new acquisitions, that had morphed into donations and discards, then into secondhand sale items, and then into evidence of illegality, now changed back into legally charitable offerings.

And yet this latest transmogrification was not without its own ambiguities. As one church worker carefully explained to me, Spanish-speaking customers now notice the absence of a price tag on an item and ask, in broken English, "How much?" English-speaking church workers now struggle to explain that the item is "open for a donation," or as a last resort, that "well, we *used to* get 50 cents for that one." Moreover, since many of the mission's goods are donated by folks at the conclusion of their own garage sales, many still have garage-sale price tags affixed—and so church workers now must take the time to find and remove these as well.[4] Still, the legal resolution of Jenna's Hope seems to have worked out well enough for everyone: secondhand goods are still being put in the hands of those that need them, the little church is able to meet its tithes and apportionments from donations to the mission—and excess goods given to the Mission are, in yet another transition, bagged and donated to Goodwill or the homeless shelter.

Except that, recently, walking past the church as I often do, I noticed a problem. As it turns out, the church members hadn't so much removed the word "shop" from their sign as they had taped a piece of cardboard over it—and now the cardboard had weakened with the weather and fallen off, leaving a stained outline around "shop" and two pieces of balled-up tape still attached to the sign. For all the world to see, "Jenna's Hope of Grace: A Mission" had been resurrected as "Jenna's Hope of Grace: A Mission Shop," if only by the recent rains. The folks at the church promised me they would get right on retaping the cardboard over

"shop." In the meantime, I thought to myself, Enid and Nadine had best pray that code enforcement doesn't roll by.

As a criminologist, I've long thought that labeling theory offers some of the most important insights into the nature of crime. In brief, labeling theory suggests that to understand crime we must understand the social processes through which crime is constructed. From this view, neither acts nor persons are inherently criminal; they are constructed as such by whatever laws define them in this way, and by others who react to them in a variety of ways. Firing a gun, throwing a punch, driving a car faster than the speed limit, offering secondhand goods to the needy—none of these carries innate meanings or spawns predictable consequences. Instead, their meaning remains in motion, awaits negotiation by observers, code-enforcement officers, police officers, lawyers, and others. A gun fired, a punch thrown can become assault or self-defense, murder or heroism, a speeding car evidence of recklessness or just another rush hour, a secondhand sweater evidence of illegality or grace. What we take to be crime—for that matter, what we take to be justice—emerges from an ongoing social process, a process that criminologists must account for as surely as they account for crime and criminals.[5]

And if this is true of people and the situations in which they find themselves, it seems to me, it's also true of objects. The empire of scrounge suggests a sort of labeling theory of objects lost

New York City block transformed into a bazaar of salvaged ironwork, October 2004.

and found, a sense that the process by which they and their meaning move about matters more than the objects themselves.[6] In this sense, it is perhaps appropriate that this process—this flow of objects in and out of people's lives, this ongoing renegotiation of their meaning and value—doesn't end when the objects find the Dumpster, or even when a scrounger jumps in to extract them. As this chapter shows, salvage operations large and small are underway throughout the empire of scrounge,

operations meant not just to reclaim and reuse discarded objects, but to reinvent them as something else. After all, a sweater bought— excuse me, charitably acquired—from Jenna's Hope may someday end up donated or discarded once again, or if not, then converted again into a yard sale item, or relegated to dog bedding, or stolen. The process of change that defines the empire of scrounge ends only with the landfill— and maybe not even there.

Sometimes, lost in a postapocalyptic reverie, I imagine that even the landfill may not be the final resting place in the empire of scrounge—that someday, when the present world of mindless hyperconsumption has finally failed, those thousands of tools and bicycle parts and lengths of copper pipe that I know are buried there will be dug up, reclaimed, reinvented. In that regard I figure that, as an urban scrounger, I'm practicing for the apocalypse. But until such time as that practice pays off and the Great Postapocalyptic Salvage Festival rolls around, the little salvage operations that already animate the empire of scrounge will continue.

Hecho a Mano

I found that often my own salvage operations emerged on the move and in the moment. Many times I pulled cans of corn and boxes of macaroni and cans of beer from the Dumpster, lining them up on the Dumpster's lip or stacking them beside it so that someone might make use of them; as often, I found and extracted shirts and pants and blouses and, if they had been thrown away while still on their hangers, as they often had, I enjoyed hanging them for public display from the Dumpster's side. I regularly found and salvaged discarded shoes—especially half-worn-out sports shoes and running shoes—and set them out for others to find, or as seen in the previous chapter, put them on and pedaled away. In a Dumpster off University Boulevard I found two working bicycles, and left them leaning on their kick stands in front of the Dumpster. Hell, driving across the Deep South to the meetings of the American Society of Criminology, I found a box of cool old railroad "gimme caps" in a bar ditch alongside some railroad tracks, and passed them out to colleagues once I arrived in Atlanta. Like the author of *Evasion*—who scrounged a bag of cherry pies while hitchhiking and, after eating one, left the remainder "organized in a neat stack for the next hitchhiker"[7]—I was often able to convert the empire's bounty, on the spot, from trash to useful treasure.

Out on a ride in March of 2002, for example, I spot something I want to record, but then realize that I am carrying the second and smaller of my two scrounged backpacks; the first one, the one holding pencil and paper, I've left at home with a broken zipper. Cycling a block and a half to the nearest Dumpster, I find a storehouse of paper in the form of discarded computer repair orders. I fold one and put it in my pocket—but I'm still without pen or pencil. A few minutes later, sorting through a curbside trash pile, I find two like-new mechanical pencils buried in a black garbage bag. Now I can write down what until now I've been repeating in my head so as to remember.

"I work fine but am quite loud and dirty. Yo trabajo bien."

These bilingual phrases, and a big smiley face, I had earlier seen written on the back of an old refrigerator that had been set out on the curb, backwards, so that its message would be broadcast out into the street. The smiley face had been drawn such that a mechanical protrusion on the fridge's backside formed a sort of nose; the word "quite" had been written in above the phrase "am loud," perhaps an afterthought meant to assuage the concerns of those who might be disinclined by the unmodified "loud" to haul the fridge away. And this isn't the first time urban discards have talked to me, by the way—on my rides I regularly encounter little curbside signs that say "Please take" or "Works fine" or "Everything here free."

Later, riding home with more than I can comfortably carry, I stop by my neighborhood grocery and ask the checker to double-bag my orange juice, oranges, and bananas. In this way I acquire an extra plastic bag to supplement my bike basket, rear deck, and second-string backpack in hauling home the day's take. During the course of the ride I've left behind a big lawn sprinkler, a garden hose, and a watering can for lack of carrying capacity. Even so, I now carry along with my juice and fruit: four lawn sprinklers, copper pipe and wire, brass shower fixtures, aluminum cans, a Homedics Professional Percussion Massager with Heat, a Currier and Ives canister, a variety of knobs and handles, an Exacto knife, sand paper, a small wheel, two small chains, a door stop, lead weights, a brass key, a numeral "4" refrigerator magnet, a container of nails and screws, three metal buttons, six pennies, three wooden pencils—and those two mechanical pencils. Hey, when I go out scrounging, *yo trabajo bien.*

Three days later, I've just filled my second-string, secondhand backpack with some scrap metal from a Dumpster when I come across a big, clean-out-the-garage trash pile on a homeowner's curb about a mile away. Riding along today, working that Dumpster, I've been thinking that I do need to fix the zipper on my better backpack, because, as evidenced the other day, the one I'm using isn't really big enough for daily scrap hauling. Now, stopping at this curbside trash pile, the first item I spot is a big, sturdy canvas Wilson sports bag. To hell with trying to fix the zipper on my old bag—this one's bigger, better, and as of this moment my new scrounging bag. Actually, though, it takes this new scrounged bag, my smaller second-string bag, and the remainder of my bike's carrying capacity to make it home with all that this pile and the remainder of the ride produce. From this one trash pile I pull little colored cut-glass serving dishes in the shape of hearts, diamonds, clubs, and spades; a Romance brand covered glass box; a children's Melamine drinking cup; a Budweiser/Texas Parks and Wildlife Foundation lapel pin; a Millard Fillmore commemorative coin; an "Ask Me What's News, Today's Star-Telegram" button; an oversized black rubber fly with suction cup; a rubber bungee cord; a pair of pliers; a 1951 Texas license plate; a Pro-Am fishing reel and new package of fluorescent pink fishing bobbers (96 cents, from Wal-Mart); a U.S. Army mess kit; a brass light fixture, a brass lamp part, a heavy brass stapler in the shape of an airplane, a brass doorknob, and a brass-colored aluminum ashtray; a tiny Swingline Tot 50 stapler; aluminum cake decorating disks; two pairs of tongs; a twelve-inch ruler; a package of screws; two small wooden rings; and a single red die.

The pile also provides me with some new reading material: *Monsters Collectors Book #3*, *Historical Christmas Stories 1990*, *The Hardy Boys: The Arctic Patrol Mystery*, *The Essential Darkroom Book*, and a little *Muir Woods National Monument* photo book. And it offers up toys, most of which I'll later pass on to one kid or another, including seventeen plastic chess pieces, various Leggo components, a children's microscope, two yo-yos (one labeled "Boy Scouts of America Longhorn Council Ft. Worth Texas"), a toy monster truck, two "superballs," a green camouflage Delta Force kid's watch, a plastic jointed male action figure whose chest opens to reveal machine innards, a wind-up dragon, two toy cars, a "Batman Returns" button, and a Troll doll. Later in the ride, already hauling this odd ensemble, I add to it a Louisville Slugger aluminum "Senior Youth" bat, aluminum cans and scrap, more brass parts, copper wire, a toy power drill, a paint roller, a penny, and a large wooden Montesino brand cigar box—made in the Dominican Republic, "434-0280" scrawled in ink on the front, and imprinted on the front and the back with a little statement about cigars and scrounging.

"Hecho a Mano." Handmade.

Oh yeah, and when a few months later the Wilson sports bag finally wears out from hauling scrap, I scrounge a big SportCraft croquet set bag to replace it. It works well, too.

Empire of Tools

While on-the-fly salvage operations like these regularly emerged during scrounging rides and walks, others required a bit more time and accumulation. Often I did leave clothes and food outside Dumpsters—but if I could afford the space on my bike, or if a particularly big find merited a return trip by truck, I would haul them home. After enough days of returning home with scrounged clothes and shoes, a truckload was ready to be hauled to the homeless shelter. When the canned goods began to stack up in my shed, it was time for a run to the food bank. A few good discoveries of discarded blankets and towels, and it was off to the animal shelter. As for myself, I kept and stored away a few food items—and in the fall I gathered peaches and the ubiquitous Texas pecan, and after shelling and eating all the pecans I could, sold the remainder at a yard sale.

The accumulation most essential to my scrounging and to my ongoing salvage operations, though, was not the scrounged materials themselves, but the tools with which to continue scrounging and salvaging them. Early on, I was amazed by the number of tools that I was finding and beginning to accumulate. I suppose there are all sorts of gendered scripts at play here, but I've always been fascinated by the practical aesthetics of hand tools, by their solid integration of form and function, and so hand tools quickly emerged as some of my favorite items to find and keep. In addition, I've always taken pride in at least a certain degree of handiness and self-reliance when it comes to repairs and material modifications, and so each newly scrounged tool made this sort of work more plausible and enjoyable as well. Soon enough, friends began to stop short as they entered my shed. Hanging from the walls, strung from the rafters, were whole collections of flat-head screwdrivers and Phillips-head screwdrivers, assortments of open end and box-end wrenches in absurd redundancy, handsaws and hacksaws stacked one on another, and such a vast array of specialty tools, old and new, that, to be honest, some of their uses still escape my understanding. Each time I walked into my shed I entered the empire of tools—and it was good.

As personally gratifying as it was to discover and scrounge the next screwdriver or wrench, it was hardly an uncommon event. The streets themselves offered one fairly steady supply, with wrenches and sockets apparently bouncing off the backs of repair trucks or out of pickup truck beds with such regularity that I seldom went more than a week or so between found tools. Curbside piles resulting from garage cleanings provided the other. A homeowner too tired to sort through those last few old boxes in the back of the garage before discarding them, a new owner eager to get rid of the last owner's belongings left behind in the garage or shed, a son or daughter getting the

home of a deceased parent ready to sell—these and others sent a steady stream of tools out to the curb. As seen in the previous chapter, one curbside pile produced screwdrivers, locking pliers, wire cutters, and an adjustable wrench. Another, after some digging, offered up two wrenches, a West German–made wood-handled brush, a heavy cylindrical metal rasp, two Allen wrenches, an adjustable angle/square, two old chisels, a grinder drill attachment, a wire-brush drill attachment, a variety of drill bits, a custom handsaw, a number of small specialty tools, and an old turnkey—as well as assortment of band clamps, screws, nails, rubber washers, brackets, bolts, and plumbing fixtures. As before, the pile even provided a way to carry all these tools and parts home—this time, a heavy canvas L.L. Bean tote bag. I was a junkie for tools, and the empire was an endless fix.

Soon enough, though, as I learned more about scrounging and the practical dynamics of living as a scrounger, I came to realize that these tools were more than trophies, albeit practical ones; they were the key to sustaining myself as a scrounger. The limited scrap-hauling capacity of a bicycle meant that the on-the-street ability to extract the most valuable components from discarded goods was essential—and the right tools were essential to this extraction process. Then again, lugging a big set of tools around with me on the bike was largely self-defeating in terms of hauling capacity, and so after a while I evolved a compact set of scrounged tools that I carried, and still carry, in a little belt pack while on scrounging rides. Wire cutters, channel-lock pliers, a reversible flat-head/Phillips-head screwdriver, a miniature flat-head/Phillips-head screwdriver, a little piece of hacksaw blade, and whichever among the endless supply of Allen wrenches I had scrounged lately—with these few tools and the old Swiss Army knife I always carry, I could field strip just about anything I came across. I couldn't bike home with a water heater—but with the channel-lock pliers I could remove the heavy brass spigot, and with the wire cutters twist and cut away the aluminum and copper tubing. I couldn't haul home an old sink, but I could remove its brass fixtures and copper pipe. I couldn't manage an old door on the bike, but I could certainly manage to remove the brass door knobs, lock set, hardware, and hinges.

The sheer abundance of scrounged tools allowed me also to outfit my old truck, and though these tools were less important because less often used, they did on occasion come in handy; at the scrap metal yard, for example, I learned that a set of tools could be invaluable for the last-minute disassembling of multimetal objects into their component parts. Far more important were the scrounged tools hanging in my shed. When not working the streets, much of my time was spent using these tools to disassemble found objects into their usable or salvageable components, or to repair and rebuild found objects for later reuse. This repair and rebuilding process was in turn aided by another sort of found tool: the professional reference book and the repair

manual. While out scrounging I discovered and hauled home discarded books like *Handyman: Complete Guide to Home Maintenance*, *Basic and Advanced Plumbing*, *Blueprint Reading for Welders*, *Electrical Wiring Residential*, the electrician's *Pictorial Workbook of the Code*, *The Watch Repairer's Manual*—and of course my favorite, the always popular *Flowers for Funerals*. Well, actually, I didn't put *Flowers for Funerals* to much use—but I did many of the others. Guided by these scrounged repositories of practical knowledge, equipped with a full armamentarium of scrounged tools, I was able to learn all sorts of practical procedures, and in so doing to move myself toward long-term scrounging self-sufficiency.

Skinning and Harvesting, Stripping and Ripping

Reclaiming scrap metal taught me a series of rituals, little configurations of skill and practice that mostly emerged out of the metal itself. Certain skills I brought along with me from years of semicompetent handyman work and general tinkering around; mostly, though, it was the physical design and fabrication of particular products—rooftop TV antennas, ceiling fans, door locks, window frames—that taught me the deconstruction rituals necessary for transforming them into salvageable scrap metal. In *Waste and Want*, Susan Strasser employs a lovely sort of materialist analysis in noting that "fixing and finding uses for worn and broken articles entail a consciousness about materials and objects that is key to the process of making things to begin with. Repair ideas come more easily to people who make things."[8] This materialist method worked in the other direction, too: the more time I spent with worn and broken articles, the more they taught me about how to disrepair them, about how to break them down into clean, cash-friendly categories of recyclable brass, aluminum, and copper.

Take, for instance, door-knob skinning. When I first began to accumulate discarded door knobs in large numbers, I figured I had hit a gold—or at least brass—mine. Here, in remodeling trash piles and elsewhere, were all these easily scrounged heavy brass doorknobs, and accompanying brass hardware and lock plates, ready to be cashed in at the relatively high prices offered for clean scrap brass. But my magnet—always the arbiter of truth in the scrap metal world—soon told me differently; a magnet only "takes" to ferrous metals, not to copper, aluminum, and brass, and yet it was attracted to many of these "brass" doorknobs. As it turned out, and as any old-time carpenter or handyman could have laughingly told me, "brass" door knobs actually vary widely in the amount of brass they incorporate; as a general rule, the older the doorknob, the thicker and heavier the brass portions of it. Some old doorknobs are in fact pure brass—but most present-day door knobs are, for reasons of structural strength and corporate economy, constructed from steel or tin or die cast, then wrapped in a thicker or thinner skin of brass.

So, after a bit of trial and error, I taught myself how to skin the brass shell from these fraudulent "brass" doorknobs. Clamping the knob or its shaft tightly in my big vice, grabbing a big pair of scrounged wire cutters or tin snips, I'd begin to cut and pull at the outer layer of brass. With a bit of torque, a small cut would become a bigger one, and eventually a flap of brass would pull loose, to be grabbed in the wire cutters and torqued away from the knob. With enough repetitions of this ritual, the knob is entirely skinned of its outer brass layer; the knob's guts go to the scrap tin and steel bin, the skin to the brass bin, and the next knob to the vice.

My salvaging of big rooftop TV antennas developed along the lines of a similarly organic metaphor. These old antennas, now regularly consigned to curbside trash piles with the ascendance of cable and dish television, really are remarkable constructions: big, square, extruded aluminum shafts affixed atop twenty-foot-long steel poles, with smaller aluminum tubes angling out from the shaft to a wingspan of ten or twelve feet, all in hopes of snagging one TV signal or another out of the ether. Because of this, I found, they could be hell to haul home (especially on a bicycle—sort of like trying to wrangle a big flapping bird while rolling along on two wheels), but easy enough to deconstruct once I learned how to harvest the aluminum. Unbolting the aluminum antenna from the steel pole begins the process; sometimes a little WD40 helps loosen U-bolts and lock nuts not adjusted since Jack Parr and Jack Benny. Then, using the big wire cutters, I quickly rip and clip off the light-weight aluminum tubes, harvesting them like little leaves of grass, and leaving only the big aluminum shaft behind. (This task can also be done more slowly, bare-handed, when wire cutters aren't available.) Finally, clamping the shaft in the big vice, the wire cutters and the hacksaw separate the extruded aluminum from the steel mounts and bolts that punctuate it.

Over the months and years, I developed a real affection for these processes. Finding a big antenna, a box of discarded doorknobs, a pile of ceiling fans on the curb didn't just mean a little cash and a lot of metal kept out of the landfill; it also set in motion a pleasurable, straightforward ritual of learned handiwork and practical reclamation. The metaphors with which I came to make sense of these processes—skinning doorknobs, harvesting aluminum from TV antennas—seemed almost always to reference earlier, organic human activities likewise founded on rhythmic, do-it-yourself skills. But whatever human history these activities may call forth metaphorically, they're not abstractions. They're practical rituals, conceptualizations of my own ongoing activity that emerged not out of my head or my books, but mostly out of the scrounged materials themselves.

The most regular of my rituals, by the way, wasn't skinning or harvesting, but stripping. Copper is generally the most valuable of scrounged metals, and the most valuable type of copper is what scrap yards variously denote as "brite and shiny (BS)" or "bare brite (BB)"—shiny copper electrical wire without its protective, color-coded plastic coating. Because of this, I was always on the lookout for copper wire, and in fact there was much to be found in big construction site rollaways and remodeling trash piles—but once found in its "natural" state and hauled home, it had to be made into "bare brite" in order to maximize its salvage value. The result was hour after hour of stripping—securing one end of a length of electrical wiring in my big vise, pulling back on the wire to tauten it, and then stripping and scraping away the coating with a utility knife. Of course, repeatedly pushing a knife blade through heavy plastic coating and along copper wire is a quick way to wear it—and yet scrounged tools solved this problem as well. Among my most commonly found tools were utility knives—in trash piles and Dumpsters, and lost in the streets —as well as the little boxes of replaceable blades that accompany them. In fact, despite countless hours of stripping copper wire, my supply of knives and blades never dwindled; for every knife or knife blade I wore out, there were five or ten more stored away and waiting in my shop.

So, to recap, my essential tools as a self-sustaining urban scrounger were a magnet, a hacksaw, channel-lock pliers, wire cutters, utility knives, a vice—oh yeah, and a seam ripper. Given consumer culture's aggressive marketing of product lines along with products, I suppose it's not surprising that I regularly found in Dumpsters and trash piles shirts, sweaters, pants, shorts, gloves, and hats from Nike, The Gap, Polo, and other corporate pimp daddies. And, heh, I didn't mind wearing them either—actually, I couldn't afford to mind—so long as I remembered to rip off every vestige of corporate identification; damned if I was going to provide free advertising for sweatshops, or be seen diving into a Dumpster as a Ralph Lauren man. I tried corporate logo removal with and without a seam ripper, and I have to admit, without the seam ripper sometimes big chunks of material came right off with the logo, so I generally took the time to rip the seams the right way. But really, the important thing wasn't how neatly the logos come off. The important thing, the best thing, was ripping seams one way or another, and then wearing those logo-castrated clothes while engaged in a way of life that utilized Nike and Gap castoffs to create an economic and experiential alternative to the very economy from which they profited. In fact, sometimes, lost in another of my postapocalyptic reveries while Dumpster diving or stripping wire, I imagined that this alternative world might someday overtake the present one—that someday the Gap would go out of business for good, and Nike executives would be swooshed off to jail on charges of fifty-cents-an-hour factory-made child abuse.[9]

Converted to Scrounging

Scavenging bags and packs to haul home scrounged items, using scrounged tools to ready scrounged metal for the scrap yard, repairing or rebuilding discarded items with these same scrounged tools, finding pencil and paper to record field notes on the fly, wearing found shoes and clothes—all of these were certainly important steps toward self-sufficiency in the empire of scrounge, but they were also part of a larger self-sustaining dynamic. Along with Gap shirts and Polo pants and scrounged shoes, I also pulled a denim work shirt off a discarded post-Halloween scarecrow, cut the sleeves off, and wore it out scrounging. As seen in the previous chapter, I scrounged libraries worth of books—and I sold some to used-book stores and then used the cash to buy more books. I not only scrounged one of the bicycles I rode out scrounging; I later scrounged a bike rack and a front basket, and bolted them on to increase my scrap-hauling capacity. I didn't just scrounge the sports bag and the croquet bag and the L.L. Bean tote bag; I continued to find backpacks, briefcases, and travel cases, some so nice I couldn't even bring myself to fill them with scrap.[10]

Beyond this, I came to realize the self-confirming value of reflexivity. That is, I began to understand that salvage and repair weren't enough; for the empire of scrounge to operate on its own terms, it had to be continually turned back onto itself. The options, I realized, weren't limited to repairing a lamp or breaking it down into scrap; they also included putting parts of the lamp to use in fixing another scrounged lamp, or reinventing the lamp as something else, and in so doing solving one more problem without recourse to cash or consumption. A found faucet could be taken apart and used to repair the leaky faucet in my house. A found CD carrying case could of course hold all those found CDs I was accumulating. A found book case could hold what scrounged books I didn't sell or give away. My extensive stock of found ceiling fan components could be used when, time and again, one of my own ceiling fans broke a blade or threw a bolt. Scrounged WD40 was useful for loosening rusted bolts on found machinery, scrounged silver cleaner for polishing found silverware and candleholders, a found magnifying glass for identifying the markings on old silver and other found antiques, a found hardwood silver service box for storing it all.

But it was even better than that.

When a section of my wood fence rotted away, I had only to go a couple of blocks to find enough discarded slats to fix it. Building some window shelving to hold my collection of scrounged insulators such that the south sun might shine through them, I ran out of 1 x 4 stock—and so drove my pickup six blocks away, to a Dumpster where the day before I had noticed remodeling debris, and scrounged what I needed. Finding a metal frame for a small wall-mounted shelving unit, I outfitted it with found wooden boards and displayed on it various found treasures. Needing a work table on which to mount my big industrial vice, I used scrounged tools to construct it out of scrounged 2 x 4s held together with scrounged nails and scrounged wood screws—and then used the table and the vice to strip found copper wire and to disassemble various found appliances and machines.

Of course, working at that table into the night, I needed light—and so as the months went by I scrounged enough light fixtures and working light bulbs to outfit my shed, and much of my house as well. As I discovered, people not only regularly discarded working lamps and light fixtures, but left the light bulbs in them when they did so—and despite being tossed into a trash pile or Dumpster, the great majority of these discarded bulbs still functioned. The ongoing process of scrounging, stripping, and disassembling also necessitated storage for accumulations of machine parts and scrap metal—a problem also solved without recourse to retail. I scrounged a variety of hangers and hooks from which I hung parts, tools, and supplies; likewise, I scrounged peg board and peg board hardware, installed it throughout my shed, and so organized collections of plumbing parts, tools, and door and window hardware. Scrounged file cabinets and a scrounged metal hutch became storage bins for golf balls, window screens, brass parts, and copper scrap; a scrounged medicine cabinet installed on my shop wall held a collection of shower heads and faucets. The smaller scrounged containers in which I collected scrounged parts, copper wire, and scrap metal were almost as varied as their contents: cat litter buckets, old garbage cans, ice cube holders, plastic plant pots, old metal chests, glass jars,

gar boxes, single-malt Scotch tins, and old
midcentury aluminum canisters whose raised
lettering revealed that they originally held coffee,
tea, and sugar.

Back in the house, it wasn't only found lamps
and light bulbs that were obviating the need for
cash-based consumption. A set of blinds
discovered curbside now nicely covered my living
room and bedroom windows; wooden shutters—
found, cut to fit, painted, and outfitted with
scrounged knobs—filled my kitchen window.
Finding a box of ten stylish 1950s tubular sconces,
I installed two in my living room, squirreled away
a few more, and gave the remainder to a friend for
her own interior remodeling job. In fact, I
discovered, the range and amount of household
furnishings available in the empire of scrounge
was so great that I could afford to specialize, and
so I set about redecorating my house in my
favorite mode, the one suggested by those
canisters and sconces: 1950s and 1960s
Americana, or "midcentury modern," as the
design magazines like to call it. A lovely gold and
black sunburst wall clock and a black and green
flower-patterned TV tray from that period made it
to my living room. To complement the clock and
the tray and the sconces, I scrounged more of the
midcentury: a long, low-slung green vinyl couch
(with fold-out bed); a turquoise vinyl and blonde
wood casual chair; an orange Paul Klee–patterned
pillow; a lovely little glass and gold wire pedestal
bowl; and a two-tiered, green and black onion-
skin lamp.[11]

For all the pleasure that these scrounged
furnishings provided, though, there was
something I enjoyed even more: imagining ways
to convert scrounged objects from their original
use to my immediate need, and so to close once
again the circle of self-reliance. Disassembling a
found boat ladder, for example, I tossed its
aluminum tubing into the scrap aluminum bin—
and then realized that its three nicely varnished
wood steps would make good wall shelves. A few
days later, mounting these shelves to my study
wall with found angle braces, I was forced to stop
when I discovered I was two angle braces short.
On the next day's ride, I found more angle braces,
and came home to finish the job.

If my house and shed in this way came to reflect
the rhythms of ongoing reuse, my backyard
became a veritable garden of conversion. I found
discarded landscaping plants in construction site
rollaways, hauled them home, and replanted them
—in the ground, or in any of the dozens of clay
pots, some quite large and elaborately decorated,
that I regularly pulled from Dumpsters and trash
piles. Scrounged wrought-iron side tables and
shelves became outdoor stands for these potted
plants. A pile of discarded window burglar bars,
secured end to end with scrounged band clamps
and wire, staked to the ground with found
camping stakes, became a decorative fence. One of
my gardens I bordered with found metal edging,
held down with salvaged-metal lawn chair cross-
straps reshaped in my vice. Tomato plant cages I
built from found fencing; a two-stage compost

heap I constructed from scrounged wood, fencing, plastic, and chicken wire. Twigs and limbs too big for the compost heap I bundled with salvaged twine and rope. For the birds, I converted an old outdoor light fixture into a bird feeder, and built from old wooden ceiling fan blades a birdhouse—home to a pair of sparrows last spring.

All of these little handmade salvage operations, of small consequence in their own right, seem to me to suggest something larger and more consequential. Over time, I found, scrounged tools, stripped wire, salvaged plants, and fan-blade birdhouses come together to harbinger a world outside the loop of consumer society. Where the consumer economy spirals itself and its participants deeper into destruction and indebtedness, the empire of scrounge spirals in the opposite direction. Undertaken in the long run, scrounging provides the prerequisites for further scrounging. Reused materials, after a while, form the basis for ongoing reuse; accumulations of salvaged items form the foundation for salvaging a life outside the need for cash and consumption. The informal underground economy that is the empire of scrounge digs deeper, begins to sustain itself, as its products and practices coalesce. Where consumer society spawns waste, the empire of scrounge offers recuperation.

A couple of caveats, though. First, for this dynamic of recuperation and reuse to work, a certain degree of accumulation is necessary; if solutions aren't to be purchased at the store, possibilities must be kept at hand. Charles Loring Brace's 1872 description of a rag picker's shanty—"bones, broken dishes, rags, bits of furniture, cinders, old tin, useless lamps, decaying vegetables, ribbons, cloths, legless chairs, and carrion, all mixed together, and heaped up nearly to the ceiling"[12]—wasn't so much a description of poor housekeeping as of a poor man's stock of solutions. Likewise, my grandfather, a man so careful about appearances that he would change from his farm clothes to his pressed khakis before going into town for even the smallest errand, nonetheless kept a pile of tractor parts, short iron, and sheet metal behind his shed—not as junk, but as resource for do-it-yourself repair. Those who know the empire of scrounge know that its offerings must be accepted and accumulated over time—and so, as we'll see, they regularly run afoul of others who value the precision of law and appearance over the piling up of possibility.

Second, even the most dedicated of scroungers can't always get by on his or her own accumulated resources, on handmade burglar bar fences and salvaged shirts. Sometimes it's necessary to convert scrounged objects not into new material possibilities, but into a little cash.

For that there's the scrap yard.

My Junk Is My School

Scrap yards, junkyards, and junk piles—small and large repositories of metallica lost, found, and

Scrap metal yard, Tampa, Florida, June 2004.

scrounged—flourish all around the empire of scrounge. Many of the big scrap yards operate as fluid intermediaries between scrounging and subsequent reuse, each day admitting rivers of aluminum cans, cast iron, and copper tubing through the front door and disgorging bundles of sorted, compressed metal into the railcars and truck trailers waiting out the back. Other junkyards are more stagnant, with heavy accretions of worn-out appliances, cracked car wheels, broken lawn furniture, and old tools rusted into place around the property. Some big yards operate as magnificent dramas of movement and noise—oversized truck and trailer rigs loading and unloading tons of scrap metal at a time, big cranes dropping industrial magnets into towering accumulations of scrap iron, and scurrying forklifts stabbing their front tines into mountains of copper wire and aluminum cans. Others operate more quietly, sometimes even surreptitiously, out of a small garage or side yard, their scrap eased in and out by car trunk or pickup or purloined grocery cart. Some of these repositories of reuse operate as licensed commercial scrap yards, some as informal individual or neighborhood enterprises, others as part of city or corporate recycling programs. Most all operate along or beyond one legal margin or another.

At a minimum, the sheer amount of discarded metal available for everyday scrounging, and the relatively low per-pound price of this metal when eventually sold as scrap, mean that anyone serious about working the empire of scrounge for its metal must find some way to sort and store it in fairly large quantities. Even the most fluid of metal scroungers—homeless folks scavenging aluminum cans on foot day-to-day—can't afford the inefficiency of stopping the scavenging process to walk a few cans in to the scrap yard for cash redemption. Because of this, homeless metal scroungers not only employ abandoned shopping carts in which to accumulate aluminum cans and other found scrap, but typically attach plastic bags and buckets so as to maximize the cart's carrying capacity prior to it's being pushed in to the scrap yard or recycling center. Beyond this, those like myself lucky enough to have a small home benefit from setting up some system for processing, sorting, and storing scrounged scrap metal. The more elaborate the sorting and storage system, the more ecologically sound and monetarily

profitable the enterprise; a bin for every type of scrap metal means that no part of a disassembled doorknob or window or water heater need go to waste. The greater the system's storage capacity, the longer between trips to the scrap yard, and so the less gas to be burned and gas money to be deducted from scrap metal earnings.

Even a single metal, to be made profitable, requires relatively detailed knowledge of its subtypes and a system for their sorting and storing. Aluminum, the metal perhaps most commonly scavenged and sold, necessitates just such an approach. Of course the big scrap yards buy aluminum—but they buy it, and price it, based on its purity and type. A typical scrap yard price list for aluminum, with prices per pound, would read as follows:

Aluminum Cans	.45
Clean Aluminum Clips	.45
Extrusion Aluminum	.50
Cast Aluminum	.40
No. #3 Aluminum	.35
Aluminum Cooler	.45
Aluminum Radiator	.35
Aluminum Breakage	.12
Aluminum Wheels	.55
Aluminum Copper Coolers	.50
Aluminum Copper Coolers with Steel Ends	.40

The careful reader will note that an impoverished aluminum scrounger, looking to earn a few bucks for food or beer, in this way encounters a scrap yard price structure in which one sort of aluminum may be almost five times the value of another. In turn, the careful scrounger will know that, if a mixed load is brought in, the yard will pay to the lowest type in the mix; haul in a blend of breakage and extrusion, and you'll get paid the rate for the breakage: twelve cents a pound. The careful scrounger therefore also knows, long before any trip to the scrap yard, to set up a system for identifying, sorting, and storing each of these eleven types of aluminum.

But actually its more complicated than that. Since the scrounger doesn't discover aluminum lodged within such neat categories, but rather bolted or soldered together in all manner of material configurations, street knowledge of aluminum's permutations is necessary, along with the time and space for converting these permutations from scrounged material to sellable scrap. On one March 2002 ride, for example, I scrounged from a single block of a suburban street an old aluminum lawn hose caddy, an aluminum rooftop antenna, and an aluminum door threshold. A single scrounging day in July 2002 yielded variations on an aluminum theme that ranged from a vacuum cleaner hose, a window screen, a screen door, a vent cover, and a TV antenna, to a garden hose attachment, a custom aluminum car wheel, a roll of flashing, a candy dish, two heating ducts, the border of a 1950s breakfast table, window awnings, and aluminum cans. One day in early August, three bicycle trips produced aluminum cans, an aluminum rooftop antenna, an aluminum sauce pan, three aluminum window/window-screen sets, and thirty-two heavy aluminum slats from an air conditioning unit; three days later I rolled home with a bag full of aluminum cans, five aluminum pans, one aluminum pan lid, a length of aluminum tubing, and a big chunk of heavy extruded aluminum, three holes bored cleanly through it, original use unknown.

Day after day, all of this must be stored somewhere until it can be cleaned and sorted, and then stored somewhere else once it has been. And that's not to mention the other salvageable metals that arrive in various configurations: the five types of copper, the two kinds of brass, the die cast, stainless steel, lead, tin, short iron, cast iron, auto batteries, and electric motors. The economic margins of independent metal salvaging are too thin to allow the luxury of ignorance or waste; efficient reclamation of found metal is essential. As a result, over the course of eight months' intensive scrounging, I more than once ran out of time or energy, and rather than waste scrounged metal, left a half-disassembled aluminum lawn chair or a tangle of half-stripped copper wire sitting in front of my backyard shed for a day or two. Over those same eight months, I also invented an ever-more-elaborate system of storage bins hidden away in the long, narrow space between the back of my shed and the back fence. In fact, each time I learned a bit more about the subtle categorical variations in aluminum or brass or copper, the bins multiplied so as to accommodate some new subdivision in the taxonomy of salvageable metal.

The result of this process was my own secret staging area for trips to the commercial scrap yard, a home metal-salvaging system that was ecologically efficient, marginally profitable—and profoundly illegal. Section 11A-26 of the Fort Worth City Code is really quite clear on the matter; unless zoned and licensed as junk dealers, it prohibits citizens' accumulating on their property "*any* broken, inoperable, or discarded household furnishings, appliances, machines, tools, boxes and cartons, lawn maintenance equipment, play equipment, toys, and similar items," including "used or discarded building materials" and "used, discarded, or broken auto parts or equipment."[13] Besides offering zero tolerance for any accumulation of scrap, no matter how small, the ordinance makes no allowance for invisibility; to be illegal the accumulation need not be visible to anyone else, only existent.[14] Still, to shield my illegal accumulations from the same code enforcement officers who busted Jenna's Hope of Grace just a few blocks away, I was careful to keep my bins well below the top of my six-foot wooden back fence. In fact, I'd be willing to bet that no one has ever seen my illegal staging area other than by invitation.

Though Lord knows they've tried. Afraid that their code enforcement officers weren't busting enough church charity stores and spotting enough "illegal yard signs," the City of Fort Worth established during early 2004 its Code Rangers program. As publicized in the local media, the city now began to work with neighborhood associations to recruit and train residents to be volunteer Code Rangers, thereby giving the city "more eyes and ears on the street." Sending their new eyes and ears out to look for "outdoor storage of broken or discarded items" and other offenses, the city hoped that the Code Rangers might remain on the lookout even "while walking dogs, taking jogs, even taking their children to school."[15] "This is something we are dead serious on," said Mayor Mike Moncrief as the program was launched. "Give them hell," added Councilwoman Becky Haskin.[16] And in fact, when the Code Rangers program was presented at a meeting of my own neighborhood association, a number of those present were so excited by the new program, so eager to give their neighbors code-violating hell, that I bicycled directly home and pushed all my scrap metal down another foot below the top of my back fence.

Fort Worth's eyes-and-ears army of code enforcement officials and Code Rangers haven't caught me yet—but they did catch Frank Johnson.[17] They caught him, and then they called him before the Building Standards Commission on charges of violating Section 11A-26 of the Fort Worth City Code by letting washing machines, lawn mowers, and other discards accumulate on his property. Not only that—they put him on television. As it turned out, Frank didn't need to audition for the Learning Channel's *Junkyard Wars* television series that time it came through Fort Worth and staged the promotional event at the local mall. Frank got to fight his own junkyard war, right there for everyone to see on the city's cable channel.

As the cameras began recording the hearing for later broadcast on the city cable channel, Frank—an older man, black, full gray beard, wearing a stained Bugs Bunny T-shirt and a cloth hat—listened while city officials detailed the ordinance in question. Then Frank presented his case.

"I like to work on stuff," he said. "And, I've always been working since I've been twelve, and I intend to work until I go, 'cause I like to stay active. And one reason I haven't been cleaning up is—I have been cleaning up—but, I got a little arthritis, and that lifting gets me, so it's a little harder for me to do things nowadays. I'm working on it and cleaning it up."

Commission members aren't impressed, and so, noting that Frank had first been notified of his accumulating violations a year earlier, begin the interrogation.

"These items that are in the yard, can you tell us why they were brought there?"

"Well, like I said, I like to work on stuff. Plus, I didn't have a job."

"So you were trying to repair items . . . ?"

But Frank cuts off the question with a correction. "I was trying to *survive*."

"OK, so you were bringing items in, and maybe repair 'em and sell 'em and whatever you could do?"

"Right," Frank says, reluctantly.

Now another commission member's turn to paraphrase the ordinance. "OK, and how long would you say that you have permitted those items to accumulate in your backyard?"

And now Frank's turn to clarify again just what was at stake. "Well, I've been junking a long time. 'Cause like I said, I started from survival, and you can't get a job, you either steal or try to do something else."

Another commission member tries a different approach, asking if in effect Frank has been running an unlicensed lawn mower repair business from his backyard.

"No," Frank tells him, "I've been collecting 'em and I junk 'em out."

"So what have you been repairing then?"

"Mostly *my* stuff," Frank tells him. "My cars—I taught myself how to do a lot of my stuff. *My junk is my school.* 'Cause you go to school, you don't learn everything in school, so I come back and I kinda like shade-tree it to pick up on the different things that I didn't quite learn in school."

"OK, and you do them there at your house . . . that repair work at your house?"

"Yeah, so I would learn it in case I wanted to work on something for somebody."

Finally, it's commission member Robert Hawley's turn. A pudgy, middle-aged white man stuffed into a white shirt and dark suit, Mr.

Hawley seems to be enjoying the inquisition. He offers up little smiles and smirks between his questions.

"Are you scrapping any of the metal that's out there?" he asks.

"Yes, I'm getting rid of it," says Frank.

"No, but I mean over the years have you taken it up to metal scrap dealers and sold it for scrap?"

"I *have*," says Frank, emphasis on the past tense.

"And so either you were collecting it or other people were bringing it to you and then you were taking it up to the scrap dealer?"

"Sometimes people just come by and just drop off stuff. They know that I did that kind of stuff, so they'd come by and just drop off stuff."

"So you were like a little recycling area for, staging area for the scrap dealers then?" asks Robert Hawley, emphasis on the belittlement.

"Not quite what you're saying," says Frank.

"H'mmmm" says Robert Hawley.

After a few more questions, Hawley tells Frank, "You know we're gonna make you move that stuff."

Frank agrees, says he's trying to get it moved, but "I just can't go as fast as I used to."

Wondering if in fact Frank will ever get it all moved, Hawley tells him "that's a lot of stuff out there."

"Well, like I say, I just like to do different things," Frank says. "I like to try to invent different things. I've made things where I wouldn't have to go out and buy stuff. I figured out how to do it on my own."

Unmoved by Frank Johnson's resourcefulness, city staff conclude the hearing by recommending a civil penalty of $3,120 and an order to clear the property within thirty days—else the city will have the property cleared and add a bill for its services to the $3,120 penalty. Commission members are concerned, though, that Frank can't possibly pay this penalty or get the property cleared in time—interestingly, they discuss the likelihood that the city will only get its money once the property has been sold—and so decide on a more merciful resolution: only $1,040 in civil penalties, plus the order to clear the property in thirty days, and an additional bill for city clearing services if not.

A couple of months later I drive over to Frank's property in the old Polytechnic Heights neighborhood of east Fort Worth. On his street and down the surrounding side streets are modest homes, some run down, some nicely kept. A block away is the old Macabe's Supermarket, now closed and boarded up, with a sign that says "Future Home of the Cowboys of Color National Museum." Nearby, a billboard displays a different take on changing urban economics: "Ugly's OK—We Buy Houses." As for Frank's house—well, there isn't one. By the little patches of leftover lawn, it appears there once was a house on the front of his lot, but now there's only a wide driveway and a garage apartment toward the back of the property. There are also no washing machines or old lawn mowers or piles of scrap metal. Except for the bits of lawn, all of the lot's been scraped clean, right down to the dirt, including the area behind the apartment

Jeff Ferrell at the American Recycling scrap yard, Fort Worth, Texas, April 2004.

where, as best I can tell, Frank must have kept his scrap. If junk was Frank's school, then school's out. Oh, and there's one more thing: up and down Franks' block and the nearby streets are big curbside accumulations, accumulations of the very sort of items described in Section 11A-26, piling up as they await pickup by the city's notoriously inefficient trash collection program.

Ah well, at least the city got around to hauling away all of Frank's accumulations. But I wonder, did they haul all those washing machines and lawn mowers out to the city dump, or out to the big scrap yards where they could be recycled? I spend a good bit of time at the scrap yards, and I've never seen a city truck there—but I have seen plenty of folks like Frank. As with Frank, my junk is my school—

and as with Frank's now-dismantled salvage system, when my own staging area accumulates enough salvageable junk metal, my junk moves to the scrap yard and becomes my cash.

The scrap yards make up their own important enclave within the empire of scrounge. In Fort Worth, many of the biggest yards cluster in one deteriorated section of the city's far north side, out past the old Stockyards District that these days corrals more tourists than cattle with its upscale restaurants and honky-tonks. No tourist traps around the scrap yards, though—they're flanked by places like the "BarBQ Shak and Oyster Bar," as its hand-lettered sign says, by pawn shops, by little businesses like Norman's Radiator Service and Mike's Mix 'N' Match Paint and Body Supplies, by little Latino bars like El Triangulo, and by cheap motels like the Ranch Motel, featuring "AM-FM Radio," the Fiesta Inn, offering "Color TV," and the two-tone turquoise Cowboy Inn, each of its rooms the size of a good walk-in closet.

No tourists at the scrap yards, either—and few if any of the middle-class folks whose SUVs and cell phones clutter the Stockyards and the suburbs. Instead, the yards attract guys like Frank, old black men driving beat-to-hell pickups with beds full of engine blocks and spent refrigerators and broken lawn mowers. They attract folks like those described back in Chapter Two—skinny old white guys, homeless, pushing in shopping carts full of aluminum cans, or big Mohawked white guys, greasy, shirtless, sweating as they unload truck beds sagging under the weight of car batteries and radiators. Other times it's a young white couple pulling a burned-out 1970s automobile body off a trailer, or a young Hispanic couple backing in a trailer full of washing machines behind a big custom pickup with "Mary" lettered across its front. What the yards lack in social-class variation they make up for in ethnic diversity; come to think of it, they're probably among the most integrated social venues in Fort Worth.

Ten and a half hours a day, six days a week, the yards buzz and clang as one urban scrounger after another arrives with a load of scrap, the yards' forklifts pushing and piling the loads into mountains of sorted metal. And no matter what our ethnic backgrounds or haircuts or models of pickup, all of us who arrive at the yards also eventually arrive at a shared understanding, at a philosophy of scrap that I'll refer to as democratic essentialism. At the yards, you see, a metal's origins don't matter; everything, every object, whatever its existing cultural overlay, is reduced to its essentials. Aesthetics get lost, meanings get discarded as a Pier One brass vase, some old brass plumbing fixtures, a bucket full of brass doorknobs, and a brass plaque honoring someone's past achievements all end up sold into the big brass pile at forty cents a pound. The scrap yards are a democracy of the lowest common denominator, a place of essential elements; the forklifts couldn't care less about form or meaning. Now of course, like all democracies, exceptions are made; almost every scrap yard office or weigh station features some old license plate or aluminum pulley or patinaed copper part that someone thought appealing enough to rescue from the scrap pile. In general practice, though, the economy of the scrap yard demands that objects exist only as their essential metallic elements—and the purer the better.

Within this essentialist democracy, there is in turn one fundamental scrap yard truth that is both essentialist and residual: if it's not aluminum or copper or brass or cast iron, and it sticks to the big industrial magnet that the yard crane lowers into the bed of your pickup to extract large scrap loads, it's "sheet tin," and it's worth two cents a pound. No further differentiation needed; stripped of original purpose and meaning, all are equal before the giant magnet. Because of this, a distinct group can be seen at the scrap yards, operating amid those mostly bringing in aluminum cans or copper wire. These are the scroungers who focus instead on "sheet tin," using busted-up old pickups to haul in one load after another of old water heaters, washing machines, dishwashers, and auto parts, making up for the low value of their scrap by its greater quantity and availability. Seeing this, and realizing on my bike rides just how much tin scrap of this sort was scattered around the city, I at one point decided to add this dimension to my metal scrapping—until the strain of hauling a particularly heavy load of water heaters and washing machines literally pulled the main pulley belt off my old pickup's four-cylinder engine. After that, I pretty much went back to

aluminum, copper, and brass—because, let's see, at two cents a pound, how many scrap refrigerators would I have to haul to afford a plate of spaghetti and a soda, much less to replace a blown engine?

Spaghetti and a Soda

Forklifts and their Latino drivers are everywhere, constantly moving back and forth across the yard, spinning their wheels in the corn sweetener sludge that's seeped out from the mountain of aluminum cans up under the big shed, pulling loads of mixed iron scrap from the thirty-foot-high pile that towers over the outer yard, ferrying heavy square loading buckets up to the backs of pickups for customers to offload their scrap.

Some customers, lacking the time or energy to strip insulated copper wire, haul big loads of wire into the scrap yard unstripped, in the process getting paid less than half of what they would have if, by stripping the wire, they had converted into the cash queen of all scrap: "brite and shiny" or "bare brite" copper. More than a few scrappers choose this less remunerative but less labor-intensive option—sometimes I do, too, when the illicit reservoir of to-be-stripped wire behind my shed grows too big—and so enormous piles of unstripped wire accumulate around the yard, towering knots of red, black, white, and yellow plastic-coated wire. Today, waiting for a forklift to deliver the big bucket into which I can unload my pickup bed full of extruded aluminum, aluminum clips, aluminum breakage, aluminum cans, die cast, yellow brass, and mixed iron, I sit on my tailgate and watch as a driver runs his forklift up to a monumental tangle of unstripped wire. He pushes the forklift's front forks into the guts of the pile to catch hold of it, raises the forks a little, then begins backing away with his load. He now has a ragged bundle of multicolored wire, maybe eight feet in circumference, hooked on the front of his forklift—but with many of its strands still tangled up with the larger pile. As he eases the forklift back, the strands pull and stretch, popping loose from the big pile one after another, and his efforts remind me of nothing so much as a diner pulling up a mouthful from a big plate of spaghetti, trailing and slurping strands of pasta on the way to a full belly.

Another forklift now rolls up to the back of my truck, dropping off the loading bucket; the forklifts are too much in demand to wait while customers and yard employees unload scrap, so they drop off the buckets and then return for them when full. As the driver backs the forklift away, I notice an aluminum soda can that's gotten stuck in the inner rim of the left rear wheel, spinning and clattering like a baseball card in a kid's bicycle wheel as the driver hurries to the next job.

05 June 2003

Fellini at the Scrap Yard

Fellini's running the American Recycling scrap yard this afternoon.

An older white woman, worn down, darkly tanned, wearing a big cowboy hat, maybe a bit out of it, wanders around the unloading area and into the payment booth, approaching me and others, offering us the camper shell off the back of her old pickup for fifty bucks. "It's solid," she says, along with something about it's being a good rig for hunting and fishing. It doesn't look solid; the back door of the camper shell, I notice, is patched together with patriotic "USA" flag stickers. Later I see her pulling into another scrap yard up the street, still looking to unload the camper.

Meanwhile a big, muscular black guy, maybe thirty years old, is using a six-foot length of heavy extruded aluminum to beat the shit out of an old outdoor grill he's brought in, all the while mumbling and cursing. I decide not to go over and ask, but my guess is he forgot to take an aluminum or brass part off the grill before he brought it in; if he can't get the part off, and in so doing separate his scrap into its essential categories, he'll lose money on his load.

About this time a middle-aged white guy stalls out his beat-to-hell mid-1980s Ford Mustang as he's coming into the unloading area. Two of the forklift drivers watch him for a minute, then walk over and push the car into place, at which time they begin helping him unload stripped copper wire from the Mustang's trunk.

Now that he's out of my way I back in my truck for unloading. A guy I haven't met before, apparently a new employee, drives his forklift over to deliver my loading bucket, then proceeds to toss my carefully sorted aluminum clips into the bucket with my carefully sorted extruded aluminum. This is serious. The clips are worth thirty-seven cents a pound today (prices vary day to day, depending on the larger scrap metal market), the extruded worth forty-five cents a pound—but thrown together, the whole load is worth only thirty-seven cents a pound. I have more history here than he does, though, and so when I mention this, the young woman working the pay counter cheerfully solves the problem by paying me forty-one cents a pound for the now-mixed load.

As I'm leaving, I stop to photograph the entrance to the nearby Texas Industrial Scrap Iron and Metal yard next door. Then I hear a voice. It's coming over the yard's loudspeaker, the one that the weighers and cashiers inside the pay booth use to communicate with forklift drivers, and more generally to make themselves heard above the clattering din of the yards.

"Sir? Sir, come here a minute."

"Me?" I gesture.

"Yes," the voice says.

So I walk over and go inside the booth, where the woman working the scales asks me, "Was that you out there taking pictures?"

I admit it was, and explain my intentions.

"Well, hey, no problem, go right ahead," she says.

All of these images—the camper shell on offer and the stalled-out Mustang, the animated aluminum beating and the disembodied voice—seem to me like apparitions inside some shimmering, sweat-soaked Felliniesque dream sequence.

This is the result of the afternoon's temperature.

It's 102 degrees.

22 July 2003

Queen of the Holy City

Yesterday evening I loaded the truck for today's run to the scrap yard, but now I have a flat tire. Apparently the weight of the big scrapload was enough to push the air out of my right rear tire; it'd had a nail embedded in it for a month anyway, probably from a previous scrap yard run. So I jack up the truck with the load still in it, put on the spare, and go to drop the flat tire off for repair on my way to the yard.

Circling back through west Fort Worth neighborhoods on the way to the yards, on the lookout as always, I spot a promising curbside pile —if nothing else, I can see the big rectangular aluminum window frame sitting atop it—and pull to a stop across the street. I've walked back over to my truck with the big window frame, and I'm starting to dismantle it and remove the screws so I can add it to my load of aluminum, when a gruff, tough-looking middle-aged white woman comes out of her house, walking toward me.

"Who are you?" she asks.

"Excuse me?" I say, not sure I've heard correctly what seems to be an odd inquiry.

Entrance, Texas Industrial Scrap Iron and Metal, Fort Worth, Texas, July 2003.

"Who are you with?" she says by way of elaboration.

"Nobody," I tell her, smiling, "I was just checking out the trash pile for scrap metal."

"Well that's my yard . . . I was just asking."

Then, already losing her tough demeanor, she says, "Well, you ought to check out the trailer," gesturing to a homemade trailer in a side yard loaded with scrap carpet and other discards. "There might be some metal in there, you never know."

I tell her thanks, but keep on with dismantling the frame as she goes back toward the house.

A minute later she's back. "Here you go, take these too," she says, handing me three lengths of extruded aluminum.

"Thanks, I was on my way to the yards and just thought I'd grab some of this stuff."

"Oh, yeah," she says, "we save it too; it adds up fast, doesn't it?"

"Oh, you bet."

Now out at the yards, hanging around in the shade while they weigh in my 359 pounds of mixed iron, yellow brass, aluminum cans, aluminum clips, extruded aluminum, die cast, bare-brite copper, insulated copper wire, and stainless steel, I notice someone out of the ordinary. That is, I notice someone who's not a usual denizen of the yards, not like myself, not a dirty, greasy, disheveled ol' boy of one color or another. She's a beautiful working-class woman—I would take her for a working-class fashion model if there were such a thing—maybe thirty-five or forty, tight stretch blue jean peddle pushers, a white frilly stretch blouse, long curly hair. She's unloading aluminum cans from the trunk of an old red Chevy Beretta that sports an American flag decal on the side window, a little Harley-Davidson sticker in the top center of the rear window, and a cracked front windshield. And she's unloading the cans with style, by the way, one-handed, using only her left hand to reach into the trunk; her right hand holds a cigarette, eased down by her hips between drags, her fingers splayed out around it.

Walking inside the little pay office for a moment, she nods, smiles, says "hello" as she passes me on her way back out. A minute later she's back, this time carrying a skillet lid of some sort, asking me if it's aluminum. I tell her no, I don't think so—it looks like galvanized metal. Then in my best scrapper style, in what maybe passes for gentility or gallantry in the scrap yard, I get out the little magnet I carry on my key ring, just to confirm my diagnosis. Sure enough, the magnet is attracted to the lid—it's galvanized ferrous metal of some sort, not aluminum.

A little later, while we're both waiting to get paid out, she's friendly and talkative, with very much of a white working-class Texas accent and manner about her. She tells me she mows yards for a living and cleans out lots (that explains the dark tan, if not the red lipstick), and that she finds various sorts of scrap while she does so. "I don't go out hunting cans or anything like that," she explains, making sure to distance herself from the aluminum can hunters who some think occupy one of the lower orders in the empire of scrounge, "but stuff adds up." Plus, she says, there are the cans that accumulate from the Diet Coke that she drinks "damn near 24/7."

Her best recent find, she tells me, was an old National Cash Register—and soon thereafter, watching the *Antiques Road Show* on PBS, she saw a similar cash register appraised for $15,000 and went crazy, called her mom, told her, "I'm finally rich!" As it turns out, though, her cash register was only worth $350 because it lacked a brass plate of some sort, so she decided to keep it as a conversation piece. Meanwhile, I can't help but notice her necklace. Spanning her neck, just lower than a choker, maybe gold and diamonds or maybe gold-plate and rhinestones, it spells out "Robin." She also tells me about cleaning out the house of the relatives of her now-former husband, finding $70,000 in savings bonds and cash left behind by a father or grandfather, and how excited she was, toting it up on the calculator, then returning it to the family.

I tell her about finding some old doll shoes and getting good money for them, and she tells me that there's a lady out in Saginaw, a little town just north of Fort Worth, who makes doll clothes, and who might be interested if I find some more.

Then she's gone, pulling out of the yards in the Beretta, squealing the tires, jumping the gears, fast up Main to the north past 38th Street, out toward Saginaw, leaving the yards once again to the boys.

A few minutes later, sitting in the cab of my pickup across the street from the yards, taking it all in, I spot across the heavy traffic on North Main an older white guy, lying down with his head resting on his arm and elbow. He's lying up against a wood fence under a big tree, keeping to the shade on a hot day like I was earlier. His scrounger's grocery cart is in front of him, five-gallon plastic buckets hanging off each side, and a long pole—no doubt for snagging recalcitrant cans —sticking up out of it. He has some bedding secured to the push-handle at the back of the cart, and an old military-style ditty bag hanging from the handle as well. We're both just chillin' near

the yards, resting after hauling in one more load of scrap, hanging outside the gates to the Holy City of the empire of scrounge.

18 July 2002

Resurrection

Rolling up North Main, hauling another load of scrap out to American Recycling, I'm struck again by the cultural mélange that is Fort Worth's old north side, with its "western wear" stores and other vestiges of cowboy culture, little family-run Mexican restaurants, windowless Latino bars and dance halls, storefront offices for transferring hard-earned cash back to family in Mexico, and all of it bastardized by hard use and proximity into a sort of disheveled urban beauty.

Arriving at the yards, the mélange gets richer. Beside me in the weigh-in area is an elderly black man, unloading a big pile of sheet tin and short iron from an old white Custom Deluxe 10 Chevy pickup, its sides smeared with oil and dirt, its listing bed wrecked and rusted from hauling scrap —and every window in its cab, save the windshield, broken or busted out. Out at the edge of the yards, another elderly black man in a brown jacket and a faded baseball cap is simultaneously pushing a shopping cart full of aluminum cans and pulling an old rusty lawn mower, cutting now across 38th Street toward the Texas Industrial Scrap Iron and Metal yard next door. As for me, the skinny white boy, there's my load of scrap today—15 pounds of aluminum clips, 35 pounds of extruded aluminum, 13 pounds of aluminum cans, 21 pounds of #1 copper, 39 pounds of bare brite copper, and 208 pounds of electric motors and short iron—which turns out to be worth exactly $62.87.

Heading back down North Main toward home, this mélange gets me to thinking. How can the guy in the old Chevy pickup survive on loads like that? After all, a 500-pound load of sheet tin earns you ten bucks, a big load of short iron maybe twenty. How can the guy pushing the cans and pulling the mower make it day to day? For that matter, how can I afford to invest the number of days and weeks that I have—bicycling city streets, sorting and cleaning aluminum, stripping copper wire—in a load that will ultimately yield just over sixty dollars?

The answer, of course, is that we can't—unless, by chance or choice or necessity, we learn to embrace the politics of low-cost living. You can't keep the balance sheet in the black hauling sheet tin in a shiny new extended cab pickup—but you can, at least for a while, if you're willing to drive a rolling wreck with no windows, and probably no insurance. You can't survive on a shopping cart full of aluminum cans—unless that and a bedroll are about all you have, and so the eight bucks the cart brings you all goes to food. You can't make it on a sixty-dollar load once every few weeks—unless you're lucky enough to have a little house, and willing to stay away from the shopping malls, willing to keep the pickup parked, except for

hauling those loads, and to scrounge instead by bike and foot. In turn, the yards can't afford to pay even the eight bucks or the sixty they do if they're surrounded by those same shopping malls or caught up in pricey urban redevelopment; they require the degraded urban ecology that encases them as surely as we scroungers require our own daily degradations.

And in this ugly personal and political economy of scrounging is its ongoing beauty. Without the ugliness of sweat-stained scroungers and old pickups and dirty scrap yards, all those tons of aluminum and copper and tin, hauled in one hard load at a time, would instead make their way to the eternal ecological degradation of the landfill. For those lucky enough to consume and discard amid the clean beauty of the better parts of town, yesterday's consumer items and last year's industrial waste simply disappear. And yet, because of homeless cart pushers and old men in broken-down pickups, because of noisy scrap yards surrounded by seedy bars and cheap motels, they don't disappear at all. They're scrounged, accumulated, and resurrected—reborn, ultimately, as next year's automobile frames or plumbing supplies.[18]

In this sense, the vast, disorganized army of impoverished scroungers that every day wanders the city, on the lookout for aluminum cans and copper wire and old washing machines, operates as an essential counterforce to the ecological overload offered up by consumer society. Whatever their individual circumstances or motivations—

desperation, independence, survival—their willingness to sacrifice the standards of cleanliness, comfort, and consumption that others require allows them to operate as the gleaners of consumer society, outcasts who mine the aftermath of others' affairs, salvaging what others abandon.

Those who frequent scrap yards in this way function as working-class, often subworking-class, environmentalists—and among the most important and effective environmentalists around.[19] For every brass lamp a homeowner stuffs into a garbage bag and sends to the landfill, scroungers salvage another one down the street; for every aluminum can a concerned college student tosses in the campus recycling bin, scroungers haul in a thousand. Sans organizational structure or city-sponsored programs, independent scrap haulers go about their business, forming as they do a last soiled safety net for catching the culture's waste short of the landfill. In this light I remember—we might all remember—that mortgage payments and car loans are not so much obligations as privileges. And, I think to myself, we might consider celebrating these seedy parts of town, and supporting those who perform this essential social service, rather than criminalizing their down-and-dirty efforts at accumulation and resurrection.

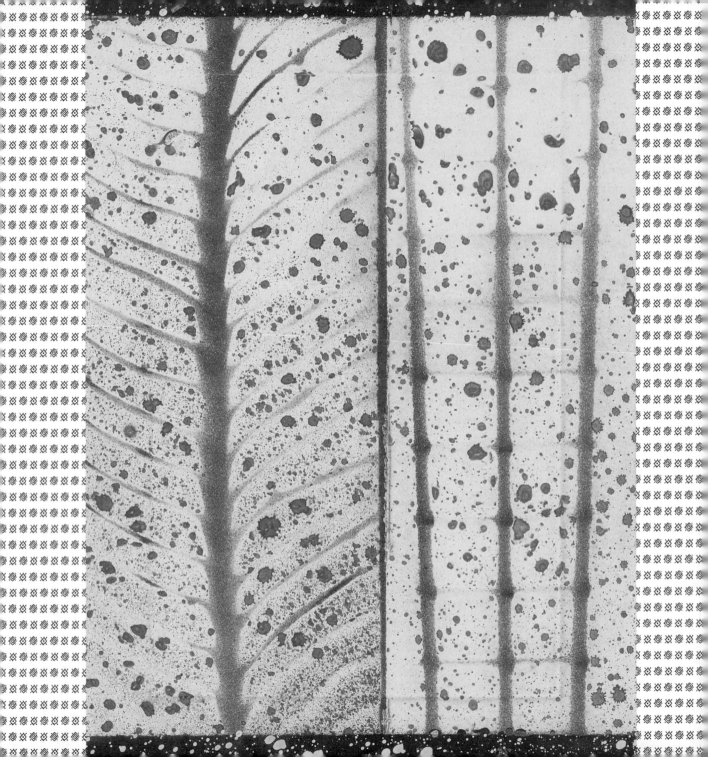

Scrapped Together

The current of mutual aid . . . flows still even now, and it seeks its way to find out a new expression which would not be the State, nor the mediaeval city, nor the village community of the barbarians, nor the savage clan, but would proceed from all of them, and yet be superior to them in its wider and more deeply humane conceptions. —Peter Kropotkin, 1902[1]

Mutual Aid

If the empire of scrounge is populated by a ragtag assemblage of cart pushers, scrap haulers, and everyday environmentalists, it's held together by an equally irregular network of mutual aid. In fact, this tattered web of mutual assistance answers, in another way, the question of how scrounger's can survive on eight-dollar loads of aluminum cans. With varying degrees of intention and endurance, many scroungers don't go it alone; they scrounge with and for one another, and in so doing invent new possibilities of collective sustenance and autonomy. As I found time and again, this mutual aid can occur on the spot, as scroungers share a trash pile or trash bin, sorting through their needs and their finds, handing clothes or food back and forth as they uncover them. At times, networks of mutual aid can emerge around some shared focus within the empire of scrounge, and so continue beyond a particular space or situation. Sometimes these efforts at collective survival are approved of, even supported, by legal and political authorities; more often they're not.

Within the empire, yard sales and garage sales operate as part of this spiral of mutual survival. At a minimum, such sales provide scroungers situations in which their salvaged materials can, as needed, be turned into cash. This dimension was more than once confirmed in conversations I had with other scroungers at scrap yards or trash piles; while working one curbside pile with a guy who introduced himself to me as Randy Pac Rat, for example, Randy described the way he supplemented his job's hourly pay by selling scrounged items at yard sales and flea markets, and suggested I do the same. Like the scrap yards, yard sales in this way offer scroungers like Randy not only cash for their efforts, but a different dynamic than that of their hourly wage—a dynamic by which cash can be acquired with a maximum of personal autonomy and temporal flexibility. For me—free during my months of daily scrounging from jobs and wages—yard sales offered yet another opportunity for conversion and reinvention. After all, I was not only recirculating scrounged items. I was pricing them with found price tags, advertising their sale with signs made from found cardboard and printed with found markers, attaching these signs to telephone poles around my neighborhood with found nails driven by a found hammer, and keeping my proceeds in a scrounged Steelmaker Cash Box, complete with interior coin trays.

While yard and garage sales in this way function as midpoints in the process by which individual scrounging and salvaging become broader secondhand reuse, their essential mutuality emerges from another midpoint: the one where the scrounger's need to convert found commodities into a little cash meets others' need to convert a little cash into necessary commodities. For many who share the economic margins with scroungers and scrap haulers, yard sales and garage sales exist within an everyday universe defined also by flea markets, thrift stores, and charity shops—that is, a universe of acquisition that operates somewhere beyond and below the shopping mall and the retail store. The Mexican immigrants and minimum-wage workers who patronize Jenna's Hope of Grace, the little secondhand church mission a few blocks from my house, also frequent the yard sales that I and other neighbors hold; such sales are an essential source of children's clothes, household furnishings, and work tools. At these sales, cheaply priced secondhand goods, scrounged and otherwise, find their way into the lives of those who most need them; the sales constitute key moments, key situations, in which the scrounger's self-made autonomy becomes also the basis for the relative economic autonomy of others.

The mutual aid offered by these neighborhood sales is more than a matter of economic calculation, though. An all-day yard sale produces a slow-paced, come-and-go community of neighbors, independent antique dealers, collectors, gawkers, conversationalists, and kids, and, like the scrap yard, a community often more ethnically integrated than most around town.

Folks meet one another, barter, trade ideas and addresses, and help each other load purchases into cars and pickups. At my yard sales, and at others I've visited, a "free box" sits out front, filled with items to be taken as needed.[2] At my sales I also price items absurdly low (low overhead, you know), drop prices even lower if someone appears to be in need, give away clothes to moms and toys to kids, and otherwise run the "sale" more like a festival of redistribution. In turn, a guy at one sale had decided to buy from me a scrounged magnifying glass, but after showing me how I could use it to check the gold content in scrounged eyeglass frames, decided I needed it more than he did and declined to buy it. At another sale a neighbor took the occasion to bring over some hyacinth vine beans; today the vines that grew from those beans shade our side porch in a canopy of green leaves and fluttering purple blooms—and the beans from these vines have in turn been passed on to other friends and neighbors.

Midpoints between scrounger and secondhand shopper, between neighbor and neighbor, yard sales and garage sales are also moments in the ongoing process that shapes the empire of scrounge. Many times, I have scrounged items discarded after the close of a yard sale and left in a pile on the curb, their homemade price tags still on them; many times, if I couldn't put them to use, I've sold these same items at my own yard sale —sometimes with the earlier price tag still intact— or else donated them to a charity. Likewise, it will be remembered, many of the donations to Jenna's Hope of Grace are yard sale leftovers, and so, to avoid violating city code, the church volunteers must remove the yard sale price tags before they can offer them to the mission's patrons. Out in Portland, Oregon, scrounger extraordinaire Leslie Hemstreet remembers a similarly circular process; growing up in Texas, she and her siblings "cut our teeth on Goodwill donation huts, tiny and overflowing compared to the semis they park now. Something was always to be had there, played with a couple of times and put back in six months when we were forced to clean our rooms right before Christmas."[3] As for my part in this process, I must admit I've wondered what my neighbors might think, coming to one of my yard sales and discovering that the items they put out for the trash have been surreptitiously rescued, and are now put up for sale—and selling. And I must admit I've sometimes wondered what I think of them, collectively if not individually buying back their own trash.

An essential part of the self-supporting rhythm that runs through the empire of scrounge, a key step in the mutually beneficial flow of scrounged goods between trash pile and secondhand consumer and charity store, the yard sale is in most cases also illegal—and decidedly so. In fact, cities like Fort Worth see their opposition to the independent yard sale as something of a crusade. The Fort Worth code enforcement officer who stumbled on Jenna's Hope of Grace Charity Shop, and subsequently forced the church to close it, wasn't actually on patrol for such shops; the officer was "out looking for illegal yard signs." The city's citizen Code Rangers, while happy enough to search for damaged fences or front yard parking or scrap accumulations like the one behind my shed, are actually most interested in yard sales. Announcing the new Code Ranger program, the local paper noted that "chief among the problems" the Code Rangers will be investigating are "households that hold more than the two garage sales allowed each year"—a focus backed by the city's code compliance director.[4] Lest any potential garage sale scofflaws plead ignorance of these codes, the city regularly publicizes them in the local paper as well. Along with limiting each household to two garage sales a year, the city requires a permit for each sale (to be obtained at least seventy-two hours in advance of the sale), requires that items be displayed only "on the patio or garage areas," and allows only one sign for advertising the sale, with this sign to be placed only on the property where the sale is to be held. "Don't wipe out your garage sale proceeds by receiving a code violation and subsequent fine," warns the city.[5]

For folks living off what they can scrounge, and occasionally sell, such fines are serious business indeed. In Fort Worth, those holding "unauthorized garage sales" can be fined "up to $2,000 per ticket"; posting "any sign on any structure, tree, pole, curb, or elsewhere within rights of way on any public street or on private property" can generate a fine of up to $200.[6] In neighboring River Oaks, where yard sale permits are required and signs are allowed only if taken down by one hour after sunset on the sale's last day, Patricia Odell found herself facing a $600 fine, fielding collection agency calls, and confronting an arrest warrant when she left two of her signs standing for two days after her yard sale. A municipal court judge ultimately reduced the fine to $450, but Odell still maintained that "the police should be more worried about crime than some yard-type sign," and noted her plans to start a petition drive to get the ordinance changed.[7]

Back in Fort Worth, thinking about the possibilities of plausible deniability in court, I take to posting signs for my yard sales that simply say "Yard Sale Today" and provide a directional arrow, sans street address or other identifiers. Friends and I kid that we could always just post signs for our yard sales that give the address of some neighbor we don't like—and that we might need to rotate our sales among sympathetic friends and family to circumvent the two-a-year rule and the $2,000 fine.

Still, all kidding aside, as a criminologist it's my job to report on crime, and to analyze it. So, a report from a crime scene, from the biggest yard sale—that is, the biggest crime scene—I staged during my months of scrounging. Permit not acquired seventy-two hours prior or otherwise, illegal homemade signs posted all over the neighborhood (and retrieved by that evening, I might add), and as for that two-a-year rule . . . well, this was the first yard sale at my *brother's* house that year, anyway.

My brother Joel and I are holding a yard sale mostly on behalf of an old friend now in New York City. A bunch of his belongings that he left behind were piling up monthly charges in a storage facility, so we agreed to retrieve them for him, sell off what we could, and send him the cash. As long as we're at it, though, I figure I may as well piggyback some of my scrounged items. So we set up the sale down the length of Joel's driveway. Down one side are our friend's abandoned items, mostly residues of high-end retail shopping: golf balls and golf equipment, kitchen ware, clothes, books, tools, cassette tapes. Down the other side of the driveway are the parallel residues of my past months' scrounging: golf balls and golf equipment, kitchen ware, clothes, books, tools, cassette tapes. But there are also hand-painted straw cowboy hats discarded after a fund-raiser of some sort, antiques, old knobs and handles, license plates, chandelier crystals, brass knickknacks, old record albums and "45" singles, bathroom sinks, plumbing parts, and an assortment of light fixtures.

The night before, as we were setting up, a small-time antique dealer had come by, inquiring about old photographs and any "girly stuff" we might have. Now, as the sale gets underway, an older Anglo guy asks me about old fishing lures and tackle, and gives me his card for future reference. A young and apparently affluent Anglo woman is interested in some circa 1950s doll items I've found; I tell her I have to get five dollars apiece for them. Finally she puts them down and leaves, but a couple of hours later she's back, rolling up in her BMW, hurrying to see if I still have them. It seems she drove all the way home, some twenty miles away, logged on to eBay, verified the worth of the shoes and lockets, and is now eager to buy them. As she hands me the cash, she tells me this is how she makes a little money—buying secondhand items and then selling them on eBay—while she's "stuck at home with the kids."

By this time we're attracting quite a crowd, working-class Hispanics mingling and talking with middle-class Anglos and others. A sweet, heavy-set Anglo kid from two doors down shows up, buys one of the painted hats and some other trinkets. Now he's back, and so I give him another hat and some playing cards, no charge. And now he's back again—says everybody in his family has decided they want a painted hat—and I sell him four more at fifty cents apiece, a solid $9.50 off the original $10 fundraiser price still marked on the hats.

Joel's neighbors from across the street—the working-class Hispanic family living in the little duplex that backs up to the freeway access road—come over and buy a big Sony Trinitron television for the neighborly price of ten bucks. A little later I look across the street and see them loading it into the back seat of their car. Or are they loading their old TV to take to a friend, now that they have a new one? I'm too busy talking and selling and giving stuff away to investigate further.

Closing down, exhausted, Joel and I put some remaining items on the curb, intentionally leaving them displayed in plain sight. There's the couch I bought a while back at a secondhand store, now replaced by the couch I found on the street; a hat rack; the remainder of the hand-painted hats; bags of clothes; and boxes full of assorted leftovers. We drive off to get some food and to deposit the remainder of the sale remnants at the Goodwill collection center, and when we get back, the next-door neighbors have a story to tell us. It seems that as soon as we pulled away, folks from "the meth house" down the street, as our neighborhood association leader is fond of calling it, had swooped in and taken everything. And indeed, the curb is clean as a whistle.

Heading home in my truck, hauling some of our friend's leftover items that I'll now reduce to scrap metal—most predictably the ubiquitously disused home exercise machine—I'm almost too tired to drive. Still, I can't resist stopping to rescue a big brass light fixture from a curbside trash pile.

Bottles, Bicycles, and Mule Deer—But Not Bombs

My scrounged bounty of cast-off consumerism was such that it took more than yard sale free boxes to give it all away. As documented in earlier chapters, I regularly took scrounged bedding to the local animal shelter, scrounged clothes and shoes to one of the city's homeless shelters. Food I pulled from Dumpsters and trash piles, leaving it for others to take, or hauled it to the food bank —but had I known of a local Food Not Bombs

group, I would have taken most of it there. Founded in 1980 on the principles of nonviolent direct action, Food Not Bombs strikes me as a group well worth supporting; it salvages and cooks surplus or discarded food, then serves free vegetarian meals to the homeless and other hungry souls. Food Not Bombs generally serves without a permit, too—and so, like yard sale outlaws and others, faces ongoing legal harassment. In 1988, Food Not Bombs servers were confronted (and in some cases beaten) by helmeted riot police in San Francisco's Golden Gate Park, with fifty-four arrested for serving food in public without a permit. By 2000, one of Food Not Bomb's founders could count over one hundred arrests "for serving free food in city parks" since 1988 alone; in 1995 he faced a sentence of twenty-five years to life under California's "Three Strikes" statute. Because of this ongoing problem, Food Not Bombs distributes, along with its recipes for potato pea curry and scrambled tofu, guidelines for what to do "if the police start taking your food." In brief: have some more food hidden away as backup, and "don't stop because of the police."[8]

Absent Food Not Bombs, I did have Bikes Not Bombs. In fact, a local chapter was just getting underway during my most intense months of scrounging. The Bikes Not Bombs organization began two years after Food Not Bombs' founding, originally for the purpose of rebuilding scrounged and donated bicycles and shipping them to Nicaragua. A quarter century later, Bikes Not

Bombs continues to rebuild salvaged bicycles, and to organize collective bicycle shops, bike education programs, and bicycle giveaways in local communities around the United States and Latin America. Working in Fort Worth with "1919," a local progressive space, we got Bikes Not Bombs going by accumulating and storing scrounged bicycles, with the intention of rebuilding them and giving them away to kids in the community—and more than one of those bikes I simply pulled from a Dumpster and took directly to 1919.

Other folks do the same, by the way. In Brooklyn, the Black Label Bike Club converts scrounged bicycles into custom-made, oddball bikes like the tall bike (multiple frames welded together) and the bronco (can't be ridden). In the Bay Area, the progressive bicycle movement Critical Mass maintains the Baatt Cave Bicycle Library, an expansive collection of old bicycles and parts available free of charge to bike enthusiasts. In Chicago, the Critical Mass–affiliated Rat Patrol rides self-customized "chopper" bicycles, and invites others along: "Do you have a penchant for choppers and alley scavenging? Join the Rat Patrol for a wild ride."[9]

Scroungers are finding other ways to move toward mutual aid as well, and in the process to turn social scrap into some sort of social change. Like many other progressive organizations, 1919 now runs a "free store" for getting salvaged clothes and other everyday necessities back out into the community; in Hawaii, artist Gayle Chan even offers a "Free Mobile Art Store." Begun in 2003 by a Tucson, Arizona, nonprofit recycling organization, Freecycle utilizes the Internet to give away surplus furniture, clothing, and toys to any who need them. By 2004 Freecycle had chapters in 253 cities, and had become a sort of Web-based free store, or maybe an empire of Internet scrounge. Having given away her doghouse and her kids' old clothes on Freecycle, for example, Christine Gianadda noted that "it makes me feel a little better knowing that it's going directly to someone who is going to use it rather than going to a thrift store. I don't need a tax write-off. It's just junk."[10] Back out on the streets, Lars Eighner not only scrounges a life for himself out of Dumpsters; he donates some of what he finds to AIDS shelters, food banks, and friends. Working at one point to liberate malnourished foxes from a fur farm near Chadron, Nebraska, caring for some baby foxes herself, Leslie Hemstreet even learns to glean roadkill, and so finds herself cruising Chadron with a big mule deer strapped to the top of her little pickup. "Many assumed we had been poaching and many approved," she recalls. "There's nothing that makes you feel a temporary merging of the parallel universes more than being a vegetarian driving around with a dead deer on top of your truck, getting kudos from yokels for poaching. We really won the admiration of those with whom we were able to share the truth. 'Poaching? Hell no. Roadkill!'"[11]

Meanwhile, Habitat for Humanity manages to merge its own parallel universes of construction and deconstruction as it continues to build low-cost housing around the United States and other countries. Habitat is well known for its largely volunteer work crews, some of them affiliated with churches or corporations, who work together on new home construction. But Habitat's ability to provide low-cost new housing rests on scrounging and salvaging old housing as well. In Fort Worth as in other cities, a Habitat-run "ReStore" accepts donations of secondhand and surplus building materials, then sells them to raise money for new home construction; many times I hauled in to the ReStore aluminum windows, wood shutters, doors, sinks, and other materials I had scrounged. And Habitat generates its own salvaged materials, too. Working in the shadow of Habitat's better-known construction crews are its volunteer "deconstruction" crews; when a homeowner donates to Habitat a home facing demolition, or the contents of a home scheduled for remodeling, this crew moves in to strip the house of salvageable materials and get them to the local ReStore for resale.

Figuring this might be a place to put my proclivities to use, I volunteered with these crews off and on during my months of scrounging. Compared to my usual solo alley rides, this was an odd outpost in the empire, a sort of organized, permission-granted, indoors scrounging. Not too organized, though; I was pleased to see that the crews worked for the most part organically, a fluid division of labor emerging from differences in skill, strength, and preference. As the Habitat coordinators emphasized, the materials salvaged and sold from these old houses were an important part of Habitat's income, and so we carefully extracted anything of value: cedar closets, doors, door frames, moldings, baseboards, wood paneling, shelving, cabinets, glass knobs, pedestal sinks, plumbing fixtures, medicine cabinets, antique light fixtures, casement windows, brass fireplace decorations, and brass mail slots.

Amid this range of salvaged materials, though, the big money salvage was the hardwood flooring. Employing a massive, multiperson disassembly line, we would pry up the flooring, move it outside, pull the remaining nails, sort the flooring by length and quality, then hand it back inside through an open window for further sorting and temporary storage. This inside storage was also meant to protect the flooring from overly eager entrepreneurs or secondhand thieves; its value was such that a batch had in one case been bought out from under a deconstruction crew while they were still pulling nails.

Once, bent over with my pry bar, leveraging up hardwood flooring, I had a vision. Maybe it was the early morning and the fact that I was still half asleep. Maybe it was because this big, vacant house was about to be razed, having been dealt a knockout blow the year before by the same tornado that bounced into downtown Fort Worth and damn near knocked down the Bank One Tower. Whatever the reason, hard at my work, listening to my crewmates talk about how our "deconstruction" was off to a good start, I swear I saw Derrida. That would be Jacques Derrida, the French philosopher who promoted "deconstruction" as a sophisticated analytic approach to taking apart the certainty of text and argumentation—except now he was standing here, off to the side, all decked out in his tool belt, his claw hammer and pry bar for pulling up flooring, a little ironic smile on his face.

See, as it turns out, it's not just Derrida who used the term "deconstruction" back in the day, nor Habitat now. "Deconstruction" has been popularized all over again in the new century, has taken on another layer of meaning in a way that Derrida might appreciate, today employed less as an epistemic orientation than an ecological strategy among architectural recyclers and salvage companies. Advocates for local self-reliance now speak of the "careful disassembly of buildings to recover valuable materials"; even the U.S. government now issues reports on "deconstruction [as] the process of selectively and systematically disassembling buildings that would otherwise be demolished to generate a supply of materials suitable for reuse in the construction or rehabilitation of other structures."[12] Derrida would be proud—for some, anyway, the multiple meanings of deconstruction have overcome the destructive metanarrative of the bulldozer.

Yet despite my early morning deconstructive hallucination, despite Habitat's practical vision of affordable housing, despite even the federal government's dream of deconstructive rehabilitation, local officials increasingly view Habitat as a problem, and so design zoning regulations that block Habitat's ability to provide low-cost housing. In Fort Worth and neighboring Arlington —as in Atlanta, or Burlington, Vermont, and other cities—officials argue that the sort of small, affordable houses built by Habitat volunteers don't "add to the quality of the housing stock," as Arlington's director of planning and development services puts it. In this light, Arlington and other cities have now increased mandatory minimum new home size to 1,500 square feet, and have often added requirements regarding brick facing and lot size as well.

Habitat officials counter that these requirements, which "we're seeing, unfortunately, more and more," pose problems for the volunteer work crews, and more importantly that they price the homes out of the range that those "doing important work that happens not to pay well" can afford. It seems that Habitat's typical house—1,100 square feet, two bedrooms, one bath—is simply not up to the standards of cities run by those whose work happens to pay better. Of course, I call such a house home; those specifications precisely describe the house in which I now live, and in which I lived during my months of scrounging. But Fort Worth councilwoman Becky Haskin, who was earlier heard urging the city's Code Rangers to "give them hell," calls houses like these something else: "Instant slums."[13]

Sometimes, though, local officials put aside the derogations and the zoning laws, call off the Code Rangers and the code enforcement officers, and actually help folks scrounge up some mutual aid—well, at least for a little while, and so long as they can do it on the cheap. In early June 2003 the local media began publicizing a new City of Fort Worth initiative: an eight-week pilot program designed to pay homeless folks three cents for every bottle brought in off the streets. The city had secured $3,000 in federal neighborhood development funds; the bottles would be redeemed at the big homeless shelter that sits atop a hill on the city's near east side; and for once, "civic leaders," the neighborhood associations, local businesses, and the homeless shelters were all in agreement. Together, they hoped that the program might "help clean up the streets and perhaps provide a little pocket money to area transients and others." Still, one city official did express a concern: "We're not sure how many bottles will come in."[14]

Of course I have to head over to the shelter and find out.

Walking around the shelter complex, looking for the parking lot where the bottles are to be redeemed, I come upon a group of women and children sitting on concrete steps in the shade of a doorway.

"You looking for a place to stay?" one woman asks me, friendly—gently, in fact.

"No, thanks, I just need to talk with someone at the center."

"Well, the men's shelter is over there across the street. This is the women's shelter."

Walking down and across the street to the men's shelter, I pass a long row of homeless folks, men and women, their possessions piled around them, their clothes hanging on the fence as they wait for the shelter to open for the night. I locate the parking lot in part by the sound of breaking bottles, and arriving first notice two big, mixed-breed dogs wandering around a big chain-link pen situated behind the parking lot. Freight trains are also rolling by, maybe two hundred yards behind the parking lot and the pen; the shelter and its parking lot are across town from the North Side scrap yards, but share with them the same down-market urban ecology.

Jimmy Silcox is in charge of the parking lot. A friendly middle-aged white guy, once homeless himself but now living and working at the shelter, he's busy counting bottles and paying out cash to those who've hauled them in. Assisting him is a young, wiry Latino fellow, out of prison for just a week now, and a small, thin black guy—who, I can't help but notice, is wearing a country-club-insignia crew-neck shirt, a residue I suppose of scrounging or secondhand shopping or some past minimum wage job. In my first few minutes there, those pushing in shopping carts full of bottles include a big black guy, arriving with his third load of the day; a small fellow who seems to be South American, wearing long sleeves and long pants in the heat, pushing a cart he's modified with a large plastic container so as to carry more bottles; and a Pakistani man who, a few days later, feels comfortable enough to tell me of the banking job he once had back in Pakistan. Like its scrap yards and its yard sales, the empire's bottle redemption program tends to generate a certain democracy of scrounge, a degree of ethnic diversity interwoven at the margins.

The parking lot resonates with the rhythmic smashing of bottles, the result of the redemption system that Jimmy has set up. Jimmy or his assistants count each bottle as its owner unloads it from the cart and throws it downward into a Waste Management Dumpster; "deposited" in this way, the bottle disintegrates and so makes room for more bottles than if left intact. As the count is completed, Jimmy carefully records it in a hand-ruled, hand-lettered ledger he's created from a white legal pad, noting the number of bottles, their value at three cents apiece, and the name of the payee. The payee signs the ledger, Jimmy reaches in his pocket and pays out the money, and the process repeats—until at the end of the day the Waste Management truck comes by and picks up the Dumpster full of broken glass.

As for the city official's concern as to how many bottles would be brought in, Jimmy tells me what the Dumpster full of glass suggests—that the response has been far greater than the city imagined. After all, he says, everybody around here knows where the bottles are, knows some of the out-of-the-way places where homeless folks gather to drink 40s and cheap wine. His log confirms it. As he shows me in the log, one guy who collected bottles all weekend carted in 1,064 of them on the Monday the program started; another rolled in with a load that Jimmy put at 1,799. On the other hand, "I've had people bring in seven at a time," Jimmy tells me.

"These people are doing this for three cents a bottle, and it's hot sometimes," Jimmy explains. "They're working instead of panhandling or going out and stealing something and selling it. And a lot of 'em have become regulars. It's working as far as getting people to work and getting the bottles off the street. . . . A lot of people say 'we want to work' but a lot of people can't just go up and fill out an application, cause of something sometimes in their past. And this makes it easy. . . . When they come up time after time with these shopping carts, they've trudged some of 'em up the hill. . . . Bottles are heavy—you start putting 125, 150 in a cart, and you're tired from the day."

Thirsty, too. "There's not that many hydrants that are available," Jimmy tells me, since store owners and others turn them off so the homeless won't use them. As a result, Jimmy and his assistants hand out donated and purchased water to the bottle scroungers, and a few weeks later I notice a new feature: City of Fort Worth bottled water. "Ft. Worth Water, 100% tap," says the label. "Fill with tap water. After use: Wash, rinse, refill."

But there are disincentives other than heat and thirst to overcome if one's to make it hauling loads of three cent bottles. The bottle haulers tell me about the mosquitoes, ants, spiders, and summer burrs that share vacant lots and alley ways with discarded bottles. They talk about their already lengthening routes as the supply of bottles near the shelter is exhausted, and how these longer routes add time and effort and subtract from what little they can make in the first place at three cents a bottle. And then there's the little poster the city put up in and around the shelter to promote the program. "A bounty of 3 cents per bottle will be paid to Bounty Hunters rounding up bottle bandits," it says, beneath a cartoon of dancing wine and beer bottles, and then goes on to describe a "bottle bandit" as "any empty glass container . . . just sitting there, up to no good, looking disreputable." Just the sort of condescending tone most appealing to folks already scrounging out a hard life on the streets.

Still, "It's all right . . . puts some money in your pocket," one homeless scrounger tells me while cashing in his bottles, perhaps accustomed to such condescension—and when I return a couple of days later, a new way to put some money in your pocket emerges.

Hanging around with Jimmy, I get to talking scrap with a street-tough white guy who's waiting for his cartload of bottles to be cashed out. I mention hauling scrap metal in my old truck, he mentions some skids of pig iron he's come upon, and now we're rollin'.

"Like next Thursday, man, you got a pickup truck, right? And you're ready to work, right?" he

Bottle scrounger's cart, Fort Worth, Texas, June 2003.

asks me, warming to the subject. "OK, we'll load that bad boy down, man, and make a day's wages with one load. I got two skids down the street. . . . See, I usually do scrap metal. It's hard for me to haul, 'cause I don't have a car anymore, don't have a truck, to haul that kind of iron. But, a pickup truck is the ideal situation. I can't push that stuff around, I'm getting too old."

"Think you can give me lift down the street to the metal shop?" he adds. I haven't heard that term before, but I figure I know what he means—there's a small scrap metal yard a few blocks away. So I tell him I'll do it and then I'll come back to the parking lot.

"Can I leave my shopping cart here?" he asks Jimmy.

"Yes, uh huh, I'll look after it," Jimmy tells him. At any given time, five or ten bottle-hauling carts are parked off to the side of the lot, awaiting their owners' return.

"I got another one so I can just like transport heavy metal with that one," the guy tells me. "We'll work out some kinda deal. I'm kinda new in this business, this bottle business. . . . There's one place that takes it out on the North Side, but I just can't tote all that glass—too dang heavy."

Then he turns to Jimmy again. "I'll try to make it back here with another load, it's only early, and you will take those twelve-ounce bottles, then, huh?

"Oh yeah, anything glass."

"OK—maybe I'll do another load then."

"I'll round that penny off to a nickel," Jimmy tells him, laughing, as he finishes calculating the guy's bottle payment. It comes to just over two dollars.

"OK, good enough, brother," the guy laughs.

On the way to the metal shop, he explains a bit more about our plan, and about the attractions of scrounging. "I'll start puttin' that pig iron in here and we can make about twenty bucks a day, a piece. No problem—all we got to do is load it up," he tells me. "So, you don't have to work for nobody or nobody, you can do your own thing. . . . See, like that fuckin' car and that wheel and shit," he says, pointing out the window to an abandoned car. "It's all scrap, man."

As we arrive at the scrap yard he thinks of one more way in which "it's all scrap," looking ahead perhaps to the end of the bottle redemption pilot program.

"We can sell our fuckin' buggies here, man."

Back at the parking lot, another bottle hauler confirms my buddy's perspective on scrounging. "Better than nothing," he tells me when I ask him if three cents is enough for each of the bottles he's throwing into the Dumpster. And besides, "You can quit when you want to."

Then Terry rolls in with a big buggy load of bottles. He's wiry, tan, shirtless—and, as I come to find out, fifty-five years old. "I did cans twenty-three years ago, when I first came to this town," he tells me, recalling decades of scrounging aluminum cans—but at the moment he's doing bottles. In fact, a week or so ago, when a local television station came out to do a story on the program, the cameraman decided to shoot Terry as he arrived with a huge haul of bottles—his shopping cart full and "like twenty trash bags hanging off my cart."

"That camera man says, 'You're fifty-five, and you're pushing two hundred bottles?' Yeah I'm pushin' two hundred bottles 'cause I can't get no work no place, so I gotta do something," Terry tells me. Already, though, the supply of discarded bottles near the shelter is thinning, and so now "we gotta go farther and farther away and that means less and less trips. . . . They need to put these stations around, in the bad neighborhoods, where the bottles are, you know."

Besides that, Terry tells me, "sometimes my legs give out" while pushing a big load of bottles up the hill. Terry and Jimmy kid that if Terry had a cell phone, he could just call in the number of bottles in the load he's pushing and Jimmy could have his money ready when he got up the hill; Terry adds that it would be nice to "rig up a lawn mower engine on a go-cart frame with a little seat and a steering wheel" to get himself and his bottles up the hill.

"But I love it," says Terry. "Heh, it's a great way to make an honest buck, at least I ain't out panhandlin'. . . . If I can't earn it I just go without it, that's just the way my pappy raised me, like that. . . . And I don't believe in beggin' and borrowin', if I can't earn it I just don't get it." In fact, Terry says, "I wish somebody'd thought of this a long time ago," since it's working so well to "clean up the neighborhood. . . . Back where I'm

from, back in Northern Michigan, you got ten cents, on any kind of a container. And you *know* you ain't gonna throw that stuff away!"

While Terry, Jimmy and I are talking about the need for more recycling programs in Fort Worth, Otis arrives. Otis is Jimmy's young assistant—kind, bespectacled, smoker and provider and cadger of cigarettes, and friend to the two mutt dogs who live in the big pen. Otis has just scrounged a nice pair of athletic shoes from a Dumpster, but they're wet, and so Terry and I both offer the same scrounger's advice: for a better fit, put them on your feet while they're drying.

As Terry parks his cart and heads off by foot on a grocery run for himself, Jimmy, and Otis—a can of refried beans, a bag of potato chips, and a two-liter bottle of Big Red—two guys roll in with a load of bottles so big that the decision is made to toss and count them two at a time, just to speed the process along. "Watch your eyes, man," one of the guys warns those around the Dumpster as he throws bottles in with both hands.

When I next hook up with Jimmy and the crew a week later I don't find my buddy, and so our pig iron plan falls through. Jimmy, though, is still hard at it. In fact, despite Terry's concerns about fewer bottles and longer trips, Jimmy tells me that he took in 9,040 bottles yesterday alone—a Monday, after the redemption center had been closed for the weekend. It's early yet, but Jimmy's handwritten ledger already documents a growing total for today as well:

352	$10.56
110	3.30
63	1.89
66	1.98
251	7.53
240	7.20
100	3.00
270	8.10
164	4.92
8	.24

Jimmy tells me the bottle redemption program, now up and running for about a month, has been a "learning thing" for all involved. Realizing the strain that bottle hauling puts on some of the older scroungers, watching the Texas summer get hotter and hotter, Jimmy and others working with the program are considering changing hours of operation. The existing hours of 8 A.M. to 5 P.M. leave too many scroungers exposed to the late afternoon heat, Jimmy says, and so 6 A.M. to 2 P.M. is being discussed.

"I was kidding ol' Caesar the other day," Jimmy tells me. "He had to go to JPS [hospital] the other day because he didn't keep himself hydrated. . . . If you stay open till five they'll push themselves." And Jimmy has another idea as well: "As it gets hotter, take a little wire and tie it to their basket and tie a bottle of water to it. You may not want it now, and one person says, 'I don't like water, it dilutes my beer.' OK, but just kinda have it there."

Mostly, Jimmy says, the learning curve emerged out of city officials underestimating the scroungers' need for money—and maybe from underestimating the scroungers themselves.

"The city . . . didn't understand . . . when the program was first allocated with $3,000, they thought that was gonna last eight weeks, and they figured there would be like two hundred bottles coming in a week. First of all, I guess honestly they didn't understand the need for some people, wanting to have money. Some of them, you'll see 'em put it in their sock, and then they'll put some in their pocket. That's their little bank, and this is their spending money for the next hour, they don't want to pull out the whole wad. You know, it's not a terrific wad, but you're down there sitting around the shade tree, the other guys are gonna say, 'Well, you got it, buy us some cigarettes, buy us some beers.' 'Oh, I had to work for this, you go down and work for your own. Don't panhandle off me, I mean I might have been a panhandler at one time, but I *work* for *my* money.' These people are starting to tell the other people on the curb, 'You get up and work.' They've come in and told me that, they've said, 'Can you believe these people out here on the curb, they're bummin' off me!' Because now they've earned it and it feels good to 'em."

Given the program's unexpected success in attracting scroungers and in cleaning up the neighborhood, Jimmy and I also talk about other possibilities: using the homeless shelter's stretch van to haul bottle scroungers and bottles, or expanding the on-site program to include plastic and aluminum. At one point, Warren, an elderly black man, pushes in a cart full of bottles, full black plastic bags hanging off the side as well, and I notice that one of the big bags does indeed hold aluminum cans rather than bottles. "Can't let all that money go to waste," Warren tells me, laughing, and so once he's cashed out his bottles he's off to the nearby scrap yard to cash in the cans as well.

A little later a black man and woman, each maybe thirty years old, push a couple of grocery carts into the lot. This is the first woman I've seen involved in bottle scrounging, which Jimmy explains in reference to the heavy carts and hard physical labor in the heat. Both carts are heavily loaded with bottles, with full black garbage bags hanging from their sides; one cart also has a plastic milk crate wired to the front to increase carrying capacity. He's all but silent; she's talkative, rambling, seemingly a bit disconnected from the moment.

Soon enough, a second black couple rolls up in an old Ford Aerostar Van, "106.1 KISS FM" and "United Christian Alliance" decals on the back, radiator fluid leaking badly out of the front. Jimmy tells me they've been given special permission to haul in bottles in their van; the general rule is walk and cart 'em in. The van holds their kid and a full load of bottles stuffed into black garbage bags; as the man begins unloading the bags from the van, a pool of radiator fluid is already forming under the engine. Jimmy goes in

and gets a couple of containers of water for the radiator.

"Gettin' hot," I say to the guy from my spot in the shade.

"*Gettin'* hot?" he says, sweating in the sun.

Otis is also away at the moment, and now the guy has the van unloaded and is ready to get the bottles turned in and get paid. Big, shirtless, muscular, dripping sweat, with cut-off jean shorts sagging a good eight inches below his boxers, he turns to me.

"You count?"

"OK," I say, wanting to be useful, and to cover for Jimmy and Otis if they need it, but knowing that I'm taking on a serious obligation. My count will determine how much this couple earns for untold hours of collecting dirty, sticky bottles in the hot sun, might even determine whether they have money to feed the kid or fix the radiator.

So I bear down and concentrate as he begins to toss the bottles into the big Dumpster. I soon realize that the shattering of each bottle provides me an auditory count to confirm my visual count, should I look away for a second; but I also notice it's easy to get distracted, to let the shattering rhythm lull me off my count, and so I concentrate harder. At around 185 or so Jimmy walks back up; not wanting to usurp his authority, and not minding some backup, I nod at him and mention my running count, and he begins to count as well. We're both counting silently, but I notice that at each hundred, at each century mark, he takes his pen and makes a little line on the palm of his hand; I'm reminded of my grandfather and other old men playing dominoes and marking the count with lines and X's. At the end, I have 465, but I keep it to myself, first asking Jimmy what he has. He says "a very rough 473," and I agree that's about right.

Of those 465 or 473 bottles, the big guy has tossed 464 or 472 cleanly into the bin—but one hit the rim, bounced off, shattered on the cement. So as he finishes, with no urging from Jimmy or me or anyone else, with his woman and kid waiting in a hot van that's leaking fluid fast, and having just collected and loaded and unloaded and tossed nearly five hundred bottles for a take of just under fifteen bucks, he picks up a big push broom and sweeps up the broken glass before he comes over to get paid.

On my last visit to the parking lot, with the program running out of money, Jimmy and I and others hang out in the heat and talk about the sweat it takes to be a bottle scrounger, sure, but also the knowledge and innovation.[15] As I walk up, Jimmy is in the middle of counting down a big load brought in by the quiet guy I met a while back; this time he's here without his female companion. "Five or six buggies" worth of bottles, the guy tells me while he's waiting to get paid, a weekend's worth of work. Terry's back, too, and we talk about the need to rotate the program through various neighborhoods so as to allow the supply of bottles to rebuild. But still, Terry says,

this sort of crop rotation model won't completely replenish the supply of discarded bottles, because after all, "some of these bottles I'm bringin' in I know are twenty years old. Hell, some of them I know I put there myself!"

Jimmy adds that "everyone has their own little hideaway" in terms of knowing where to find bottles for redemption, and talks about a guy who recently managed to accumulate a big load by walking his cart all the way to some shade-tree drinking areas on the south side of town. A little later I laugh when I see a somewhat more efficient model in play: a guy waiting in line to cash in his bottles leaves his cart for a minute, then returns with a 40 a friend has just finished, the foam still fresh in the bottle, and adds it to his cart.

But there's more to it than knowing where the bottles are. Gesturing to the carts parked nearby, Jimmy acknowledges that "it may look like I have a parking lot out here" as he notes the various models on the lot. There are "small ones, from Family Dollar [discount stores]"; "dinosaurs," old carts that the grocery stores don't want back because "they don't want a ten-year-old one that destroys their image"; and "lowriders," carts so old and broken down under the weight of bottles that they sag toward the ground. Some of the bottle scroungers, Jimmy explains, "have started off with small shopping carts and decided they want a big one, and so they just abandon them here. . . . I want to keep some around for somebody walkin' up . . . use it and bring it back.

Bottle scrounger's wheelchair, Fort Worth, Texas, June 2003.

. . . Certain ones I know that they're not easy to push and we need to get rid of those."

Other carts not easy to push have been modified rather than gotten rid of. Jimmy tells me how one guy added two custom wheels to the front of a cart for smoother and more efficient bottle hauling. Some folks have attached scrounged milk crates or buckets, in addition to the ubiquitous black garbage bags, to increase carrying capacity; another cart even has a scrounged dress belt attached to the front for holding excess bottles. One bottle hauler uses an old rolling trash bin he fished out of a gully; another employs a scrounged wheelchair that he's customized with scrounged wheels and a strapped-in bottle bin.

Of course, none of this compares with the *cartoneros* of Buenos Aires—the Argentina cardboard scroungers who, as noted in this book's first chapter, utilize specially customized steel push carts that can accommodate five hundred pounds of scrap cardboard and cans. Such carts would certainly be useful to the bottle haulers, the *botellaros*, of Fort Worth, struggling their loaded-down lowrider shopping carts up the long hill to the cash-in line. But really, cross-cultural comparisons like this can be dangerous. After all, commentators argue that the *cartoneros* of Argentina constitute a "growing labor force that is off the books and on the margins," a "potent symbol of the sudden increase in poverty," even "the most painful and visible symbol of the disintegration of a country"—and that certainly couldn't be the case with bottle haulers and other urban scroungers in the United States.[16]

Here, it will be recalled, city officials were enthused about the three-cent bottle program and the way it could clean things up on the cheap, concerned only with the number of bottles the program might bring in. Well, that and one other concern. As Jimmy tells me, city officials and the Fort Worth Police Department also initially worried about the possibility of theft, what with all those homeless folks rolling in and Jimmy out there in the parking lot with that pocketful of cash.

Jimmy wasn't worried.

"To me, I look at it as the people that are selling their bottles to me are gonna protect me because I'm their buddy, I'm their banker . . . and also I'm probably more than fair with them and they know that," he explains. "But, yeah, if you take my money, then I don't have money to pay them, and so I think it's sort of like don't mess with this person because he's a friend of all of us, and we want to sell our bottles. If you rob from him, you're robbing from me . . . nobody really wants to. . . . Now there might be somebody that might, but he probably wouldn't be a regular neighborhood person, cause everybody would turn him in. The thing about it is, they work hard for their bottle money, and if it's gone . . . I feel comfortable because they trust me and I trust them. . . . With the bottle count and this and that, I flex with them, I laugh with them."

Time and again, Jimmy and Terry and others emphasize this notion. This constellation of homeless shelters, railroad tracks, freeways, and shade trees is their *neighborhood,* and the three-cent bottle program has given them at least a temporary method for collectively cleaning it up. So scroungers customize their carts and sock away their money; Jimmy looks after their carts, their bags and clothes as well when needed, and passes out water to stave off the heat; and a bottle scrounger grabs a push broom and cleans up broken glass.

"In a sense," Jimmy says, "we're a family operation."

Aesthetic Salvage

As scroungers we are all of us in the gutter—but some of us are looking at the stars.[17] Certainly bottles and cans are collected and cashed in, clothes and tools accumulated, survival scratched out, but for many, beauty is found and created as well. As seen in a previous chapter, my scrounging acquaintance Elaine wraps her yard, trees, and front porch mannequin in scrounged decorations appropriate to each holiday season. As for me, I scrounge, sell, and give away hand-painted cowboy hats, and scrounge discarded calendars and photographs that I use to decorate my storage shed. Other times, I scrounge art books. Years ago in Denver, I salvaged from a curbside trash pile 1950s, 1960s, and 1970s editions of *Horizon,* a hardcover "Magazine of the Arts," and I still treasure them, especially the Winter 1970 edition featuring big color plates of Matisse's cutouts. During my more recent months of intensive scrounging, I find books like Paul Renner's 1964 *Color: Order and Harmony*, Christopher Darling's 1977 *Kain & Augustyn*, a photographic study of the ballet dancers Karen Kain and Frank Augustyn, and my favorite: Gwen Frostic's *A Walk with Me*, a book of lovely nature lithographs printed on handmade paper back in 1958. In one big trash pile, I find so many copies of books featuring the works of artists Stuart Davis and George Bellows, books published in the 1980s by the local Amon Carter Museum, that I'm still trying to give them away. I have fifteen scrounged copies of the tape *Musical Highlights from the Ninth Van Cliburn International Piano Competition*, too, if you're interested.

Other residues of the lush life show up in the trash piles and Dumpsters as well.[18] In one I find a little leather-bound 1972 *Wine and Food Diary*, published in London by the Confrérie Saint-Etienne, with its maps of Bordeaux and the Côte de Nuits, its wine and wine glass recommendations, and its calendar and little hardwood pencil for keeping track of it all. In another I discover an elegant writing pad, its gold-tinted aluminum case embossed with "The Statler Hilton 1956"—though apparently it's been used more recently, since its top sheet shows indentations from a torn-out page that read "e-mail Juno main number." And in a remodeling Dumpster outside All Saints Episcopal Church—the church just west of the exclusive River Crest Country Club, just east of the Baldrige House mansion and the discarded first-edition books described in a previous chapter—I find an expensive lamp, its arched chrome shaft some ten feet long, its chrome orb shade bigger than a basketball, its solid marble base almost too heavy to lift into the bed of my truck. The lamp now illuminates a friend's living room; the three elaborate wrought-iron candelabra I also hauled from the Dumpster now serve as bird perches in my backyard.

For me, though, the most aesthetically appealing discoveries haven't come from lush lives lived and lost, but from the scrounged beauty of everyday material culture. Old glass bricks catch the light on my back porch; antique glass doorknobs sit on a shelf near my desk. A heavily chromed 1940s clock that I extracted from an abandoned GE kitchen stove also resides in my study; the black and gold 1950s sunburst clock I pulled from the bottom of a trash pile still keeps time from my living room wall. The lovely, oversized 1950s TV tray, black with a mint green and gold floral design, also still graces my living room; touching old photos—a child's first birthday, twin baby boys laughing—shine down from walls throughout the house, secure in their scrounged frames. Old, imported phonographic albums that I found—*Tuff Guitar Al Caiola, The Blue Trumpet of Roy Etzel/Spanish Brass, The Music of Ernesto Lecuona/Trio Los Panchos*—are perhaps more pleasing visually than sonically, pressed as they were in translucent orange, red, and lime-green vinyl. Scrounged maps like a *Map of New York World's Fair and Rapid Transit Lines* and *Lowell Thomas' War Map of the World* mark time as much as place. Scrounged postcards likewise intertwine notions of tourism with ironies of beauty and degradation—as with a scrounged "Giant Post Card," mailed July 31, 1959, and featuring a gaping open pit copper mine, located outside "Santa Rita, New Mexico . . . one of the most interesting scenes in Southwestern New Mexico."

And that's not to mention all the scrounged chandelier crystals and old Bakelite knobs, or my collection of salvaged wooden windows. Or the afternoon before Valentine's Day, when I pulled all the roses, tulips, daisies, and lilies I could bike home from a wonderfully fragrant Dumpster behind Joy Florists, and had the pleasure of assembling a bunch of happenstance bouquets for my sweetheart. Or the fact that Leslie Hemstreet found more than that. "I even fell in love in a Dumpster," she remembers. "I knew it was true love when my then-friend-now-partner Matt dropped the Dumpster lid on my head and then kissed it to make it better."[19]

Artists of the Empire

In the 1920s and 1930s, in Weimar Germany, the rapid emergence of the "photographically illustrated press . . . spawned a new image-based culture"—a newly image-saturated world that Dadaist artists like Raoul Hausmann, Max Ernst, and Hannah Hoch embraced and subverted through techniques of photomontage, cut-up, and collage.[20] The profligate production of images in the popular press provided the material—Hannah Hoch's job with a large publishing firm gave her direct access to stacks of the firm's nineteen newspapers and magazines—and the Dadaists provided the countercultural aesthetic. Human heads, guns, lips, machinery, nudes, apes—sorted into categories of conventional meaning in the media, they were reassembled into unconventionality and critique in the collage art of the Dadaists and others. A world now awash in mass-produced images made possible an aesthetic confrontation with mass production and mass society itself; the emerging machinery of cultural production spewed forth the seeds of its own critique.

As this mass-marketed visual culture has continued into the twenty-first century, so have the critiques that turn it back on itself. In the 1950s and 1960s, for example, the French Situationists famously converted the mass-produced comic strips and cartoons that littered mass society's everyday life into a critique of everyday life in mass society. Attempting to launch a "revolution of everyday life," they substituted subversive slogans for the usual banalities of cartoon dialogue, literally rewriting the scripts through which such cartoons spoke to their audiences. To the Situationists, this constituted a process of *détournement*—that is, a theft of everyday meaning, an undermining of understandings mass produced for mass consumption. Today, this use of secondhand images and dislocated language in progressive visual and performance art continues—so commonly, in fact, as to have become all but a postmodern cliché.[21]

But of course the twentieth century has produced as many consumer items as it has mediated images, and this overwashing flood of material culture has in turn spawned the perfect aesthetic parallel to the reassembled image art of Dadaists and Situationists. Artists variously denoted as "folk artists" or "outsider artists," or more specifically "junk artists" or "scrap artists," have little need for easel or oil paint or the potter's wheel; as with the mass visual culture available to the Dadaists and Situationists, they have the entirety of cast-off consumer culture at their disposal, and so utilize it as art. As importantly, such artists often exist not simply as "outsiders" to the traditional art worlds of the studio and commercial gallery; instead, like the Dadaists and Situationists, they exist outside the conceptual boundaries of everyday culture. For them, the pace and experience of consumer culture are inverted, subverted, maybe even détourned. What others discard they reclaim and reinvent; what others denigrate as trash they construct as spirituality and art.

Vagabonding across America, in and out of jail, George Daynor saw just such a vision in 1929, a scrounger's hallucination that directed him to a desolate dump in Vineland, New Jersey. Squatting there, he erected over the next few years the Palace of Depression as a monument to the human spirit, an object lesson in creating something from nothing that might counter the hopelessness of the Great Depression. And the architecturally magnificent palace was indeed something from nothing; Daynor built it without tools, converting the dump's abandoned auto chassis into floor beams, its auto fenders into gables, its bed frames into doors. Likewise, African American outsider artists like Eddie Williamson and Tyree Guyton have created over the past decades "yard shows" that embody African spiritual traditions, Williamson's from discarded bottles and found hubcaps on a squatted embankment, Guyton's from "voraciously collected cast-off consumer objects" affixed en masse to the fronts of old houses.[22] In Houston, Jeff McKissack some years ago created the Orange Show monument from objects scrounged on his postal route and on his road trips through the American South; John Milkovisch meanwhile paved his Houston yard in found objects and built a house from 50,000 aluminum beer cans. Over three decades, Simon Rodia built the soaring Watts Towers in Los Angeles from "discarded pottery, glass, tiles, mirrors, and other neighborhood detritus."[23] During the same period, James Hampton, Jr., a janitor in federal buildings in Washington, D.C., built the Throne of the Third Heaven inside an old, rented garage. Hampton's throne now sits in the Smithsonian—but, at the time,

you might have seen him walking from a government
building with a trash bag full of used light bulbs; or
maybe out on the street with a burlap sack, asking
bums if he could buy the foil off their wine bottles.
He'd dig through Dumpsters to get green glass,
sandwich foil, cardboard. And of the course the best
thing about working for the American government
was how wasteful it was, throwing perfectly good
material away because someone didn't like the way it
looked. The best thing about cleaning up after the
people who ruled the world was that they didn't see
the real value in things.[24]

Today, the cleanup and the aesthetic reconstitu-
tion continue. In Philadelphia, the Dumpster
Divers, a group of some forty "junk artists," trace
their heritage to the found-object art of Marcel
Duchamp and Pablo Picasso; in New York City,
artist Brian Matthews constructs puppets,
pneumatic wings, and catapults from scrounged
objects; and in South Carolina, these and other
junk artists get together at the big Revival Design
Camp Meeting.[25] San Francisco maintains an
artist in residence at the city dump. Out in
Washington State, they don't have a resident junk
artist, but Gary Vig welds a three-ton, twenty-
two-foot-long bull out of scrap metal and plants it
in a horse pasture. In Gage, Oklahoma, federal
regulations put Jim Powers's scrap metal yard in
jeopardy, so he decides to just start welding life-
size dinosaurs and elephants out of the scrap
metal; over in Leedey, Oklahoma, Joe Smith
prefers to build forty-four-foot-tall cactuses out
of water heaters and oilfield pipe.[26] Folks send

Davy Rothbart grocery lists and lost love notes
they find in the streets; Rothbart publishes them
in *Found* magazine and his *Found* book, and tours
with a multimedia *Found* show.[27] Meanwhile,
Caribbean steel drum bands continue to play;
Vancouver's Scrap Arts Music ensemble keeps
staging concerts; and Leslie Hemstreet writes a
song about it all, set to "Ramones-style three-
chord head-bopping rock":

> *I'm a radical, bad-ass dangerous babysitter*
> *(repeat three times)*
>
> *You feed your poor children Burger King*
> *And all sorts of Styrofoam things*
> *I wanna teach your family about surviving*
> *So I'm taking your babies Dumpster diving.*[28]

Around Fort Worth and its suburbs, scraps of art
continue to emerge, too. Ed Schaefer—one of the
top luthiers (guitar makers) in the country, whose
jazz guitars run from six to nine thousand dollars
apiece—admits he got his start thirty years ago
scavenging guitar necks and bodies from a
Dumpster behind a Fort Worth guitar importer's
store, building guitars from the pieces, and selling
them to pawn shops for fifty bucks apiece. "I'm a
true criminal," he jokes, "but I think the statute of
limitations has kicked in."[29] Brian Larsen's Fort
Worth friends have learned to bring him any
industrial parts they find; he turns them into wall
art and camshaft-legged coffee tables.[30] When
he's not making a living driving a shuttle bus out
at Dallas/Fort Worth Airport, Congolese

immigrant and art school graduate Augie N'Kele digs around in the airport's Dumpsters for scrap metal, which he converts into "some of the world's most acclaimed African-themed art."[31] And then there's Ron Drouin. He builds some amazing scrap sculptures. Well, he used to, anyway.

Ron Drouin's original inspiration for turning scrap metal into art was as much aggravational as aesthetic. When his neighbors in Arlington, Texas, turned him in to the city over an old 1937 International pickup he had in his yard, he reluctantly got rid of the pickup—but retaliated by replacing it with homemade yard art. City officials assured him that while the old pickup wasn't legal, the yard art was—and so now the neighbors' continued complaints to the city got no results since, as Ron told me, "you can't touch art."[32]

Over the next year and a half, though, Ron found that as he continued to turn motor mounts, bunk bed frames, bicycle seats, car bumpers, ladders, wheelbarrows, and other scrap metal into turkeys, dragons, giraffes, and turtles, his creations "came to life" in a way that transcended any sense of retaliation. The artistic momentum continued to build in other ways as well. He broadened his work, now constructing, along with the animals, windmills and whirligigs, using bicycle bearings and oversized light housings to create pieces that would swing and sway in the wind. He discovered a favorite junkyard in nearby Balch Springs, Texas, where he bought quirky pieces of metal scrap by the pound to supplement what he found along the roadside. Friends began to drop off chain-link fencing and other metal scrap they thought he might be able to use. School buses full of kids stopped by his yard to enjoy the art; cops, too. Folks noticed a scrap sculpture he had put out in front of a friend's shop, and he was invited to display a scrap metal dinosaur at an Earth Day celebration on the University of Texas at Arlington campus. He even began to supplement the money he made as a carpenter by selling a few of the pieces—a hundred dollars for a turtle, three hundred for a dragon.

But then the legal problems that precipitated Ron Drouin's career as a scrap artist came full circle, and with a vengeance. This time it wasn't as simple as a pickup in the yard and a city code violation; it was major drug charges. So, sadly, when I finally catch up to Ron and have a chance to talk with him in person, it isn't out in his yard, under a shade tree, beside one of his lovely dragons or giraffes; it's inside the distinctly unlovely Green Bay Correctional Facility out in north Fort Worth. Amid the chipped green paint and the cacophony of visitors' hours, he tells me that the worst parts of jail are not being able to stay busy with his scrap art or otherwise, and so his tendency to sleep all day—well, that and being separated from his two Chow dogs. Where he once saw a growing scrap art business, he says, he now hopes to pass his prison time teaching some GED classes, using his engineering skills on something other than turtles and turkeys—and maybe imagining future scrap art projects, someday, back out in the free world.

The last time I saw Dan Phillips there was prison in the air, too—but then there always is in Huntsville, Texas, what with the big Texas prison complex and the Texas death house.[33] Still, Dan's a free man, or as free as any of us can be down here in the death penalty state, and so he cruises around Huntsville, checking on the progress of his salvage-built houses, and once a week he heads south out of Huntsville, pulling his trailer down I-45 to the Houston lumber warehouses to pick up scrap materials that would otherwise go to the landfill. Instead of the landfill, these and other salvaged materials go to Dan's sprawling Huntsville scrap and storage yard, a scrounger's wonderland located just down the road from a little pit barbeque joint and the Mt. Zion Baptist Church. There, sheds and outbuildings—one of them roofed with discarded license plates—house stack after stack of lumber, doors, windows, shutters, sinks, faucets, light fixtures, and tile; the big shade trees provide cover for other collections of rough timber and building materials. Across town, a friend provides a tractor trailer and an old house in which Dan stores still more windows and doors. As Dan says, joking about the title of my book, he and his friend both reside *deep* inside the empire of scrounge.

From deep inside the empire, Dan Phillips uses these scrounged and salvaged materials to hand-build houses. As noted in Chapter One, though, these aren't just any houses—they're houses whose architectural innovation and structural integrity is such that they show up in magazines

Dan Phillips's license plate roof, Huntsville, Texas, April 2002.

Dan Phillips's scrap yard and shed, Huntsville, Texas, April 2002.

A Dan Phillips home, Huntsville, Texas, April 2002.

like *People* and *Fine Homebuilding*.[34] In building these homes, Dan is as playful as he is skilled, and so he consistently invents oddball possibilities while converting the detritus of industry and consumption into fine architectural detail. Hundreds of 2 x 4 cutoffs are interlaced to form a turreted spiral stairwell; stacked like bricks, nailed together, they form a sturdy outside wall as well. A part from an antique woodworking machine makes a deadbolt for an interior door; an antique shoe last functions as a step lever for a cedar-lined laundry shoot. Bits of porcelain from a broken toilet become elegantly curved tiles to finish the top rim of a shower stall; a beer tap functions as a faucet. Sliding glass doors reappear as sturdy skylights. Hickory nuts make good drawer pulls, and hickory shells become the raw material for fretwork over a front porch. And then there are the secret compartments, tucked away inside stair newel posts and elsewhere. "I like secret compartments a lot," says Dan.[35]

He likes folks on the margins a lot, too—unskilled workers, Wal-Mart employees, people with few prospects. He hires them at minimum wage to help build his houses, teaches them the skills of carpentry and craft work, then helps them find jobs that will reward these new skills. And he sells his houses to them, finances their home purchase if needed. Back in the mid-1990s, he remembers, "I got to thinking that I'd always wanted to build houses, and I'd always been incensed that too much stuff went to the landfill . . . and now I'm building houses for low-income families. It just rankles me that carpetbaggers come in and exploit the poor with their mobile homes, and then they're in worse shape than when they started." When a lawyer walked up while Dan and I were standing in front of one his houses and asked Dan to build her a fine home, he explained his approach. "You're way too cultivated; I don't build for people like you," he told her, friendly enough. "I build for the people who quit school in the seventh grade, single mothers, five kids, four jobs . . . and have miserable credit. Everybody has to live somewhere."[36]

In this way, Dan Phillips integrates the empire of scrounge with a do-it-yourself effort to assist the poor—and he does so by way of art and craft. With a background as a trained dancer and professor of dance theory (as I did at the beginning of my scrounger's life, he "got tired of the bureaucrats and said adios" to academia), Dan brings a sharp aesthetic analysis to his work. Prior to the Industrial Revolution, he argues, the notion of craft "grew from intrinsic, organic shapes and availability of materials, one's ability to work and join natural materials, and the clever achievement of the intended—or discovered—shape."[37] Now, however, standardized building materials and bottom-line, efficiency-driven building procedures operate "to *obliterate* all organic texture and human gesture." "We're frozen into the Wal-Mart mentality," Dan says. "We're allowing Wal-Mart to dictate artistic principles. . . . It's spiritual suicide." Worse, this aesthetic assembly line requires an endless supply of raw materials for conversion into newly formed board feet and prefabricated bricks—and it requires a rationalized legal apparatus to perpetuate it. "All the building codes are predicated on standard materials," Dan notes, and yet "standard materials are at the root of why we're denuding the planet. It's just insidious. And our culture is bleeding across the world. We've got to stop this!"[38]

But if standardized, mass-produced materials and modern building codes together operate to enforce an aesthetic of straight lines and square boxes—an aesthetic as individually vacant as it is environmentally destructive—what's to stop it? Dan proposes a return to imaginative craftwork—that is, to art—within the contemporary ecology of scrounging and salvage. Referencing John Dewey's 1934 treatise *Art as Experience,* he argues that artists always engage a creative dialectic, letting "the external shaping of materials concomitantly shape the interior landscape so they grow together. And the nice thing about building a house from salvage is, yeah, you start off with blueprints, but don't stick to them. The materials point in new directions, so it's an extremely organic process, and to me, that's what art is. If you let materials speak to you, whatever the materials are, they foment imaginative design adventures into directions you never could have foreseen."[39]

In this alternative model—and in Dan Phillips's houses—formulas of preplanned precision give way to an aesthetic of playful possibility intertwined with the found world. Routinized assembly is replaced by craft skills and practical

Scrounged stencil art by Jeff Ferrell.

art, a Wal-Mart job by work that builds both high quality homes and a sense of hope. The wastefulness of mass production and cheap efficiency becomes instead a commitment to reclaim what has been wasted, a willingness to work with what's available, and a pleasure in inventing out of it what's not. The exportation of American-style production and consumption across the world stops short, too, turns the other way around. "Every poor country that doesn't have access to standardized materials, they use whatever is available in their backyard and they make it work," Dan argues. "Well, that's what we could all do; in fact, that's what we could do here in America, and maybe tidy up our backyard just a little bit."

Sharing with Dan Phillips this scrounger's aesthetic, but absent his architectural skills, I've discovered other ways of using whatever is available and making it work as art. Out by my backyard shed, under the pecan and hackberry trees, I've built little lawn sculptures out of scrounged bicycle wheels, custom curtain rods, and scrap metal, and mixed these in among scrounged solar yard lights. I've even built a few little mobiles out of old telephone bells, metal filters, and wire—scrap sculptures that hang and flutter, sometimes ring, in the wind. Still, these

he says, "you don't really know 'til you see what Mother Nature does." The poet Carl Sandburg, paraphrasing the artist Hokusai, allowed near the end of his life that "if God had let me live five years longer I should have been a writer." Now in his early 80s, surrounded by his monumentally soaring whirligigs, Vollis Simpson has the same thought. "I would have liked to have started this ten or twelve years sooner," he said. "I could have really built some nice things—some big things."[40]

If Vollis Simpson is humbled by his creations, you can imagine how I feel about my dinky little scrap mobiles—and so despite constructing a few mobiles, mostly I just stick to spray paint. During my years in the hip hop graffiti underground, I learned how to handle a spray can—how to use it to create fades, splatters, shadowing, and other special effects—and I learned from graffiti writers how to scrounge objects for use as on-the-spot stencils while painting city walls.[41] As a full-time scrounger, I resurrected these skills in order to produce my own version of scrounged art—art for my own pleasure, and to sell on occasion as a supplement to my scrap metal monies. To do this, I scrounged canvases, card stock, envelopes, and spray paint; I even scrounged a stamp pad for inking my signature on my artwork. Best of all, I scrounged the stencils.

As I soon learned, the ongoing scavenging of stencils demands close aesthetic engagement with the empire of scrounge. It teaches the scrounger to reconsider, reimagine really, the assorted detritus of the urban environment. And it fosters

are nothing in comparison to Dan Phillips's turrets and fretwork, and they're certainly nothing in comparison to Vollis Simpson's monumental wind-powered scrap metal whirligigs out in North Carolina.

While stationed on Saipan during World War II, Vollis Simpson built his first wind-powered whirligig and rigged it to run a washing machine; now he builds towering, intricate scrap sculptures that turn this way and that with the wind, since, as the very sort of creative tension between external possibility and aesthetic intentionality proposed by Dan Phillips. For a scrounged object to make a good stencil, it of course needs to offer something of artistic use: a clean straight edge, for example, or an interesting exterior shape. But, I discovered, it also needs a sort of flat dimensionality, an absence of warps and ridges, so that it can hug the paper or canvas and produce sharp resolution when sprayed over and around. It also needs to be heavy; a steel square, for example, holds its place far better than a paper square against the aerosol bursts of the spray can, and so produces cleaner and more reliable images. And in this regard, yet another lesson learned about what the empire of scrounge has to offer: a flat heavy chunk of scrap aluminum, a finely toothed gear or an old metal gasket pulled from an auto shop's trash bin, makes a better and more precise stencil than anything I can cut, no matter how carefully, from cardboard or paper.

With the accumulation of these found stencils over time, the interplay between aesthetics and availability continued. After a while, my shed came to contain not only collections of found tools and plumbing supplies, but an ever-widening pallet of artistic possibilities in the form of found stencils. Lengths of scrounged wire twisted into circles and spirals and squares, curved bits of broken guitar body and decorative molding, wire mesh of varying densities, slotted drain covers, pieces of board games, old picture frames, metal punch-outs, washers, clock springs, saw blades,

Scrounged stencil art by Jeff Ferrell.

clean edges, fluted edges, torn edges—all offer distinct options when composing a piece of stenciled art. And then, at the moment of creation, some selection of these stencils mixed with various techniques of spray painting, layers of color and texture laid down and sprayed over, some imagined shapes and forms available at arm's reach, others not, and all of it producing an

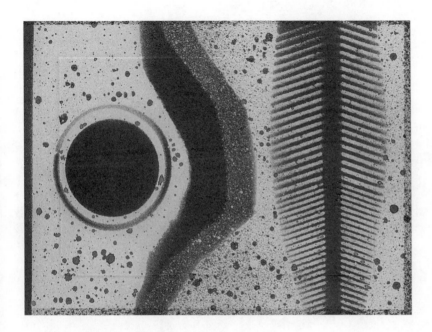

image that is ultimately equal parts imagination and uncertainty.

As I continued to refine my techniques and produce this sort of stencil art, the empire of scrounge emerged as an empire of accidental images. Searching for objects that might make good stencils retrained my scrounger's eye, taught me to see the city differently, to sort amid its effluvia not only for clothes and cans, but for aesthetic possibility. In this sense, the process of looking became itself a sort of performance art, an ongoing appreciation of unintended urban beauty that enlivened every scrounging ride.[42] The subsequent conversion of these found objects into working stencils, and the occasional selling or bartering of this stencil art to help finance my continued scrounging, added yet another turn to the spiral of reflexive use and reuse that kept my scrounging viable and virtually autonomous. With the inclusion of found stencils, salvage operations all but came full circle. Nothing need go to waste or be left behind; an appliance part or piece of metal that couldn't be used elsewhere might well be of use aesthetically. The meaning of the material world shifted once again, this time from new to old to art, as consumer culture's castoffs became possibilities that couldn't be imagined.

6

city scrounge

This book's first chapter argued that urban scrounging is a social activity shaped by ambiguity and uncertainty—that scrounging, both in its historical evolution and contemporary practice, embodies dynamics of meaning constantly in motion. My months and years of daily scrounging confirmed this. Day after day, I and other scroungers negotiated the porous boundaries between private property and discarded public resource. We read and misread transitory signs that suggested scrounging opportunities, and in doing so wandered back and forth between legality and illegality. As we dug in Dumpsters and accumulated scrap and reinvented what we found, we watched the status of everyday objects drift between wished-for possession and forgotten waste, useless castoff and usefully reconstructed tool, trash pile discard and outsider art. And rightly so, by the way—the ambiguities of urban scrounging, confirmed in my own experience, seem essential to its very viability, and to the ongoing viability of the urban environment in which scrounging occurs.

Yet for all its ambiguities, I did discover in the empire of scrounge one straightforward problem, as troubling as it was pervasive. It certainly didn't come from the scroungers themselves, in whose ragged company I mostly found moments of common purpose and outlaw community. It didn't originate with the owners of the trash bins and Dumpsters, either. Though I certainly ran into harsh words and hard looks, I more often encountered home owners who encouraged me to take what I needed, who brought out more of their discards for my perusal, who even sorted and arranged their trash for the sake of better curbside shopping. And it didn't come from the street cops and security guards, whom I mostly avoided, and who mostly rolled by with little more than a glance when I didn't.

No, the trouble materialized elsewhere.

Everyday Economy and Social Change

The trouble was there each time I opened some big black garbage bag to find inside the course of a life—baby shoes, diaries, framed diplomas, fancy wedding albums, birth announcements, employee awards—now discarded with the death of a loved one, a divorce, or the sale of a house. Even more, it was there during that episode I described in the first chapter, when on the street behind a big West Fort Worth mansion I found all those thick black trash bags full of baby shower party favors and baby gifts, still new in their packages. It was

certainly there the day I was scrounging a trash pile nearby, close to the exclusive River Crest Country Club, and found not only a working sewing machine thrown away, but a framed poster, "Poverty Sucks," a blonde model posed next to a Rolls Royce. It was there over and over again, with me day after day, as I found in one trash pile after another new clothes, shoes without a scuff, appliances in working order, golf clubs, televisions, antiques, jewelry.

The problem I kept discovering in the streets and alleys, the trouble I kept encountering in the Dumpsters and trash piles, was unambiguous: an American culture of endless consumption and growing inequality, a global economy mass producing the culture's material foundations, and a world of waste and indulgence in consequence. Certainly consumer culture is predicated on programmed insatiability, on the constant construction of needs and desires that can never quite be met, and so remain ready for the next new commodity. In this sense, consumer culture creates and sustains among its adherents a sort of existential vacancy—a personal void, a material longing promoted by the same corporate advertisers whose products promise its resolution. But in the same way that consumer culture empties individuals of their identity, it fills their trash bins and Dumpsters with its waste. We can interrogate consumer culture by viewing its advertisements, visiting its engorged shopping malls, even investigating our own closets. We can interrogate it just as well in its aftermath, peering into its packed Dumpsters, digging in its trash piles, touring its landfills.

Thorstein Veblen saw this trouble coming a century ago. He understood it decades before I ever noticed it, understood the rhythms of what he called "conspicuous consumption"—rhythms that roll, always, toward the next new commodity. As Veblen argued famously (and, always, acerbically), consumption functions not only as a mechanism for acquiring necessary goods, but as a social and cultural practice; as such, consumption is undertaken as much to acquire social status as to fulfill innate need.[1] In fact, with the development of late capitalist consumer society, consumption quite clearly comes unhinged from necessity, and doubly so. Corporations and their advertising agencies continually work to invent new needs and desires, layered one after the other over the basics of everyday survival, and with these new wants new markets for their consumer goods; consumers in turn acquire such goods for the emerging status they bestow, for their promise of up-to-date cultural identity. Ideally—ideally for the machinery of consumer culture, that is—neither party cares to stop the process; new and improved goods bestow new and improved social status, and conspicuous consumption continues.

But how to make room for the new? And what then to do with no-longer-new commodities whose value was primarily in their acquisition anyway, once the next round of consumption rolls in, as it always will, and soon? Certain trends in American culture provide one set of answers: proliferating rented storage facilities, larger homes and bigger mortgages for the middle class, the new National Association of Professional Organizers (for closets, that is, not unions), and four-car garages stuffed full of SUVs and last year's purchases.[2] Trash piles and Dumpsters offer another sort of answer, and so an archeology of conspicuous consumption and its consequences. The trash pile and the Dumpster offer something else, too: the arrival of those left to pick through them, and perhaps to be made social outlaws for the degraded circumstances under which they acquire the materials with which to make a life.

As one of those social outlaws, I came to understand quite well the culture I was uncovering, especially in the trash piles of the affluent. Finding an unopened box or a blouse with price tag still attached once in every fifty trash piles might suggest the unfortunate overlooking of a valued gift in the rush to clean up after a birthday party, or a new purchase accidentally discarded in the aftermath of a shopping spree. Finding such items time and again, buried in one trash pile after another, suggests something more: a pattern of conspicuous consumption—and of ostentatious giving and duplicitous receiving—among the leisure classes that were Veblen's original focus. Among those classes, Veblen argued back in 1899, consumption takes on a "ceremonial character"; it becomes "honorific," both ostentatious display and material evidence of one's wealth. But ironically, this ongoing display of wealth and leisure itself often becomes hard work, a demanding daily task of mastering proper manners and consuming all the right commodities. And so, "the aid of friends and competitors is therefore brought in," Veblen noticed, "by resorting to the giving of valuable presents and expensive feasts and entertainments."[3]

If indeed this giving of gifts exists for both giver and recipient as a symbolic display of manners and privilege, what might we expect of such gifts once the party has ended? Certainly nothing so mundane as actual utilization in the household—putting the gift to use might imply that one was actually *in need* of it. Certainly not conspicuous disposal, either; a lovely gift, left atop the trash pile the day after the party, invites scandal if seen by the giver, and worse, attracts the attention of whatever scroungers or scrap metal haulers might be menacing the neighborhood. So, best to bury it deep inside a big tear-resistant black plastic trash bag; it's conspicuous utility served, it can rest there comfortably on the ride to the landfill—unless, that is, its liberator comes along.

Near the end of my eight months of daily scrounging, less than a week before Christmas, I came upon a big trash pile that Veblen would certainly have appreciated—a trash pile big enough to hold all the trouble that is contemporary consumer society. Cycling through Fort Worth's elegant Monticello neighborhood—

once again, near River Crest Country Club—I stop to investigate a curbside trash pile in front of an expensive home with a "For Sale" sign out front. As I'm bent over sorting through it, the woman of the house—slight, blonde hair pulled back, late twenties—comes out carrying another trash bag, so I stand up and say, unapologetically, "I'm sorting through your trash—I find stuff and resell it." She seems taken aback, says, "Well, let me think is there anything particularly good in there—I don't think so," and quickly retreats to the house.

But of course there's plenty of particularly good stuff in there.

To begin with, there's a big hardback book, slick high-quality pages, "Texas International Fine Arts Fair, NorthPark East, Paintings, Sculpture, Furniture, Jewelry, Silver, and Objects, November 1–7, 2001" embossed on the cover. It's a veritable catalog of leisure-class acquisition habits, a found archive of conspicuous consumption. The book includes letters of greeting from Texas governor Rick Perry and Dallas mayor Ron Kirk, and features color plates of items for sale at the fair, among them original art by Joan Miró and Marc Chagall, yachts (Atlantis Yachts is a fair sponsor), a "Complete Billiard Room Suite" (London, c. 1890), and a "Magnificent Pair of Antique George III Silver Wine Coolers" (not to be confused with the wine coolers available down at the convenience store). Among the advertisements in the back are those for similar fairs in New York and Palm Beach.

While the pile holds this sort of straightforward evidence of conspicuous consumption, it also contains more than one of consumer culture's many malodorous ironies. Some trash piles stink of rotting food and old clothing; this one smells of consumption's contradictions.

In a single black trash bag are perhaps a hundred or so compact disk cases, sans disks: Beck, Dave Matthews Band, Bob Marley, The Beatles. And then there's the Snoop Dogg *DoggyStyle* case, its cover featuring a clothed dog straddled over a doghouse, tail erect and wagging, and crawling into the doghouse a black woman, pink ankle wraps and pink fluff on her tail, butt in the air, naked but for this and a g-string, and a character off to the side saying, "Snoop is always on top of things." Listed song titles include "Murder Was the Case," "Serial Killa," "For All My Niggaz and Bitches," and "Pump Pump."

Immediately I start laughing to myself, thinking of that scene in the movie *Office Space*, the one all my students love: the white boy stuck in traffic on the way to his office cubicle, window down, rappin' loud and proud along with a gangsta rap song on his car radio—and then seeing the black guy approaching him, the one selling flowers in the median, and down goes the tune and up goes the power window. I can just envision this woman and her husband (he's evident in the trash pile by the discarded men's athletic shoes), turning down the Snoop and powering up the windows on the Lexus as they're approached by some Niggaz or Serial Killaz at a

stop light—or maybe heading back inside when confronted by a dirty white boy scrounger in their trash pile. Maybe I can even see hubby telling her, shit bitch, I likes it doggy style, especially when hubby's back home from a few drinks at the country club. Or, like the little cartoon in the CD liner notes, tellin' her, just like Snoop tells his bitch, "Beeitch, if you ain't got no kinda chronic yo punk ass gots to go! Ho!" and later, when the chronic turns out to be no good, Snoop's buddy C-style, urging "Let's kill da ho!"[4]

Ah, Snoop and C-style and their misogynistic Christmas cheer. But there's more. Still new in its box is a KSA Collectibles Limited Edition "Christmas Treats" figurine, Santa emptying out his bag of toys, part of the "Visions of Santa" series, "a new series of limited edition figurines from KSA Collectibles. Each is individually numbered in an issue of 7500 pieces." This one is number 1770. "These Santas represent the magical memories of childhood," the box assures me. "They are beautifully sculpted in cold cast and hand painted with exceptional detail. Destined to become a treasured keepsake for your annual yuletide celebration."

Well, hand painted with exceptional detail, yes— but as the box says, in finer print, "In Indonesia for Kurt S. Adler, Inc." So now I'm envisioning another scene, and I've long since stopped laughing: child laborers, young Indonesian women, at work twelve, fourteen hours a day, earning a pittance for creating "Christmas Treats" but with no treats of their own, not to mention no childhood and no "magical memories of childhood," all of which have been quite systematically and efficiently stolen from them by Kurt S. Adler and his suppliers. Then I have another Christmas vision, that this inhumane hand-painted residue of the global economy might in fact be "destined to become a treasured keepsake" for some middle-class American family that receives it as a gift and doesn't throw it out, for them a cheap reproduction of cultural memory and tradition, and all of it a dirty little fraud, a trick of fabricated authenticity.[5]

And then there are the two hand-carved wooden *matryoshka* Santa dolls, each with its smaller dolls nested inside in the Russian folk art tradition . . . except that both have "Made in China" printed on the bottom. Another trick of manufactured meaning, and a predictable one; as sociologist William Greider reports, "Over the last generation, toy manufacturers and others have moved around the Asian rim in search of the bottom-rung conditions: from Hong Kong, Korea and Taiwan to Thailand and Indonesia, from there to China, Vietnam, and Bangladesh, perhaps on next to Burma, Nepal, or Cambodia."[6]

As it turns out, this leisure-class trash pile offers not only copious evidence of conspicuous consumption; it offers a world tour of global capitalism's rush to the worst of work conditions and wages—and maybe in next year's pile, outside some other affluent American family's home, we'll get to visit Burma and Nepal, too. All of this consumption, all these contradictions,

coagulating in those big black trash bags, just a few days before Christmas, in with the scraps of food and the disposable razors.

Scraps of Hope

Yet for all that, a trash pile like this one contains, amid the discarded degradations of consumer culture, scraps of dignity and hope as well—and one more contradiction. As I discovered, the same global economy that drives down wages in the United States, and exports its work life to sweatshops in China and Indonesia, spews forth waste in sufficient amounts to provide a modicum of relief for those very Americans whose jobs and wages it has destroyed. Under contemporary conditions of global consumerism, a complex alternative economy—a widespread enterprise of everyday survival within the empire of scrounge—has emerged amidst the excesses of American consumerism itself.

Of all the discoveries I made, this understanding of the empire's diverse population was among the most important, and surprising. Minimum-wage earners heading home in their work uniforms, immigrants lacking a green card, poor folks without a driver's license or steady home address, homeless men and women with their shopping carts, disabled folks supplementing a pension, old boys living rough by choice or chance or necessity—all were there with me at the trash pile and the Dumpster, all piecing together economic and physical survival one discard at a time. But lest this sound like the invisible hand, weaving a social safety net from the dynamics of free enterprise, let's be clear: The global economy hasn't provided these folks an alternative existence. They've invented it out of its contradictions, against all odds, against one law and another meant to stop them, using their courage and innovation to extract survival from dirty Dumpsters and tightly tied garbage bags.

While this sense of the empire as an alternative, underground economy emerged throughout my time there, it became especially clear while hanging out with the folks scrounging bottles for three cents apiece. At the reclamation center in the homeless shelter parking lot, Jimmy Silcox and others talked over and over again about how such a program gave folks without a regular job a chance to earn a few bucks, gave them the freedom to make their own decisions, to set their own hours, to work as little or as much as they could. And as folks kept rolling in with cartloads of bottles, talking about a revoked driver's license or some other impediment to wage slavery, laughing about their own scruffy independence, it hit me: We were all a bunch of urban prospectors, riding the urban frontier for bottles or copper or aluminum cans.

In my own experiences as well as theirs, this urban prospecting offered a self-defined, self-employed way of survival for those of us unwilling or unable to submit to corporate employment's increasingly demeaning constraints. Riding an old bike instead of a horse, serving as your own pack mule while pushing an abandoned shopping cart, you embrace the blessed uncertainty of prospecting: adventure, danger, disappointment, elation. Sometimes you strike it rich with a Dumpster full of copper tubing; other times you strike out, returning with nothing but a few aluminum cans or lead weights. Sometimes you stake a claim, even defend it, while working a big curbside trash pile; other times you share the claim, or just walk away and wander, restless to see what the next alley holds. Sometimes you discover and work a secret vein, until you run the construction Dumpster out of scrap aluminum or the hidden drinking spot out of cast-off 40s. Sometimes you hide what you find up under the weeds or behind a wall, till you can come back for it; sometimes you just give it away to someone who needs it more. All the time, you negotiate the heat or the cold or the rain, even learn to like it, to embrace it, as part of the freedom and the adventure—which in any case, as the bottle scroungers emphasized more than once, sure as hell beats minimum wage work at Wal-Mart.

Like all prospectors you also have to come in now and then, find a way to convert all that damn ore into cash, and hope not to get cheated or robbed as you do. With Jimmy in charge, the bottle program was easy; sometimes the scrap yards aren't. In fact, one scorching August day, while a veteran street scrounger and I were sitting out the worst of the afternoon heat in the shade of a rundown little convenience store near the North Side scrap yards, he took the time to school me in this nicety of urban prospecting. A big burly gray-bearded white guy, maybe fifty-five years old, he sat on the sidewalk next to his prospecting gear: an old grocery cart with white collection buckets wired to both sides, and a long wooden pole tipped with a bent nail. A North Side native, he knew a secret history and politics of its many scrap yards, knew which families owned more than one yard, knew who'd sold out to whom over the years.

Mentioning to him that I often took my scrap to the nearby American Recycling yard, his eyes—bloodshot, shimmering, piercing—narrowed a bit. He used to take his scrap there, he told me, until one day a cashier tried to pay him $1.79 for what he figured was five bucks worth of scrap—as he said, you push in enough cartloads, you get to where you know about what each one should be worth. When he told her "just keep the $1.79 as a tip," the yard owner came out from behind the counter and challenged him—and even though the matter was resolved without fists, he now takes his scrap over to the J&E yard on 29th Street. "The guy who runs that yard is a street person like we are," he told me, a guy who came from the streets and understands the difficulties of street scrounging, a guy who'll sometimes "cut you a little slack on a dirty load"—that is, pay full price even when a load hasn't been completely cleaned of contamination.

But if knowing how to cash out your scrap is essential to survival in this alternative economy, so is knowing when not to. As my time in the empire taught me, a scrounger is best able to craft economic autonomy from the discarded items of consumer society by avoiding the stores that sell such items in the first place. Converting found items into cash pushes the scrounger back toward retail consumption; converting them directly into solutions for everyday needs pushes the scrounger away from retail and toward self-reliance. Many times scrap yard cash or yard sale money is necessary—but in the best of all scroungers' worlds, they're no more than remunerative lubrication for a homemade economy of existential independence. It's like master Dumpster diver Lars Eighner said, commenting on those foragers who focus only on aluminum cans: "One can extract the necessities of life from the Dumpsters with far less effort than would be required to accumulate the equivalent value in cans."[7]

Whether converted into self-reliance or cash, the countless aluminum cans and lengths of copper pipe that urban scroungers salvage each day coalesce into another sort of alternative to consumer society as well: an on-the-ground practice of recycled environmentalism. Scroungers don't just live off the waste of consumer society; they collect it, contain it, and in their own practical way reverse the valences that produce it. A recent study finds that in Buenos Aires, the cartoneros each day "collect 66 tons of waste cardboard and paper products—trash that is recycled instead of added to the landfills in the suburbs."[8] In Fort Worth, a neighborhood association representative marvels at the effects

Urban scrounger, New York City, October 2004.

of even a short-term bottle reclamation program. "You just don't see the bottles anymore," she says. "There's none lying around. Before, they were knee-deep."[9] In New York City, homeless Vietnam veteran Juan Taylor calls himself an "accidental environmentalist" as he wanders the city scrounging aluminum cans. "I'm invisible to the world, but I do people's dirty work," he says. "People don't appreciate the service I'm performing."[10] If the police are, as some claim, the thin blue line between social order and crime, urban scroungers are the last thin line between consumer waste and the landfill—and every day, working one by one, they string out and save countless tons from its clutches. In this sense they certainly produce scraps of hope for themselves and their own survival, but also for the survival of a social order currently awash in its own waste.

Then again, for some, maybe the hope is not for the survival of the social order but for its transformation. Writing about the subversive potential of youth subcultures, Dick Hebdige noted that "by repositioning and recontextualizing commodities, by subverting their conventional uses and inventing new ones, the subcultural stylist gives lie to what Althusser has called the 'false obviousness of everyday practices,' and opens up the world of objects to new and covertly oppositional readings."[11] Many in the empire of scrounge work to promote a similar political dynamic, to invent oppositional readings as they go about salvaging, reconstructing, and repositioning the commodity waste of consumer culture. As their names suggest, groups like Food Not Bombs and Bikes Not Bombs undertake reclamation and reuse for the benefit of the homeless and other folks on the margins; but they also operate in opposition to state militarism, within traditions of anarchist direct action and antiauthoritarian mutual assistance. Leslie Hemstreet pointedly refers to her Dumpster diving as "a recipe for revolution" and intersperses it with activism (and arrest) on behalf of Earth First! and other environmental groups, arguing that "waste was practically written into our cultural constitution."[12] As seen in the previous chapter, Dan Phillips makes clear that his do-it-yourself plan to build fine, affordable housing from scrap is more generally meant to overthrow a modernist aesthetic that stifles creativity and spawns endless waste. In Buenos Aires, cartoneros form cooperatives aimed at increased remuneration and autonomy, and stage a Somos Todos Cartoneros festival; a trash pickers' cooperative in Ciudad Juarez, Mexico, fights for better schools and medical care.[13] Down the road from me in Dallas, Texas—home to a greasy conglomeration of televangelist ministries —activist Ole Anthony even digs through televangelical Dumpsters to get the goods on the rather too cozy relationship between prayer and profit.[14]

The growing "freegan" movement likewise mixes urban scrounging with an oppositional politics of cultural transformation. Emerging out of an underground culture of do-it-yourself anarchist, anticapitalist, and animal rights activism that today animates many outside the American political mainstream, freegans take the do-no-harm ethics of a vegan diet into the realm of consumption and waste. As they point out, "Freegan is a play on the word vegan. Freegans go farther than vegans by choosing to monetarily consume nothing so as to give no economic power to the capitalist consumer machine." Rather than shopping, and laboring to earn the money to shop, freegans "live off the massive waste of modern capitalist society," Dumpster diving vegetables, fruit, and other necessities.[15] In this way, they quite consciously withdraw from a global economy founded on the twin demands of alienated work and ongoing consumption, and try to invent an everyday politics of survival that can undermine these foundations one Dumpster at a time. In this way, they echo the author of *Evasion*, whose adventures in scrounging have surfaced more than once in previous chapters.

Determined like the freegans to avoid work in the corporate economy, the author and his friends decided on a plan by which all necessities would be "stolen, scammed, or Dumpstered"— and perhaps more to the point, a fluid approach by which "whatever we chose as our next move, *a large corporation would pay for it!*"[16] As they hitched rides and hopped freights across the United States, squatting empty houses and loitering in public squares, they did indeed construct Hebdige's "oppositional reading" out of the objects and situations they scrapped together; undertaking the sort of "revolution of everyday life" imagined by the Situationists, they converted the scraps of consumerism into a way of life that was distinctly and aggressively anticonsumerist.[17] In case this intentional unraveling of the everyday economic order wasn't clear enough from their shoplifting and Dumpster diving, they *détourned* an official antishoplifting billboard with spray paint, undermining its intended meaning to the point that its reversed message came to read, "Shoplifters have more fun; get involved in crime. Evasion." And they included in the subsequent book a postscript, written by one Holden Caulfield Commando: "To revolt against work and thus boredom, routine, wage slavery, the exchange economy with your *body* as well as your mind, to recognize and legitimize your

heart's longing to escape by *trying to*, is to declare openly that we are not crazy for wanting more than the scraps of self capitalism leave us."[18]

In this way, the author and his friends managed to create a travelogue of youthful discontent that became also a catalog of existential resistance to consumer culture, a document of decentralized rebellion against life under the material weight of the global economy. Ultimately, after enough days and months living rough out of the Dumpster, the author of *Evasion* arrived at a particularly pointed question. It's a question that Leslie Hemstreet and Dan Phillips are asking also, that bottle haulers and freegans and Food Not Bombs activists are posing as they scrounge out a mix of survival and social change. For that matter, it's a question I asked myself more than once, hanging out with these assorted urban scroungers, digging with them through the disposables of the leisure class. "I wondered who the barbarians were, the contemptible," writes *Evasion*'s author. "Those operating the machine, enslaving the people, bleeding the Earth dry. Producing things only to throw them away, digging a hole only to fill it up again. Or those who saw the absurdity of it all, and chose to humbly wait in the shadows of the machine and pick up the crumbs."[19]

Law, Crime, and the Life of the City

On occasion, the author of *Evasion* picked up the crumbs while passing through small towns, and

Leslie Hemstreet did at one point salvage some roadkill outside of Chadron, Nebraska—but in my experience and that of others, the empire of scrounge operates most commonly, and most effectively, as an urban phenomenon. As such, the everyday practice of urban scrounging intertwines with the city's other everyday features: its human ecology, its economic rhythms, its dynamics of legal and political control. In fact, scrounging seems clearly to constitute an essential component of contemporary city life—and so if it is to be investigated as an alternative mode of economic survival, or for that matter evaluated as a candidate for legal regulation and control, it must be conceptualized in this urban context.

Over the years, criminologists have sometimes taken note of the city's social and cultural ecologies: its close proximities of people and populations, its concentrations of habitation, its zones of revitalization and decay, its shifting patterns of human movement and symbolic interaction. Criminologists have also posited connections between urban ecologies and particular forms of crime and criminality. Perhaps patterns of criminality reflect the tension between social organization and disorganization as the populations of urban areas ebb and flow. Perhaps urban gangs emerge in part out of the cultural proximities and externalized standards of success that the city offers, if not enforces. Perhaps the city surrounds its residents with such sharp contrasts in lifestyle and status that relative deprivations are experienced as unbearable inequities, to be confronted through violence or other interpersonal violations.[20]

But the city's dense human ecology suggests something else as well. It's not just people and populations that exist in intimate proximity, their cultures and experiences crowded close together—it's their possessions that are crowded together, too, in many cases uncomfortably so. Just as the city's residents exist and move about in close quarters, so does the city's everyday material culture, piling up on itself here, circulating there in networks tightly woven one against the other. Housing, employing, unemploying millions of inhabitants, a large city also houses astounding amounts of personal property, generating countless items of consumption and everyday survival. Accumulating in flats, garages, closets, shopping carts, automobiles, storage facilities, trash bins, vacant lots, and alleyways, this overwhelming material culture gives the city a collective weight, a distinctive urban density and identity, as significant as the shared experiences of its inhabitants.

In the short run, anyway, this urban accumulation can only continue, it seems, and accelerate. As hyperconsumptive economies increasingly define both developed and developing societies throughout the world, their cities fill to overflowing with more people and more possessions—and the Worldwatch Institute concludes that such "economies are defective in their design. . . . Consumption oriented societies are not sustainable, for environmental or social reasons."[21] Along with noting the profound environmental harms proffered by this world culture of spiraling consumption, criminologists and scholars of the city have begun to notice some of these unsustainable "social reasons." In fact, as trajectories of increasing urban consumption collide with growing intensities of urban inequality, all manner of deformities are now emerging in the practice of everyday city life.

Elsewhere, for example, I've documented the ways in which legal and economic authorities today work not to protect the city's public spaces, but to police and privatize them—that is, to sanitize city spaces of homeless folks and other urban outsiders who might impinge on the development of new "symbolic economies" organized around seductive venues for high-end consumption.[22] Sitting atop heaps of consumer goods so acquired, the privileged urban classes in turn increasingly invest in surveillance systems, sophisticated locking devices, prickly bordering bushes, guard dogs—invest in anything they imagine might protect their growing accumulation of material wealth—and so find themselves consumers once again, this time shopping the ever-expanding urban market in avarice and fear. Tired of this tension, some of the city's more affluent residents retreat to suburban enclaves and gated communities, abandoning city life altogether. Those left behind worry over rates of automobile theft, identity theft, consumer fraud, burglary, vandalism, and shoplifting, cognizant of all the ways in which their mounting material accumulations might be protected or lost.

And yet this particular criminology of urban accumulation hardly exhausts the meaning of the city's growing material density, or its consequences for law, crime, and social control. For as much as many city residents face issues of protecting their private property, they face another problem, too: finding a place in their lives for all this material accumulation, and finding ways to dispose of that for which there is no place. A city of consumers must always follow its collective desires of conspicuous consumption to the next new commodity—and then dispose, collectively, of the old. Doing so, though, will necessitate negotiating certain cultural and economic barriers, introducing certain sectors of the city uncomfortably and ambiguously one to the other, and crossing personal and social margins that some might rather maintain, or imagine not to exist. Especially in the context of the city's ecological and material density, material disposal will offer all the contradictions and inequalities of material acquisition and protection; the flow of material goods out from people's lives will define and complicate city life as much as the flow in. And so the disposal of urban material culture—or more to the point, the ongoing exchange between privately held property and the broader domain of the city and its inhabitants—will by turns reproduce and address urban injustice and become a matter for both morality and law.

Waste collection, New York City, October 2004.

It is of course precisely these material margins, these moments of exchange between consumer goods and city life, these complications of law and morality, that make up the empire of scrounge. Scrounging's spatial ecology is also marginal, emerging as it does in the city's back alleys, in and behind its trash bins, at the margins between street and residence. Needless to say, scrounging's economic viability is no more certain. And because of this material, spatial, and economic marginality, the work of the urban scrounging must always remain *interpretive*. One interpretive dynamic occurs as scroungers sort through trash, utilizing hard-won knowledge to decide which items of discarded food might offer more nutrition than contamination, and employing elaborate understandings of personal need and market value to determine which material items merit saving, hauling, reusing, or selling. Likewise, urban scrap metal scavengers must learn fine differences between grades of aluminum, copper, brass, lead, tin, and iron; must be able to spot these differences as combined within a single material object or buried in a trash bin; and must know something of current prices for scrap metal in deciding each day what to haul away and what to leave.

A more important interpretive dimension, especially in regard to issues of law and crime, emerges around the ambiguous urban boundaries that separate individual ownership from public resource, and possession from dispossession. In the same way that trash pickers and urban scroungers must analyze the relative value of that which they find, they must analyze the spaces and situations in which they find themselves—and there is little straightforward about it. Full Dumpsters are widely considered semipublic offerings of discarded materials and are regularly utilized as such—but they are also regularly decorated with signage warning interlopers away and protected by city ordinances. Even within a single city, of course, all trash bins are not equal—scavengers' informal access to them, and the likelihood that this informal access will be policed by shop owners or security guards, depend on sight lines, temporal rhythms, traffic density, proximity to buildings, and surrounding neighborhood dynamics. Open accumulations of used goods near a street or in an alley in turn carry their own variety of messages: ongoing

remodeling project, temporary storage, house cleaning, eviction, overstock, invitation to take or invitation to trouble. And it is not just urban scroungers who must negotiate these spatial and cultural subtleties—homeowners, shop owners, and passersby must as well if they are to decide upon spotting a scrounger to intervene, or encourage, or ignore. The margins that define the exchange between private property and the urban environment, that define the world of the urban scrounger, are themselves not defined; they are malleable, ambiguous, and continually under construction.

An urban trash pile is in this sense less a collection of discarded items than a collection of symbolic codes, an amalgam of invitations, warnings, and seductions to be read, misread, and reinvented. The pile itself is a process. Left long enough, some trash piles grow as neighbors or passersby interpret the existing pile as an invitation to add their own discards; other piles slowly dwindle as scavengers haul away material by foot, bicycle, or truck. Occasionally, property owners attempt to resolve uncertainty, or at least to speed the process of diminishment, by neatly lining up shoes or small appliances on the curb, or by writing invitations and encouragements—"Please Take" or "Everything Here Free" or "Yo Trabajo Bien"—on the sides of discarded items. But even here new ambiguities emerge. Once I came upon a curbside pile of lumber, furnace filters, and floor tile, and beside it a little TV table with a note left for yesterday's scrounger: "The trunk and pictures were accidentally left on curb during move. Please page me 817 977 7942 or call my office 817 373 8444 and receive $100 cash for trunk." Indeed a complex negotiation of trash and treasure—and one still underway.

Marginality, ambiguity, interpretation—all are inherent to the informal disposal and repossession of the contemporary city's material goods. Together, they confirm what history and etymology suggest: that to scrounge is still to *scrunge*, to work the same margins between independent survival and illicit acquisition that have defined scrounging since the term first emerged. Most importantly, I discovered, such marginalities of meaning are not unfortunate residues of this vital urban process; they are dimensions of shadow and uncertainty essential to its viability. Scroungers read trash piles for subtle signs of permission, availability, and value, then mine those they consider worthwhile for treasures that otherwise would languish in the landfill. Homeowners and business owners interpret or misinterpret scroungers' intentions, negotiate with them terms of courtesy and community, sometimes reimagine in the scrounger's presence even the value of their own trash as they decide to forfeit or reestablish control over it. Particularities of legality and illegality are missed or ignored on all sides; specificities of trespass, private property, residential accumulation, rightful ownership, public order, city regulation, and proper disposal evaporate as those involved negotiate the informal, situated dynamics of urban disposal and reclamation.

In this way, important urban borders are kept open. The material margins between disposal and reclamation remain porous, allowing for shifts in meaning, for the fluid if flawed transformation of overburdening private property into public resource, for the day-to-day leakage of individually accumulated materials out into the broader needs of the city. This trash pile porosity, this steady seepage of private goods into the city's public realms, constitutes a material safety valve of sorts for consumers and city officials. More importantly, it constitutes a significant economic, political, and ecological counterdynamic within late capitalist consumer society. Amid the concentrated inequalities of the consumer city, urban scrounging offers a fluid, day-to-day redistribution of wealth—a redistribution neither mandated nor undermined by political agendas, but negotiated directly in the streets and alleys of the city. Urban scrounging offers a form of direct social and economic action for consumers and trash pickers alike, an informal secondhand commerce outside the control of charitable organizations, multinational corporations, or governmental bureaucracies.

Of course, some might celebrate this dynamic less than condemn it as an urban disgrace. After all, the vast and concentrated economic inequalities of city life not only create these material margins, but push the city's impoverished residents toward them; the same

Secondhand commerce: collecting bottles and cans, New York City, October 2004.

economic order that affords the possibilities of boundless consumption for the privileged relegates others to picking among the discards of this consumption. From this perspective, the profound economic injustices of consumer capitalism coalesce, become materially manifest, in every urban trash heap; piled together there are the residues of profligate consumption, the arrogance of ongoing waste, and the pathos of lives consigned to the dirtiest of urban margins. Worse, in a world socialized into consuming always the next new thing, the stigma of yesterday's old trash rubs off on those who pick among it; they are imagined to be filthy, parasitic, out of cultural bounds. If, historically, scrounging has flourished amid the disruptions of wartime, then perhaps it does so today as well. In the class war of city capitalism, scrounging proliferates— and the urban trash pile exists as an uneasy demilitarized zone, a marginal place where the privileged can offload some of their material excess into the dislocated lives of the poor.

Yet for all this, the alleyways and Dumpsters that make up the empire of scrounge constitute one of the few borders still open between the worlds of privileged consumption and impoverished survival—not a perfect opening by any means, but at least a relatively porous one in material terms. Compared with the constipated theologies of religious charities and the enforced degradations of governmental agencies, Dumpsters and trash piles offer relatively free access to the city's necessary commodities. The widespread involvement of homeless folks, minimum wage workers, undocumented workers, disabled citizens, and independent scrap haulers in urban scrounging, and the sense of dignity and autonomy I found so often among them, suggest something of scrounging's value for individual sustenance. The essential contributions of scroungers to alternative urban economies, and to the everyday ecological reclamation of urban waste, confirm scrounging's value to the city itself. The progressive possibilities for social change and economic transformation that many find in scrounging further affirm this fundamental urban reality: Scrunge City Lives.

Salvaging Scrunge City

Unless, of course, it dies.

The careful reader will note that, in chronicling my adventures in the empire of scrounge, I have also recorded in previous chapters innumerable little moments of law and enforcement that, taken together, all but strangle the viability of urban scavenging. Scattered through the book's first five chapters, these various legal constraints perhaps have seemed little more than incidental impediments; considered as a whole, they take shape as something more.

American cities large and small increasingly outlaw Dumpster diving and the scavenging of goods from curbside trash piles; officials in Whitehall, Pennsylvania, even consider licensing scavengers, "just to make sure we know who's out there, so if a patrol car sees a particular vehicle that's licensed, we know who that guy is."[23] Fort Worth and other cities strictly limit yard sales and the signs that promote them, issuing large fines to violators. Code enforcement officials and Code Rangers target not only yard sales and signs, but even small residential accumulations of scrap materials; scrap metal yards also come under increasing legal regulation. In this climate, a wheelchair-bound can scrounger worries about open container laws, and Frank Johnson gets himself hauled before the Building Standards Commission—then to have his scrap hauled away by the city. Groups and individuals mining the empire of scrounge for its progressive possibilities fare no better. The volunteers at Jenna's Hope of Grace fight city code enforcers over the distribution of charitable aid, and Food Not Bombs suffers ongoing legal harassment over its distribution of scrounged food. Both Habitat for Humanity and individual builders like Dan Phillips get tangled in restrictive and elitist building codes as they attempt to use scrap for funding or constructing affordable housing.

Significantly, these are matters of law and legal containment aimed not at murder and mob violence, but at the little practices of everyday life —though they don't always sound that way when discussed by their sponsors. Fort Worth councilwoman Becky Haskin, it will be recalled, urges the city's Code Rangers to "give them hell" and describes the sorts of homes built by Habitat for Humanity as "instant slums." Announcing a new plan to pick up curbside trash piles, others on the Fort Worth City Council reinforce her tendencies toward moral panic. "We've got a huge problem in some sectors of this city," says councilman Jeff Wentworth—and Mayor Pro Tem Ralph McCloud agrees, adding a sense of gnawing urgency: "The trash, the bulky waste, rodents are feasting on [it] as we sit here discussing this." Councilman Jim Lane accelerates the issue from vermin to monsters and warfare. "This is a problem that grows bigger and bigger every day. It's a monster that's growing in the inner city," he says. "This is a war we can't wait to begin."[24]

Meanwhile, just down the road, the Dallas mayor—a maven of old Neiman Marcus money— admits that she will "roll down the window and yell and scream" at homeless panhandlers "to get off the street" when she's out driving, and the city "makes it illegal to possess a shopping cart off the premises of the business that owns it" as part of a clampdown on the city's homeless population.[25] (Fort Worth bottle haulers and other big city scroungers could of course have told the mayor what would happen: To get around the new law, Dallas's homeless scroungers subsequently resort to hauling scrap metal in hand-built wagons and modified baby strollers they've scrounged.)[26] As noted in Chapter One, the mayor of Newark, New Jersey, characterizes the scrounging of recyclable materials meant for municipal collection as "a national problem with enormous significance for local residents."[27] And indeed it would seem so, if judged by a similar problem across the continent

Alternative to the shopping cart, New York City, October 2004.

in Hawthorne, California. There, the city develops police "scavenger patrols" and "sting operations" in concert with the city's recycling contractor in an effort to apprehend late-night scroungers. As city official Jaime Lozano explains, "many residents . . . lived in fear" of the scroungers, since "some of these folks are not 'well' mentally." But beyond "scaring residents, their children, etc.," he argues, "the basic fact is one that we cannot avoid to come back to at the end of the day. . . . It is illegal to scavenge!" And so Lozano suggests a further step beyond the patrols and the sting operations: "Maybe cite them and impound the vehicle used in committing [the] crime."[28]

This odd mix of constipated legal containment and panicky public pronouncement begins to make sense when understood in a context already noted: the emerging "symbolic economy" of upscale urban life, the model of urban economic redevelopment predicated on carefully controlled consumption spaces and desirable urban lifestyles. As part of this impetus, urban political and economic authorities today cooperate to engineer a host of legal constraints designed to keep "undesirables" from fouling the consumption experiences of the city's better classes. Around the United States, legal authorities harry the homeless with statutes and enforcement strategies aimed at "public lodging," "public camping," panhandling, loitering, trespass—even illegal sitting and standing. Civil gang injunctions prohibit the everyday urban activities of those designated as urban street gang members, including "appearing anywhere in public view"—a preemptive strategy mirrored in Great Britain's sweeping Anti-Social Behavior Orders. Likewise, urban graffiti writers and other street artists confront campaigns to erase them and their unsanctioned art from public view, and street musicians find themselves increasingly constrained within designated spaces and sounds.[29]

Within this emerging aesthetic of antiseptic urban consumption, growing legal constraints on urban scrounging and scrap accumulation accomplish two related purposes: the protection of upscale consumption zones and upscale communities from symbolic intrusion by ragtag urban scroungers, and the rationalized control of the waste that these consumers and communities predictably spawn. Reporting on Houston's new ordinance banning "aggressive panhandling, Dumpster diving, and sleeping on downtown sidewalks during daytime hours," for example, the *Houston Chronicle* explains that "the redevelopment of downtown as a retail, entertainment and residential center has nurtured an urban spirit less hospitable to the poorest of the poor."[30] From his spot inside a Dumpster, the author of *Evasion* comes to similar conclusions. "Creating something from nothing," he says, "has side effects generally characterized as 'bad for business.'"[31] As for me, I think about the cartoneros, each night riding the Ghost Train in to Buenos Aires to scrounge its cardboard and cans. Miguel Machado, who with his five kids rides the train and scavenges the city's trash piles, explains that folks call it the Ghost Train because "it is as if the cartoneros don't exist in this world." Adds writer Hector Tobar, "Most people avert their eyes when the Ghost Train rattles past. Probably they wish they hadn't seen it. Or maybe they want to believe it doesn't exist."[32] If officials in the United States get their way, urban scroungers here will be riding the Ghost Train, too—a train so apparitional as to remain unseen.

These campaigns against urban trash piles and urban scroungers present them only as accumulating problems of petty crime and public disorder, to be contained within legal regulation or controlled by law enforcement. In this way, these increasingly common legal strategies reference and reinforce the notion of a dual city— that is, a city where official mapping and regulation work to control the flow of unofficial everyday experience. Specifically, they reveal an effort to confine scrounging—an everyday urban practice of informality, ambiguity, and porosity— within an official urban regime of bureaucratic rationality and legal regulation. Yet as urban scholars like Michel de Certeau and Keith Hayward have shown, these strategies build bad urban policy on a foundation of inadequate urban understanding; they ignore the ambiguous interplay of identities, the informal transgressing of spatial and cultural borders, essential to the life of the contemporary city.[33] This sort of dualistic model of urban control cannot "adequately grasp the social and spatial terrain of the late modern

Street sign, New York City, October 2004.

city nor the dynamics of the actors who traverse it," argues criminologist Jock Young. "It rightly suggests barriers and divisions but wrongly exaggerates their efficacy and solidity; it mistakes rhetoric for reality, it attempts to impose hard lines on a late modern city of blurred demarcations and crossover."[34]

Misguided or not, these campaigns to regulate or criminalize urban scrounging continue, operating as they do to erase scrounging's inherent ambiguity, to sanitize and contain a process whose viability resides in its messy uncertainty. To the extent that these campaigns succeed in resolving urban scrounging's legal and experiential ambiguities, and so exhausting scrounging's open-ended possibilities, they promise a nasty array of consequent social harms: the reinforcement of hyperconsumption as a monolith of late modern meaning and identity, the clogging of the contemporary city with ever-larger accumulations of material goods, and the destruction of an informally autonomous economy essential to many at the urban margins. In fact, in the context of global capitalism's ongoing deterioration of local economies and meaningful work, the outlawing of urban scrounging and the disruption of its economic and ecological dynamics portends a distinctly late modern dystopia, a dystopia defined only by the teeming shopping mall, the towering landfill—and for those at the margins, the poverty of disenfranchisement and dead-end work sans even the dignity of the do-it-yourself scrounge.

This dystopia will be distinctly antiurban as well. Legally closing down a practice like urban scrounging not only ensures that cities will overflow with consumption, consumer waste, and landfills; it erodes the sorts of interactive uncertainty that shape the city's very vitality. Even cities of vast economic and political injustice have often offered in counterpoint a relatively porous culture of collective urban citizenship; their scrounged alleyways, their open arcades, their public places have provided engaging if unsteady realms of evocative encounter and interpersonal give-and-take. In combination with other practices emerging in the late-modern city—the aggressive policing of public space, the promotion of exclusive residential enclaves, the deterioration of neighborhood economies, the dominance of automotive transit—the legal containment of urban scrounging threatens to destroy this essential urban dynamic. Given this, residents of the contemporary city might well hope that urban scroungers are able to escape increasing legal containment and so continue their work along the urban margins, salvaging not just the castoffs of consumer culture but something of the city itself.

Scrounging Zen

Empire of Scrounge has, I hope, documented some of the many ways in which urban scavenging undermines the existing order of things. As consumers set out yesterday's goods on the curb or discard them in the trash bin, and as scroungers explore these marginal accumulations, sorting and saving and reusing what they find there, consumers and scroungers alike cooperate to subvert all manner of neatly dualistic categories: commodity versus trash, public versus private, possession versus dispossession. Part of this subversion is transgressive; the daily, informal exchange of secondhand goods keeps the city's boundaries open, its situations porous and permeable, and in so doing erodes revanchist strategies for partitioning the city by social class and privilege. Other aspects of this subversive dynamic are economic. Operating as a far-flung underground economy, the empire of scrounge connects homeless scroungers, independent scrap haulers, scrap yard denizens, junk artists, and yard sale aficionados—and more remarkably, exists as an underground economy that offers for many of them a lived alternative to the very consumer economy on whose discards it operates. As a practice of boundary transgression and economic independence, urban scrounging also subverts conventional legal categories; despite the stern efforts of legal and political authorities, scrounging continues to float somewhere between property theft and ecological salvation, social problem and celebrated self-reliance. And in each of these cases, it seems to me, the subversive power of urban scrounging builds from its inherent humanity; as an ambiguous and largely autonomous human process, it's ever-shifting meanings and slippery contexts erode the certainty of law, property, and commerce.

But for all that, eight months as a full-time urban scrounger, and ongoing participation in urban scrounging and scavenging since, have suggested to me some deeper subversions as well. As seen in previous chapters, Situationists would see such deep subversions as moments of *détournement*, moments in which the taken-for-granted order of daily life unravels. I would agree, and would also call these subversions *existential*, since they seem to expose and undermine fundamental, everyday notions of existence, meaning, identity, and purpose. Similarly, these subversions might be distinguished from scrounging's economic and legal dynamics to the extent that they shape and reshape moments of *personal* experience—though, as we will see, this is not to say that they aren't soundly political and economic as well. In fact, it may well be that these

existential subversions offer avenues into social issues, and insights into issues of crime and justice, as important as those routes more conventionally taken. Whatever their broader implications, though, these subversive understandings did in fact emerge for me as an accumulation of lived moments. Walking and bicycling mile after mile, scavenging curbside trash piles and diving Dumpsters day after day, I came to realize that I was scrounging more than material artifacts.

It seemed I was scrounging time and space. Or maybe I was scrounging myself.

Time

In the day-to-day process of scrounging by foot or on a bicycle, a distinct sort of pace emerges—one that is distinctly different from the usual pace set by workday automotive commutes, office hours, and suburban mall shopping. The physiology of walking and the physics of a simple secondhand bicycle begin to set this pace; when utilized for scrounging, both move the body and the mind through urban space at a dawdler's velocity. Yet this slow, uncertain movement occurs by intention as well as by physical limitation; spotting a hidden Dumpster and easing over to it, rolling up on a curbside trash pile, walking the street's gutters while looking for coins or cans or auto parts, the scrounger is well served by a pace geared to the slow process of noticing and investigating. Certainly the low cost, do-it-yourself economy of walking or bicycling fits the cash-poor economy of urban scrounging—but in fact so does the attentive pace that these modes of transportation offer. Wandering a mile or so of street in an hour, rather than driving down that street at sixty miles an hour, offers the scrounger advantages of both time and money.

In my experience, another practical advantage accrues: The scrounger arriving by foot or bicycle presents less sense of threat or intrusion than does the scrounger arriving by pickup or car, and so elicits less concern and reaction on the part of home or store owners. On the other hand, in comparison to car travel, foot or bicycle scrounging certainly elicits more numerous informal interactions from other dawdlers, pedestrians, bicyclists, and hangers-out—and when these interactions occur, the pace of scrounging slows further still. Engaged with the particulars of the urban environment, and all but certain to become engaged with the city's varied on-the-street citizenry, the scrounger moving about by foot or bike sets a slow rhythm punctuated by pause and interruption.

As the days of scrounging accumulate into weeks and months, the ongoing process of surviving off a world of found objects replicates this uncertain rhythm. The daily zigzag through streets and alleys slowly builds into a complex personal map of the city, an accretion of little understandings about situations, tendencies, and opportunities. Favorite Dumpsters emerge from repeated

discoveries of useful items inside them; dangerous alleyways, aggressive homeowners, and fouled Dumpsters are remembered on the next ride, and avoided; routes known to yield particular types of scrap metal are replicated, if imperfectly, when needed. And even this slowly developing grid of street knowledge holds within it still other bits of lag time, other requisites of patience and pace. Big rollaway trash receptacles at construction sites contain clues as to the stage of the construction process, and so suggest a time for returning when the electricians and plumbers later arrive, with their discards of copper and brass. Thrown away in the street, beer cans still wet with warm beer and spittle are noted but not picked up, to be revisited instead when sufficiently compacted by car traffic and dried by the sun; the length of this lag time is in turn uncertain, contingent as it is on weather conditions and volume of street traffic. An office Dumpster discovered at 2 P.M. suggests a safer return visit after the 5 P.M. departure of the office workers; in the meantime, curbside trash piles in a nearby neighborhood can be visited while homeowners are away at some identical office building elsewhere.

The Dumpsters and trash bins themselves, and the items they contain, offer further moments that linger and loop back on themselves. Last Christmas's hot-selling, must-have toy is found baking in this year's overheated summer Dumpster; a little lost Cupid figurine shows up in a trash pile on the 9th of April, two months after his holiday. Some juxtapositions of then and now are more immediate. One of the most commonly discovered is the old appliance—often a microwave oven or television—tossed in the trash bin along with the box and packaging from its newly purchased replacement. Other juxtapositions are of greater duration, and tragedy. As I discovered time and again, decades-old baby photos and college annuals, century-old diplomas and first-edition books are simply thrown away, and so left to intermingle in trash bags and trash bins with soiled diapers, greasy pizza boxes, and remodeling debris; in moments of family dissolution, the long cycle of birth and death catches up to the ever-shorter cycles of contemporary consumption and waste. As a scrounger, one's own life and the lives of others are indeed lived in lag time. Momentary or millennial, the delays emerge amid the residues of past wants and aspirations, and always after the fact.

Yet my sense of living my scrounger's life in lag time took shape most sharply—though, as always, slowly—as I developed a practical rhythm for utilizing my accumulations of scrounged items. The empire of scrounge, I found, offered most everything I needed for surviving outside a cash-based consumer economy—but it almost never offered it quickly or predictably. As the weeks and months rolled by, needed items were found, little problems solved, to-do lists crossed off, if only I had the patience to let the solutions emerge. The ability of the empire to provide, in time, the particulars of my daily life I found remarkable. A locking latch for the back window of the house, fencing for the back yard, an 11 mm wrench, some additional bins for scrap storage, a carrying bag for my bicycle's rear deck, another pair of sturdy shoes, a couch for the living room, a lamp to go with it—it was all there, not efficiently, but eventually. Whether attributable to the power of selective perception or the kindness of the universe, a needed item was more than once found as soon as I began to look for it; in other cases I would find, months later, the precise part that I had all but forgotten I needed. In the end, I never wanted—unless what I wanted was immediate resolution.

Supplementing this slow-paced process were the gradual dynamics of recuperation and conversion, as I learned through experimentation and hard-earned wisdom to put found objects and their constituent parts to a range of uses never intended nor imagined. A handcrafting process running in reverse, the ongoing use of a hacksaw, hammer, table vice, and pair of wire cutters to break down found items into usable components led also to emergent understandings of sorting and categorization, and so to a growing collection of bins for holding parts with similar uses. Like the thrift store and the flea market, I found, the Dumpster and the trash bin teach—enforce, actually—patience and an openness to possibility for those who would employ them successfully.[1] Ultimately, it seems they teach a larger, leisurely lesson about life and the dynamics through which we live it: Perhaps learning to wait, and to want what you eventually find, is as important as going out to find what you already want.

Of course, I could afford to learn this lesson, to follow this pace, precisely to the extent that scrounging allowed me to acquire necessary items without benefit of money. Not needing to convert my time into money by way of employment, and only occasionally looking to sell some of my scrounged goods, I was free to reverse the usual clichéd equation: If time is money, then little need for money means little need to rush. Recalling inquiries as to how he and his Dumpster diving, shoplifting friends could continue to survive without access to cash, the author of *Evasion* explains something more of this reversal: "'Money?' they ask, the implication being that without money our system was flawed, incomplete. When in fact our lifestyle had stripped money of its value, reduced it to an inefficient and indirect means of acquiring what we just stole or pulled from the trash."[2] And while we're deconstructing clichés, there's one more that came into focus during my time outside the consumer economy, during all those days of imagining new uses for found objects and the parts they yielded. It's true, I realized, necessity *is* the mother of invention; it's a hard-worked wellspring of personal creativity and innovation. But if so, wouldn't the opposite hold true of existence *within* contemporary consumer culture —that when nothing of yourself is needed, when everything is bought new and delivered complete, convenience becomes the mother of existential complacency?

As suggested by this question, and by these reversals of cultural truisms about time, money, and motivation, I found the temporal rhythms of urban scrounging to challenge understandings at the core of contemporary economy and identity. In fact, I would argue, scrounging's slow-paced dynamics—the dawdling movement through urban space, the lag time in encountering and utilizing the products of consumer culture, the inevitable procrastination in problem solving, the looping nonlinearity of then and now—collide head-on with contemporary cultural structures of efficiency, productivity, and personal satisfaction. After all, the mass consumer culture of late capitalism operates on twin schedules—an overdriven pace of a panicked daily life, and accelerating cycles of consumption and waste— that intertwine in the presumed "right" of the consumer to the immediate and efficient addressing of needs and desires. Drive-through lattés, high-speed Internet access, on-line bill paying, grocery express lanes, speeding tickets, sales that Must End Saturday—all coalesce into a consumer culture of perpetual panic intermingled with momentary, gulping gratification. From this view, scroungers and scavengers slowly making their way through the city and its trash piles aren't just bums because of their predilection for back-alley trash or their inattention to fashion trends; they're *time bums*, unwilling or unable to keep pace with contemporary status and respectability.[3]

Except, of course, that this pace of contemporary status acquisition is all a self-perpetuating fraud. An addiction to immediate gratification guarantees no lasting gratification at all, only an itch for the next quicker fix, an insatiable desire for the faster and the more efficient. Sold like so much crack cocaine, the corporate promise of greater convenience persuades the consumer to perceive today as an unbearable inconvenience, and to pay for tomorrow's imagined resolutions. As the pace of this cycle accelerates and feeds off existing patterns of hyperconsumption, a sort of binge-and-purge panic emerges, a consumptive bulimia; consumers purchase products mostly for the immediate pleasure of doing so, then return them for a refund and repeat the cycle—or, as I regularly discovered while scrounging their Dumpsters, choose a more convenient and efficient solution, tossing them into the trash, unopened and unneeded.[4] In the process of offering a temporal alternative to consumer culture, it turns out, scrounging serves also to excavate consumerism's fast-accumulating temporal ruins.

And it is here, in the realms of individual experience and social relations alike, that we can begin to understand urban scrounging as temporal subversion—to understand that the alternative way of life that urban scrounging offers, the critique of consumer society that it provides, are as much temporal as they are practical and economic. If the plethora of purchased items scrounged from contemporary trash piles reveals something of consumer society's wasting of human and planetary potential, so does the pace with which they have arrived there. Likewise, if scrounging can be differentiated from corporate employment by degrees of autonomy and self-sufficiency, it can also be distinguished by orientations toward time and temporal efficiency. As I discovered, to become an urban scrounger is to feel, over time, the tight-wound panic of late modernity begin to unravel. To dawdle from Dumpster to Dumpster as cars and commuters whiz by, to forgo a fast trip to the store for the slow solutions offered by chance and accumulation, is to undermine in some small way the temporal foundations of the social order. Chris Carlsson characterizes bicycling, or more specifically the choice to bicycle rather than to purchase and operate an automobile, as "an act of desertion from an entire web of exploitative and demeaning activities, behaviors that impoverish the human experience and degrade planetary ecology itself."[5] If so, then slow-paced bicycle scrounging would seem a sort of double desertion, a withdrawal from both time and money.

Significantly, it seems to me, temporal subversions and desertions of this sort are hardly confined to the world of scrounging. During my years in the hip hop graffiti underground I discovered a sense of time as aggressively unconventional as the sense of art; the graffiti artists resolutely and proudly refused to be bound by the straight world's norms of temporal propriety.[6] Residing in an inner-city

Zen time, New York City, October 2004.

neighborhood in Denver, I watched working-class Latino street cruisers and low riders commit the offense of driving too slowly, not too fast. Living for awhile in Arizona, I listened time and again to Anglos honking and complaining while stuck behind slow-moving Navajo and Hopi drivers—and watched those Navajo and Hopi drivers maintain that same slow, steady pace in response.

Beyond this, food activists have organized a "slow foods" movement in response to the corporate peddling of "fast food"—and anthropologists have documented the tyranny of the industrialized world's chronometric "clock time" in contrast to longer and more leisurely temporal rhythms elsewhere in the world.[7] Time, it seems, is both cultural and political—and so a tissue of temporal resistance connects those on the cultural margins of the political order.

But if time is cultural and political, it is also personal, even existential; as we organize time, so it organizes and defines the frameworks within which we live. The accelerated pace of contemporary consumption incorporates not only the consumer's illusory right to immediate gratification, but also a sense of personal status derived from the control of time and the on-demand domination of goods and services.[8] In this sense, while the ideology of consumerism certainly defines identity in terms of successful goods acquisition, it also defines identity in terms of *control*: control of time, of pleasure, of the world and our existence in it. An existential embracing of materialism, contemporary consumerism is equally an existential affirmation of domination and control. In contrast, a practice like urban scrounging, in abandoning the accelerated pace of consumerism, at the same time forfeits temporal control over the world of material goods, instead encountering and utilizing them as they come and go. To scrounge, then, is to in some way desert time, money, control—and one's own identity, to the extent that one's identity has developed as an internalized machinery of the dominant consumer culture. Dare I say, it is to embrace a sort of Zen, a Zen of scrounging, an existential sense of not wanting what one doesn't have, a humility and patience in waiting for possibilities to emerge outside one's own control.[9] It is to develop an existential orientation that gently subverts the temporal foundations of consumer culture. After all, riding the slow, rhythmic currents of their own lives, scroungers find, amid all that consumer trash, an existential calm that others can't.

Space

As already seen, scrounging's leisurely pace allows for a slow accretion of everyday understandings as to the dangers and opportunities offered by the city's trash. While these understandings may over time develop into dislocated insights about people and their disposal habits, in the day-to-day process of scrounging they remain situated firmly in the particulars of urban space. To be an urban scrounger, I found, is not to mine the city as an undifferentiated stockpile of discarded consumer goods, but rather to encounter the city as a series of spaces and situations, each requiring on-the-spot evaluation and negotiation. Successful scrounging of course involves a daily search for discarded items—but it also necessitates a daily search for spatial arrangements, an ability to discover situations and make sense of potential linkages between them. In this way, much of the daily process of scrounging becomes a process of *mapping*, a fluid task of interpreting and coordinating the spatial possibilities offered by the city and its trash.

The scrounger maps the city as a series of subdivisions, telescoping in from broad spatial understandings to small details of street and alley. As a daily scrounger I came to understand particular sorts of neighborhood boundaries—those defined by trash pickup and Dumpster-emptying schedules, for example, and by the limits of bicycle or pedestrian accessibility. In turn, I created a set of roughly defined bicycle routes within and across these neighborhoods, often coordinating these routes with city trash collection schedules, at other times varying them with particular needs or integrating them with other errands to be run by bicycle. But riding these routes day after day was never as simple as following a predetermined time and path—nor was it meant to be. Routes were designed in part to take me by as many intersecting cross-streets as possible, so that in looking down these cross-streets as I rolled along, I could spot and evaluate the maximum number of curbside trash piles, Dumpsters, and trash bins. Depending on what was spotted, of course, the street and the route necessarily changed.

No matter what the street, though, smaller mappings also emerged. I learned to look for little triangular islands of street debris, created by the patterned movement of automobile tires through intersections; such islands often held lead weights, small auto parts, and coins. (Dawdling along in order to catch a red light affords time to examine such islands.) I came to pay special attention to the pavement as I passed large potholes or speed bumps; their concussive possibilities sometimes jar loose a lead wheel weight or dislodge a tool from the back of a service truck. In fact, such a tool found in the street merits continuation down that same street for a while, even if not initially intended; more than once, a first discovery led to others, sequentially, apparently the result of tools bouncing out of an unsecured tool box block after block.[10] On the other hand, tire-store lots offer not sequentiality but concentration, a mother lode for all those lead tire weights, with thousands used each day to balance car wheels as they are fitted with new tires. If, upon cycling up after closing time, the dealer's lot remains dirty from the day's work, lost and discarded weights will be found scattered around the lot and in front of tire-changing bays; if the lost has been cleaned, they're likely to have been swept into a pile near a Dumpster or washed together into a gutter.

In parallel parking spots along streets, or in parking lots' parking spaces, I likewise learned to look for coins (valuable in their own right) and keys (valuable because they're made of brass)—especially on the driver's door side of the parking space, or near park-and-pay kiosks. The larger mapping of lost coins, keys, and other valuables integrated time, space, and direction. Reinventing a trick I learned over the years in searching for glass marbles and glass insulators along railroad tracks, I paid special attention to the pavement while biking east into the morning sun or, more often, west into the afternoon sun. Equipped with a good pair of scrounged sunglasses—a large supply of which I always had on hand—I could use the sun's reflection to show me coins, jewelry, and other bits of shiny value. So effective was this technique, in fact, that I often changed course, at least temporarily, so as to traverse a parking lot or ride a street directly into the sun. And while we're on the pavement, I should mention one further spatial contingency: pausing to pick up a lead weight or a sunlit dime I found to be far more appealing when bicycling a flat street or parking lot than when flying down a big hill or grinding my way up it. On a bicycle, momentum is a terrible thing to waste.

Stopping to investigate a curbside trash pile or an alley Dumpster, a new sort of mapping would begin—a careful calibration of space measured not in feet or yards, but in the potential for unpleasantness and interruption. In fact, as a scrounger I developed a keen sensibility for nearness and juxtaposition—or perhaps more accurately, resurrected the same sort of sensibility that I earlier acquired as an alley-wandering graffiti writer.[11] I learned to avoid curbside trash piles or alley Dumpsters situated too close to parked cars—especially expensive parked cars—lest the owner misread my presence as a precursor to stereo removal or auto theft. Likewise, I learned to check the proximity of a business's back door to its Dumpster, and to look for windows from which someone might disapprovingly discover me in the trash pile. Forgetting this precaution in one case, too eager to investigate a full Dumpster situated between a small business and an apartment building, I was startled by a voice from above, by what at first seemed the voice of some redneck deity: "Leave that alone! I'm fixin' to bring that up here." Thankfully, as it turned out, the guy in the second-floor apartment just wanted the Dumpstered piece of furniture whose knobs and handles I was at that moment removing. As a researcher, I valued the insights offered by human interaction; as a scrounger, living off what I found, I learned how to be left alone when needed.

Moving in this way from the broad boundaries of neighborhood access to the minutiae of potholes and alleyway arrangements, scrounging created for me an idiosyncratic map of urban possibility. In a real sense this map became my method. Some forty years ago, in fact, certain sociologists began to talk about this sort of phenomenon in terms of "ethnomethodology"—that is, the practical, situated method by which people and groups construct the reality of their daily existence. Exploring what Harold Garfinkel called the "constitutive phenomenology of the world of everyday life," ethnomethodologists attempted to document the small, often unnoticed practices through which people make sense of, or "accomplish," their lives.[12] Though this documentary work could at times lead ethnomethodologists to efflorescences of excruciating detail, it did offer one profoundly humanistic insight: All of us—dirt farmers, drug users, school kids, sex workers, janitors, musicians, scroungers—develop and utilize intricate, elaborately nuanced methods for negotiating the contingencies of our everyday lives. And another important thing about this perspective, by the way: Conventional hierarchies of the learned and the ignorant, the accomplished and the incompetent, can't hold. As Hugh Mehan and Houston Wood put it, all sorts of folks develop "elegant knowledge" of their own lives and situations, knowledge saturated with "intricacies and sophistication."[13]

Previous chapters have, I hope, documented something of the sophisticated method that scroungers develop out of practical, experiential engagement with the urban environment. Close and quick determinations of on-the-spot street value, subtle interpersonal negotiations of possession and dispossession, innovative applications and material reinventions make up this method—and so do the intricate reconstructions of time and space by which scroungers learn to salvage from the city all they can. Recalibrating consumer time, remapping the city's spaces, urban scroungers invent a way of life that is extraordinary in its accomplished everyday practicality.

And yet for all its practicality, this method is surely subversive as well. It's not just that scroungers' everyday methods lead them into little confrontations with legality, into moments of trespass or accusations of theft, as they work their way through the city on their own terms. It's that their methods subvert and reinvent the city itself. For just as scrounging's dawdling pace serves to undermine consumer culture's temporal foundations, it's peripatetic remapping of the city begins to unravel forms of official spatial organization.

The practice of subversively remapping urban space is of course hardly the province of scroungers alone; others have also noted, and participated in, its transformative power. The long-standing tradition of the urban *flâneur*, for example—the unfettered individual walking the city's streets—has referenced for many not only a sort of endless urban wandering, but a special, perhaps subversive, sort of spatial knowledge. As Michael Keith puts it, the self-knowledge gained from the *flâneur*'s negotiation of the city's streets becomes also a form of valuable social information, confronting "the will to power implicit in the aerial view of the urban plan," giving lie to "the metanarrative certainties of the plan, the scheme, the totalizing view."[14] Lost to the flow of the city's streets, the *flâneur* is in reality not lost at all, manufacturing instead an emergent, microscopic map of city life—a map that, in its slow-paced human engagement, subverts the gridded certitude and hurried efficiency of city planners, law enforcers, and corporate developers. And in this way the *flâneur*'s map—like the scrounger's map always changing, always open to amendment—reconfigures the city itself, defining the city less by street numbers and property boundaries than by emergent human possibility.

As suggested in the previous chapter, urban theorist Michel de Certeau saw in informal city life the possibility of this same subversive dynamic. For de Certeau, the city of the "city planner or cartographer" was an aggressive abstraction, a totalizing arrangement of street grids, privately protected spaces, and legal regulations designed for efficiency, profit, and control. And yet, de Certeau argued, an irony emerges. The ongoing and inevitable flux of urban life within this bureaucratic city "increasingly permits the re-emergence of the element that the urbanistic project excluded"; by occupying the city, by walking its streets and sidewalks, by moving around and with one another, the city's inhabitants unravel the certainty of the planned city. Those walking the city's crowded streets write a new story of the city, a new urban "text," out of their interactions; they "compose a manifold story that has neither author nor spectator, shaped out of fragments of trajectories and alterations of spaces."

In this way, urban dwellers don't simply occupy the spaces set up for them by city planners and legal authorities; they reconstruct them as they move through them on their own terms. Likewise, urban scroungers don't simply obey or disobey the law, trespass on private property or not; they reinvent the experiential meaning of such legal abstractions, they remap the city itself, as they go about their work. Walkers, scroungers, bicyclists, loiterers—all engage a sort of collective ethnomethod that subverts the mythology of the city as a place of planned and efficient control. Together, as de Certeau says, "their intertwined paths give their shape to spaces." They "weave

places together" in a way that the authorities, with their cost-per-square-foot coefficients and spatial controls, cannot.[15]

The peripatetic remappings undertaken by scroungers, walkers, and *flâneurs* suggest transformations that are at the same time existential and collective in nature, suggest everyday practices that merge peculiarities of individual method with accretions of urban trans-formation. And for still another group of urban inhabitants, this double transformation of self and city was not only a suggestion, but precisely the point—and the point was a "revolution of everyday life." The Situationists—a disreputable collection of left intellectuals, artists, and cultural dissidents already glimpsed in earlier chapters—sought to overthrow the everyday banality of consumer society; in fact, their ideas did become the spark for the 1968 student and worker revolts in France and the insurgent British punk culture of the 1970s, and continue to animate various urban and environmental movements today.[16] Revolutionists of everyday situations, saboteurs of taken-for-granted meanings and emotions, the Situationists were radicals who didn't bother with guns or bombs. Instead, they employed two weapons designed to shoot down assumptions and blow up common sense: *détournement* and the *dérive*. As seen previously, *détournement* denoted a radical reversal of meaning, a subversive theft of understanding, such that the stultifying stability of everyday life might be disrupted. A corporate billboard transformed by graffiti into a call for

Remapping the city, Tampa, Florida, June 2004.

revolt against corporations, a banal cartoon strip illicitly reprinted as a commentary on banality, a work of art made ugly, a religious situation made sacrilege—all might offer, the Situationists hoped, a healthy shock of social and existential uncertainty, perhaps even an unraveling of the social order.

In the particular context of urban scrounging and spatial subversion, though, it's the second Situationist strategy that is perhaps more instructive. The situationists designed the *dérive* as a disorienting, drifting walk through the city, a bit of existential magic by which the vast, accumulated boredom of everyday street signs, office towers, and traffic grids might reappear as excitement and surprise. An abandonment of fixed coordinates, a discarding of the maps made by work and consumption and habit, the *dérive* offered at its best a shock of its own: a startled awakening from the somnambulant shuffle of everyday existence. In this way the *dérive* was meant to transform its participants and the city alike; as with the wanderings of the *flâneur*, it could invent new existential orientation out of personal disorientation, and sketch a new map of the city by annihilating the old.

Formulating in 1953 a Situationist "new urbanism," for example, Ivan Chtcheglov imagined a city that replaced "frigid architecture" with "changeable décors," a city in which "the main activity of the inhabitants will be *continuous drifting*. The changing of the landscapes from one hour to the next will result in total disorientation."[17] Elaborating on the *dérive*'s "psychogeographical effects," emphasizing the *dérive*'s "primarily urban character . . . in the great industrially transformed cities—those centers of possibility and meaning," Guy Debord a few years later offered a clarification uncanny in its similarity to the everyday practices of urban *flâneurs* and urban scroungers. The *dérive*, Debord argued, is not merely a matter of "chance"; instead, it is a "letting-go" mixed with its opposite, the "knowledge and calculation" of the city's otherwise unnoticed terrain.[18] The *dérive* is the cartography of possibility and surprise.

Now a half-century old, this notion of spatial subversion and reinvention continues to surface in a variety of venues. Groups like Critical Mass, a loose confederation of urban bicyclists, "dis-organize" collective bike rides featuring emergent routes and destinations, alter the pace of urban traffic and urban life while slowly riding the city's streets, and in this way work to invent a new city, to "live the way we wish it could be."[19] Tracing their lineage to the Situationists and the tradition of the *flâneur*, contemporary psychogeographers use one city's map to navigate another, set off on "algorithmic" walks defined by "directions but no map," and engage in "reverse shoplifting" by surreptitiously placing objects on store shelves—all the while promising that "when you remake your environment, or find wonderful things in it, it breaks you out of the machine."[20] Writing about her own experiences as a field researcher, anthropologist Stephanie Kane notes that "powerful insight can arise out of walking down a street by mistake. Serendipity can realign data," and goes on to argue that "we may even be able to engineer incidents of mistaken identity" in order to develop new insights into "social control and resistance."[21] Wandering the country, living out of Dumpsters, the author of *Evasion* offers a similar insight. "I always secretly looked forward to nothing going as planned," he says. "That way, I wasn't limited by my imagination. That way anything can, and always did, happen."[22]

Wandering the streets of Fort Worth, this is what I looked forward to as well, and what I found. Engaged in intensely practical activity—mapping the city on my own terms so as to scrounge enough goods to get by—I reinvented the city as a place of subversion and surprise. The conventional map of the city was reversed, read backwards, *détourned*, as I went about my work. I followed provisional routes made up of back alleys more than major thoroughfares. I looked not for the best of situations but waited to find the worst, aiming not for tourist attractions and symbols of civic pride but for demolition sites, accumulations of trash, and the residues of broken relationships. I came to appreciate stores and strip malls not by their bright signage and display windows but by the depth and quality of their back-lot Dumpsters. I judged the desirability of neighborhoods not by housing prices and school standards but by the quantity and value of curbside trash. Adopting a back-alley slouch, timing my travels to arrive not at events but at their aftermath, I found myself rearranging the city as I moved through it.

Out of this *détourning* of the city's meanings, out of this scrounger's *dérive* through its forgotten spaces, there emerged a vast landscape of possibility. Working the spatial margins of consumer society, reading the city in reverse, I found that anything was possible, so long as I didn't expect it. Culture, history, meaning collided in a series of absurd juxtapositions, by turns tragic and funny, and always surprising. Antique door knobs on top of cheap microwave ovens, lag bolts left lying next to discarded lipstick, copper wire piled on a pretty overstuffed sofa—every Dumpster, every trash pile offered an implosion of oddball surprises. Once, scaling a huge rollaway, then climbing down deep inside it,

working my way underneath a ton of remodeling debris in search of copper and brass, I found a little antique green and white bowl, unbroken, unchipped even, resting in a small pocket accidentally formed by the tossed-in cross-layering of lumber and sheetrock panels.[23] Other times it was a shiny camera found at the bottom of a dirty trash bin, foreign currency discovered inside a purse inside a garbage bag underneath a trash pile, 1950s baby doll shoes buried beneath a pile of furniture, still fresh in their little pink and white boxes—and of course the everyday chance encounters with homeowners, homeless folks, and others.

In an urban environment increasingly subject to close surveillance and control, I found myself salvaging surprise and adventure as surely as consumer discards. The tyranny of the ordinary, the tight circuitry of the city's legal and spatial control, fell away as the process of scrounging reversed everyday meanings and transformed ordinary situations into extraordinary events. As with the Situationists, this little revolution of everyday life didn't require bombs or guns—only spatial subversion. Its excitement didn't flow from a fast motorcycle or new sports car, but from the slow pedaling of an old bicycle; its endless surprises didn't come from consuming the latest product innovations, but from sorting through yesterday's consumer discards. Drifting from situation to situation, mapping the spaces between one moment and the next, I found I could escape the banality of the consumer city not by running away from it, but by losing myself in it, and so overturning it.

In fact, this realization paralleled a practical one, and together the two drew me deeper and deeper into scrounging: In the same way that urban scrounging offered all the tools and clothes I needed to remain functionally self-sufficient, it offered all the excitement and surprise I needed to remain existentially alive. By conventional terms of bureaucratic planning or commercial success, each day of scrounging was an accident, an impossibility—and a dirty one at that. And yet, for me, scrounging came to constitute a seductive sort of existential and urban magic, like the *dérive* a trick of meaning and experience that could transform the same old city into the "breathtakingly beautiful wasteland" that Raoul Vaneigem and the Situationists imagined.[24]

Come to think of it, maybe this magic trick—this transmogrification of urban banality into situations of uncertainty and surprise—explains something of crime's broader seductions.[25] Burglars, street racers, skate punks, graffiti writers, gang members—all read the everyday functionality and legality of the city in reverse, remaking the urban grid in their own image and animating it with their own illicit desires. In their worlds, the most common of urban spaces— freeway on-ramps, stairwells, alleys and alley walls, front stoops and back doors—are reimagined as illegal staging areas, entry points, escape routes. As with urban scrounging, these remappings are of course practical matters essential to the success of criminal enterprise or illicit activity. But these remappings are also epistemic, and emotional; their alteration of the city can be measured not just in broken locks and spray-painted walls, but in the illicit illumination of urban life for those involved. Moving through the city, casing houses or grinding handrails, the city's outsiders rewrite its everyday geography into a map of alternative meaning, a shifting grid of danger and excitement. The geographer Edward Soja has called for "a more flexible and balanced critical theory that re-entwines the making of history with the social production of space, with the construction and configuration of human geographies."[26] Our understanding of crime might likewise benefit from a critical theory of transgression that better integrates the making of crime with the experiential production and repro- duction of urban space.[27]

But in any case, this much I do know: In writing an illicit map of the city, scrounging made a new map out of me. In the same way that it confirmed for me the existential pleasures of slowing down, it affirmed the possibilities available in an everyday life on the margins, a life reconstructed by back alleys and abandoned urban spaces. Much of this personal transformation merged with, and emerged from, what I might call *existential ethnography*. With no research grant, no book contract—hell, with no job, academic or otherwise —I was able at least to approach the point of "becoming the phenomenon," of scrounging the city not as a research project or field experiment, but as existence. In this way, scrounging resituated me in time, in space—and in the web of social relations that constitutes urban life. Catching the scornful stares of respectable folks while digging through their trash, hearing other times offers of kindness from them or from other scroungers, finding frustration in a Dumpster locked against those of us who would add to or subtract from it—all were moments of real insight, it seems to me, precisely because they were moments of existential reorientation as well. They taught me about scrounging, and about the world of urban scroungers, by teaching me something about myself and my emotions as a scrounger.[28] Humility and humiliation, gratitude, independence, pride, pleasure—as they became part of who I was, as they animated the scrounging situations in which I found myself, I became better able to understand those who shared those situations with me.

And so, it seems, we arrive again at the urban *dérive*, or maybe at some sort of Zen of scrounging and of life . . . where wandering away is the only place to be.

Coda

Improvisations on the Everyday

Profoundly practical, a place of cast-off clothes and scrap metal and everyday survival, the empire of scrounge nonetheless constitutes an empire of alternative meaning. To live and labor there as I did is to undermine the carefully constructed cultural status of consumption and consumer goods, to muddy certainties of law and crime that others might wish to enforce, to remake even the reality of time, space, and identity. In its daily rhythms, the empire of scrounge demonstrates once again that "the cultural" is not generated only by the operations of the mass media or the machinations of moral entrepreneurs; it pervades even the most commonplace of worlds, animating the bottom of the social order as surely as the top. Beauty and tragedy, memory and emotion suffuse the trash pile, and the lives of those who find sustenance in it, as surely as they do those groups and situations deemed more worthy of popular attention.

Deep inside the empire of scrounge, among those compelled to construct alternative means of survival—to measure, that is, how many of their kids' school clothes they can pull from a Dumpster, or how many scavenged aluminum cans they can fit in their secondhand shopping cart—I found neither meanness nor mundane calculation, but instead graciousness, excitement, innovation, art—and home furnishings. The shared *culture* of urban scrounging—the situated codes of honor, the little moments of mutual aid, the common values of autonomy and reinvention, the commitment of many to progressive social change—overwhelmed any possibility of reducing scrounging to some simple category of crime or criminal calculation. In the dustbin of American consumer culture was waste . . . but flowers, too.[1]

I discovered a further criminological complexity as well: The everyday crimes of urban scrounging arrive from all directions. For every illegal Dumpster diver, a homeowner illegally tossing paint cans into a Dumpster. For every inebriated scrounger rolling her old car up to a trash heap, a trash heap holding old bullets and booze. For every guy walking in a load of cheap malt liquor bottles for three cents apiece, a liquor company targeting his neighborhood with cheap malt liquor sold in disposable bottles, and a nearby roadside awash in the discards of drinking and driving. For each building code that Dan Phillips or Habitat for Humanity break, a building code designed to break them, to enforce a narrow aesthetics of mass production or high-end housing. Any thoroughgoing criminology of urban scrounging, I found, would need to be aimed at all manner of targets.

But wandering along on my old bicycle, occupied in part with simply surviving off what I found, I didn't attempt any such thoroughgoing project. Instead, I tried to wait and watch, to see what the empire might offer me, to improvise my survival and my analysis from whatever emerged. This languid pace, this happenstance approach seemed essential to the empire itself, to its slow rhythms of discovery and reinvention, and so appropriate to my immersion in it. As my colleague Meda Chesney-Lind and I have talked about more than once, it also seems a useful approach to research more generally. Over the years, both of us have found that our best work has come from research that remains open to surprise, from a sort of shambling scholarship only vaguely aware of its own destination. Such scholarship sets up a nicely creative tension between purpose and possibility, casting the researcher as an intellectual scrounger sorting among situations and ideas.[2] At its best, it coalesces into something more than can be anticipated, approximating those moments of im-provisational jazz when shared musical structure explodes into insight and emotion.

Come to think of it, this tension defines cultural criminology as well, and distinguishes it from more conventional criminological approaches. Cultural criminology is less a stern social science than it is an open-ended jazz riff, played between cultural criminologists and those they encounter, played differently in each moment and situation—and, we might hope, played always with some exploratory sense of style.[3] For that matter, maybe these improvisations on the everyday define any sort of life worth living, scrounged or scholarly or otherwise . . . or maybe they define any sort of life worth changing. "The instant of creative spontaneity is the minutest possible manifestation of the reversal of perspective," wrote Raoul Vaneigem in *The Revolution of Everyday Life*, "it is a unitary moment, i.e., one and many. The eruption of lived pleasure is such that in losing myself I find myself; forgetting that I exist, I realize myself. Consciousness of immediate experience lies in this oscillation, in this improvisational jazz."[4]

Notes

NOTES TO CHAPTER 1

1. See, for example, Jeff Ferrell, "Degradation and Rehabilitation in Popular Culture," *Journal of Popular Culture* 24(3) (1990), pages 89–100; Jeff Ferrell, "Dancing Backwards: Second-Hand Popular Culture and the Construction of Style," in Jean Guiot and Joseph Green, editors, *From Orchestras to Apartheid* (North York, Ontario: Captus, 1990), pages 29–43.

2. See Jeff Ferrell, *Tearing Down the Streets: Adventures in Urban Anarchy* (New York: Palgrave/St. Martin's, 2001; Palgrave/Macmillan, 2002), chapter 3, on the politics of cars and bicycles.

3. Gary Fisher quoted in Bill Strickland, editor, *The Quotable Cyclist* (New York: Breakaway Books, 1997), page 35.

4. See Susan Strasser, *Waste and Want: A Social History of Trash* (New York: Henry Holt, 1999), for more on trash and spatial margins. See also Erving Goffman, *The Presentation of Self in Everyday Life* (Garden City, NY: Doubleday, 1959), on the front stages and back stages of social life.

5. Donald Cressey, *Other People's Money* (New York: Free Press, 1953).

6. The Worldwatch Institute, *State of the World 2004* (New York: W. W. Norton, 2004), pages 4–5.

7. *State of the World*, page 16.

8. See, for example, Thorstein Veblen on "conspicuous leisure" and "conspicuous consumption" in *The Theory of the Leisure Class* (New York: New American Library, 1953 [1899]); Janet Thomas, *The Battle in Seattle: The Story Behind and Beyond the WTO Demonstrations* (Golden, CO: Fulcrum, 2000).

9. See Barney G. Glaser and Anselm L. Strauss, *The Discovery of Grounded Theory: Strategies of Qualitative Research* (Chicago: Aldine, 1967).

10. *Online Etymology Dictionary* (www.etymonline.com); William Morris, editor, *The American Heritage Dictionary of the English Language* (Boston: Houghton-Mifflin, 1979), page 1168.

11. *Oxford English Dictionary Online* (OED Online, www.oed.com and www.askoxford.com).

12. *Time* correspondent Frank White describing his encounter with photographer Jean Roy in Port Said, circa 1956, in Russell Miller, *Magnum: Fifty Years on the Front Line of History* (New York: Grove, 1997), page 133.

13. Morris, *American Heritage*, page 1168.

14. Strasser, *Waste and Want*, page 116.

15. Charles Loring Brace, *The Dangerous Classes of New York, and Twenty Years Work among Them* (New York: Wynkoop and Hallenbeck, 1872), pages 147, 152, 153, 154.

16. Strasser, *Waste and Want*, pages 73, 77, 115.

17. Stuart Henry, *The Hidden Economy: The Context and Control of Borderline Crime* (London: Martin Robertson, 1978), pages 4, 12.

18. www.allthingsfrugal.com.

19. Gertrude Chandler Warner, *The Boxcar Children* (Niles, IL: Albert Whitman and Co., 1942), inside back cover and pages 47–48.

20. Franz Lidz, *Ghosty Men* (New York: Bloomsbury, 2003), pages 7, 11.

21. Lars Eighner, *Travels with Lizbeth* (New York: Fawcett Columbine, 1993).

22. "'Junkyard' Junction," *Fort Worth Star-Telegram*, 12 June

2003, page 3E; Robert Caldwallader, "Scrappers," *Fort Worth Star-Telegram*, 14 June 2003, page 18B.

23. Alexis Swerdloff, "Pop Trash: French Photo-Journalists Go Dumpster Diving with the Stars in a New Exhibit," *Papermag* (www.papermag.com), 2004. See also, for example, Joe Rhatigan, *Salvage Style* (New York: Lark Books, 2001).

24. Houston, Texas, City Councilman Mark Ellis, quoted in Rachel Graves, "City May Tell Homeless to Move Along," *Houston Chronicle*, 14 May 2002, pages 1A, 10A.

25. Quoted in "Search and Seizure—Garbage Searches," *Harvard Law Review* 102, no. 143 (November 1988), page 193; see pages 191–201.

26. Quoted in Dave Ferman, "Trophy Club Town Council Votes to Make Scavenging in Trash a Crime," *Fort Worth Star-Telegram* (www.infoweb.newsbank.com), 20 January 2004. See relatedly Steve Jusseaume, "Trash-Takers to Land in Heap of Trouble," *Hampton Union* (www.seacoastonline.com), 30 July 2002.

27. "Newark Targets 'Poachers' of Curbside Recyclable Trash," *U.S. Water News* (www.uswaternews.com), October 1995.

28. C. T. Butler and Keith McHenry, *Food Not Bombs* (Tucson, AZ: See Sharp Press, 2000), page 1, italics in original; see pages 29–34. See also Richard Edmondson, "The Permit Game," *SFLR News* (San Francisco), 31 October 1999.

29. "Know Garage Sale Guidelines," *Fort Worth Star-Telegram*, 24 February 2003, page 2B. Fort Worth city code also prohibits the public posting of "lost pet" and other homemade signs. See Martha Deller, "Sign Fine Spurs Petition Plans in River Oaks," *Fort Worth Star-Telegram*, 11 June 2003, page 7B.

30. Of course, whatever small profits accrue from cashing out scrap metal or selling scrounged goods are themselves subject to a most stringent form of legal regulation: IRS oversight. But like other underground economies, the empire of scrounge generally operates in the shadows, outside the IRS's sight, and so in a state of perpetually questionable legality. See Henry, *The Hidden Economy*.

31. Associated Press, "Police Nab Coin-Fishing Man," *Fort Worth Star-Telegram*, 7 August 2002, page 9A; "Woman Caught Scooping Money from Fountain," *Fort Worth Star-Telegram*, 10 August 2002, page 10A; see *Three Coins in a Fountain* (film, 1954), directed by Jean Negulesco.

32. Ed Johnson, "Pond Diver Trapped in Jail for Salvaging Lost Golf Balls," *Fort Worth Star-Telegram*, 3 May 2002, page 5A; "Golf-ball Scavenger Won't Go to Jail," *Fort Worth Star-Telegram*, 21 May 2002, page 5A.

33. Michael DiGregorio, "Recycling in Hanoi," *Southeast Asia Discussion List* (SEASIA-L@msu.edu), 5 February 1995; "Vietnamese Scrap Metal Collecting," *Mine Action Information Center* (www.maic.jmu.edu), 17 June 2002; Lisa M. Vanada, "GERGERA: Mine Action Activities in Vietnam and Laos," *Journal of Mine Action: Landmines in Asia and the Pacific*, Issue 5.1 (Spring 2001), page 49; "Nine Kyrgyz 'Metal Hunters' Die in Dump Collapse," *Reuters* (www.planetark.org), 12 April 2001; "Scrap Metal Thieves Raid Nuclear Lighthouse," *Thomas Crosbie Media*, Ireland (www.archives.tcm.ie), 24 May 2001.

34. Quoted in Hector Tobar, "Scavengers Are Gauge of Rising Poverty," *Los Angeles Times* (www.latimes.com), 19 November 2002. See also Jon Jeter, "Scrap by Scrap, Argentines Scratch Out a Meager Living, *Washington Post* (www.mre.ogv.br), 6 July 2003; Jonathan Goldberg, "One Man's Trash," *The American Prospect* (www.prospect.org/webfeatures), 21 January 2003.

35. Jack Kerouac, *Lonesome Traveler* (New York: Grove Press, 1960), pages 5–6.

36. Eighner, *Travels with Lizbeth*, pages 117–118, 121.

37. Anonymous, *Evasion* (Atlanta: CrimethInc., 2003), pages 21, 64, 119, emphasis in original.

38. See Glaser and Strauss, *The Discovery of Grounded Theory*.

39. During the long hikes between insulator finds, other accumulations of railroad detritus can be scrounged, including what scavengers call "railroad marbles"—small orbs of green glass often found along the sides of railroad tracks. An old railroad man once told me that raw glass is transported in this way, and so bits of it are occasionally lost along the tracks; in any case, these railroad marbles seem to fascinate those who scrounge them—or those who later discover them for sale at a yard or garage sale.

40. One of the more famous and photographed structures along old Route 66 is a large northern New Mexico shed, its weathered wood festooned with an array of old

hubcaps. As I've grown increasingly disenchanted with car culture over the years, I've continued to scrounge hub caps on occasion, but mostly as fossils of a dying world; see Ferrell, *Tearing Down the Streets*.

41. Strasser, *Waste and Want*, page 116.
42. See Dan Phillips, "Making the American Dream Affordable," *Fine Homebuilding*, no. 136 (January 2001), pages 94–99; Jason Lynch and Gabrielle Cosgriff, "Surreal Estate," *People* (25 March 2002), pages 81–82.
43. Jean Genet, *The Thief's Journal* (New York: Grove, 1964), page 19.
44. Jeff Ferrell, *Crimes of Style: Urban Graffiti and the Politics of Criminality* (New York: Garland, 1993, and Boston: Northeastern University Press, 1996); Jeff Ferrell and Clinton R. Sanders, editors, *Cultural Criminology* (Boston: Northeastern University Press, 1995).
45. Jeff Ferrell and Mark S. Hamm, editors, *Ethnography at the Edge* (Boston: Northeastern University Press, 1998); Jeff Ferrell and Neil Websdale, editors, *Making Trouble: Cultural Constructions of Crime, Deviance, and Control* (New York: Aldine de Gruyter, 1999); Jeff Ferrell, *Tearing Down the Streets: Adventures in Urban Anarchy* (New York: Palgrave/St. Martin's/Macmillan, 2001/2002).
46. See, for example, Stephen Lyng, editor, *Edgework: The Sociology of Risk* (New York: Routledge, 2005); Jack Katz, *Seductions of Crime* (New York: Basic Books, 1988); Ferrell, *Crimes of Style*.
47. Among recent offerings, see, for example, *Theoretical Criminology* 8, no. 3 (2004), Special Issue on Cultural Criminology; Jeff Ferrell, Keith Hayward, Wayne Morrison, and Mike Presdee, editors, *Cultural Criminology Unleashed* (London: Cavendish/Glasshouse, 2004); and any issue of *Crime, Media, Culture: An International Journal* (London: Sage).

NOTES TO CHAPTER 2

1. See Michel de Certeau, *The Practice of Everyday Life* (Berkeley: University of California Press, 1984).
2. Not her actual name.
3. See *The Discreet Charm of the Bourgeoisie* (film, 1972), directed by Luis Buñuel.

4. See REM, *Automatic for the People* (album/CD, 1992), Warner Bros. As the story goes, this phrase originates with a restaurant/restaurant owner in REM's hometown of Athens, Georgia.
5. Susan Strasser, *Waste and Want: A Social History of Trash* (New York: Henry Holt, 1999), page 101.
6. Loudon Wainwright III, "Dead Skunk," *Album III* (album, 1972), Columbia.
7. The white box also contained a new-in-the-package .44P Bore Brush, Pro-Shot, priced at $1.19.
8. Lars Eighner, *Travels with Lizbeth* (New York: St. Martin's Press, 1993), page 121.
9. Anonymous, *Evasion* (Atlanta: CrimethInc., 2003), page 68.
10. Zoe Bake-Paterson, "The Art of Dumpster Diving," *Martlet This Week* 56, no. 17 (8 January 2004) (www.martlet.ca).

NOTES TO CHAPTER 3

1. Unnumbered front pages, emphasis in original.
2. Pages 90–91.
3. An early September 2002 ride produced yet another collection of instructions, pulled from a pile that included a bottle of boot conditioner, a fanny pack, and a Navy-style cloth belt: *The Outdoorsman's Emergency Manual*, *Oklahoma on the Rocks* (rock climbing guide), *The Wilderness Handbook*, and J. Fenimore Cooper's *The Last of the Mohicans*.
4. Supplement to *St. Louis Post-Dispatch*, Section X, January 16, 196-.
5. See relatedly Jeff Ferrell, "Speed Kills," *Critical Criminology* 11 (2003), pages 185–198; Jeff Ferrell, *Tearing Down the Streets* (New York: Palgrave/Macmillan, 2002).
6. Susan Strasser, *Waste and Want: A Social History of Trash* (New York: Henry Holt, 1999), pages 77–78.
7. Barbara Ann Kipfer, editor, *Roget's 21st Century Thesaurus* (New York: Delacorte, 1992), page 739.
8. H. L. Mencken, *Supplement II, The American Language* (New York: Alfred A. Knopf, 1948), pages 722, 782.
9. Katherine L. Lipscomb and Virginia B. Chamberlain, editors, *Fort Worth Social Directory 1981–1983* (Fort Worth, TX: Fort Worth Social Directory Association,

1981), pages 45–46, 196. All names and identifying information in this chapter have been changed.

10. My thanks to Bob Young for the notion of "identity scrounging."

NOTES TO CHAPTER 4

1. Jeff Ferrell, "Degradation and Rehabilitation in Popular Culture," *Journal of Popular Culture* 24, no. 3 (1990), pages 89–100; Jeff Ferrell, "Dancing Backwards: Second-Hand Popular Culture and the Construction of Style," in Jean Guiot and Joseph Green, editors, *From Orchestras to Apartheid* (North York, Ontario: Captus Press, 1990), pages 29–43.

2. Gregory Lee Cuellar, "Unheard Voice" (letter to the editor), *Fort Worth Star-Telegram*, 9 July 2003, page 10B.

3. In Bud Kennedy, "Church 'Shop' Given a Second Chance," *Fort Worth Star-Telegram*, 28 June 2003, pages B1, B13; Bud Kennedy, "Church Women Could Use a Little Grace from the City," *Fort Worth Star-Telegram*, 31 May 2003, pages B1, B5.

4. My thanks to Janice Culpepper at Grace United Methodist Church for this information (telephone interview, 29 October 2004). Culpepper also explained that the mission takes its name from Jenna, a little girl and third-generation church member whose hope it is that the church and its mission can continue.

5. Howard S. Becker, *Outsiders: Studies in the Sociology of Deviance* (New York: Free Press, 1963).

6. See, for example, Judy Attfield, *Wild Things: The Material Culture of Everyday Life* (Oxford, UK: Berg, 2000), pages 121–148.

7. Anonymous, *Evasion* (Atlanta: CrimethInc., 2003), page 20.

8. Susan Strasser, *Waste and Want: A Social History of Trash* (New York: Henry Holt, 1999), page 10.

9. See Naomi Klein, *No Logo* (New York: Picador, 2000) (and www.nologo.org); William Greider, *One World, Ready or Not: The Manic Logic of Global Capitalism* (New York: Simon and Schuster, 1997).

10. Taking this to the realm of the absurd, I at one point even discovered someone else's collection of scrounged materials (though I declined to haul it home). Among the items piled on the curb in front of a duplex with a "For Lease" sign was a large collection of street and highway reflectors—the sort affixed to the road itself to mark turn lanes and the like—all gathered in a big straw basket. They had apparently been scrounged on road trips, state by state; the back of each reflector featured a person's name, a state name, and a date.

11. A number of these furnishings can be seen in the photos included with Jeff Ferrell, "How I Skipped Work and Found a Secret World," *The Times* (London), 18 November 2004, pages 4–5; and Thomas Bartlett, "The Emperor of Scrounge," *Chronicle of Higher Education*, 26 March 2004, pages A10–A12.

12. Charles Loring Brace, *The Dangerous Classes of New York* (New York: Wynkoop and Hallenbeck, 1872), pages 152–153.

13. Fort Worth Municipal Code, Sec. 11A-26, "Storage of Discarded, Used, and Broken Items" (Ord. No. 12931, 3-25-97, emphasis added).

14. Separately, the ordinance in addition prohibits "materials or items stored on rooftops or porches of buildings when visible from the public right-of-way or neighboring property."

15. Anna M. Tinsley, "City Code Watchers Are Hitting the Streets," *Fort Worth Star-Telegram*, 5 May 2004, pages 1B, 9B.

16. As quoted in Tinsley, "City Code Watchers Are Hitting the Streets."

17. Name changed. Building Standards Commission Hearing, 24 March 2003.

18. Following 9/11, some victims' families expressed outrage at how quickly and efficiently the twisted steel of the World Trade Center was hauled away to the scrap yard, to be anonymously resurrected as auto chassis and otherwise.

19. See Andrew Jacobs, "The Accidental Environmentalist," *New York Times*, 25 September 2004, page A24.

NOTES TO CHAPTER 5

1. Peter Kropotkin, "Mutual Aid," in Peter Kropotkin, *The Essential Kropotkin*, ed. Emile Capouya and Keitha Tompkins (New York: Liveright, 1975), page 207.

2. Dumpster diver Leslie Hemstreet notes that she maintains a "permanent 'free/gratis' box in front of my house," which has had the additional benefit of helping her overcome her tendency toward "squirreling away"

scrounged materials. And thus Lars Eighner's insight: "All the Dumpster divers I have known come to the point of trying to acquire everything they touch"; Eighner, *Travels with Lizbeth* (New York: Fawcett Columbine, 1993), page 118.

3. Leslie Hemstreet, "Out of the Dumpster," unpublished manuscript.

4. Anna M. Tinsley, "City Code Watchers Are Hitting the Street," Fort Worth Star-Telegram, 5 May 2004, page 1B.

5. "Fort Worth City Page," *Fort Worth Star-Telegram*, 25 August 2003.

6. Tinsley, "City Code Watchers Are Hitting the Street," page 1B; "No Posting on City Poles," on the "Fort Worth City Page," *Fort Worth Star-Telegram*, 13 September 2004.

7. Martha Deller, "Sign Fine Spurs Petition Plans in River Oaks," *Fort Worth Star-Telegram*, 11 June 2003, page 7B.

8. C. T. Lawrence Butler and Keith McHenry, *Food Not Bombs*, rev. ed. (Tucson, AZ: See Sharp Press, 2000), page 96 and unnumbered pages.

9. Joshua Bernstein, "Trash Clan," at www.infoshop.org, 1 March 2004; Chris Carlsson, editor, *Critical Mass: Bicycling's Defiant Celebration* (Oakland, CA: AK Press, 2002), page 22. See Jeff Ferrell, *Tearing Down the Streets* (New York: Palgrave/Macmillan, 2001/2002), pages 91–147; Garth Batista, editor, *Bicycle Love* (Halcottsville, NY: Breakaway Books, 2004). Bikes Not Bombs members have at times been forced to ride their refurbished bicycles across national borders one at a time, rather than truck them across, due to the fine points of importation tax law.

10. In Aman Batheja, "Web Service Gives Altruists a Home Page," *Fort Worth Star-Telegram*, 7 March 2004, pages 1B, 4B. Thanks also to Meda Chesney-Lind for information on Hawaiian free stores.

11. Hemstreet, "Out of the Dumpster."

12. Neil Seldman and Mark Jackson, "Deconstruction: Deconstruction Shifts from Philosophy to Business," at Institute for Local Self-Reliance (www.ilsr.org), July 2000, page 1; Urban and Economic Development Division, U.S. Environmental Protection Agency, "Building Deconstruction and Material Reuse in Washington, D.C.," at www.smartgrowth.org, 6 March 2003. And . . . RIP, Jackie Derrida.

13. Karen Brophy, Joedy Isert, Michelle Kennedy, and Becky Haskin, as quoted in Mike Lee, "Zoning Puts Dent in Habitat Homes," *Fort Worth Star-Telegram*, 28 March 2004, pages 1B, 6B.

14. In Anna M. Tinsley, "Program Offers Incentives for Glass Bottles," *Fort Worth Star-Telegram*, 2 June 2003, pages 1B, 9B.

15. Supplemental monies kept the program running off and on over the next few months.

16. Jon Jeter, "Scrap by Scrap, Argentines Scratch Out a Meager Living," *Washington Post* (www.mre.gov.br), 6 July 2003; Hector Tobar, "Scavengers Are Gauge of Rising Poverty," *Los Angeles Times* (www.latimes.com), 19 November 2002.

17. Apologies to Oscar Wilde.

18. Apologies to Billy Strayhorn.

19. Hemstreet, "Out of the Dumpster."

20. Leah Ollman, "The Lives of Hannah Hoch," *Art in America*, April 1998, pages 101–105.

21. See, for example, Raoul Vaneigem, *The Revolution of Everyday Life* (London: Rebel Press, 2001 [1967]); Greil Marcus, *Lipstick Traces: A Secret History of the Twentieth Century* (Cambridge, MA: Harvard University Press, 1989).

22. Bill Donahue, "Roadside Relic," *Metropolis* (www.metropolis.com), March 2002; Judith McWillie, "(Inter)Cultural (Inter)Connections," *Public Art Review* 4, no. 1 (1992), pages 14–15.

23. Lucy Lippard, *Mixed Blessings: New Art in a Multicultural America* (New York: Pantheon, 1990), page 66.

24. Greg Bottoms, "The Gospel According to James," *Utne Reader* 110 (2002), pages 77–80; see Lynda Roscoe Hartigan, "From Garage to Gallery: James Hampton's Capital Monument," *Public Art Review* 4, no. 1 (1992), pages 20–21, 26; Charlene Cerny, Suzanne Seriff, and John Bigelow Taylor, editors, *Recycled Re-Seen: Folk Art from the Global Scrap Heap* (New York: Harry Abrams, 1996).

25. David Biddle, "Dumpster Diving for Profit and Passion," *In Business Magazine* (www.jgpress.com), May/June 1999; Bernstein, "Trash Clan."

26. James Sullivan, "Trash Turns into Treasure as New Art Form Evolves," *San Francisco Chronicle*, 22 April 2004, page C17; Amy Nevala, "Welder Recycles Scrap into Bovine Pasture Art," *Seattle Post-Intelligencer* (http://seattlepi.nwsource.com), 15 January 2000; Jim

Powers at www.powersville.net; Robyn Hoffman, "Farm Junk as Art," *American Profile* (www.americanprofile.com), 17–23 March 2002. See also Ferrell, *Tearing Down the Streets*, for other examples of contemporary scrap art; and Michael Wallis and Jack Parsons, *Heaven's Window* (Santa Fe: Graphic Arts Center Publishing, 2001), on Los Alamos scrap turned into art.

27. Davy Rothbart, *Found* (New York: Fireside, 2004).

28. Hemstreet, "Out of the Dumpster."

29. In Barry Shlachter, "Guitar Man," *Fort Worth Star-Telegram*, 28 July 2003, pages 1C, 8C. Sadly, Schaefer has now moved to Minnesota.

30. Amber Nimocks, "Pet Projects," *Fort Worth Star-Telegram*, 26 July 2003, page 3E.

31. Bryon Okada, "Heavy Metal," *Fort Worth Star-Telegram*, 20 May 2003, page 12B.

32. Interview with Ron Drouin, Green Bay Correctional Facility, Fort Worth, Texas, 5 August 2003. Unless otherwise noted, all subsequent quotations from Ron Drouin are taken from this interview. See also Jenice Johnson, "'Junk' Turns to Earth Day Treasures," *The Shorthorn* (University of Texas at Arlington) (www.theshorthorn.com), 17 April 2002.

33. See Steve Earle, "Ellis Unit One," *Sidetracks* (album/CD, 2002), E-Squared.

34. Jason Lynch and Gabrielle Cosgriff, "Surreal Estate," *People*, 25 March 2002, pages 81–82; Dan Phillips, "Making the American Dream Affordable," *Fine Homebuilding* 136 (January 2001), pages 94–99.

35. Interview with Dan Phillips, Huntsville, Texas, 10 April 2002. Unless otherwise noted, all subsequent Dan Phillips quotations are from this interview.

36. Phillips's work has now expanded into a "Trash into Plowshares" program in conjunction with the city of Huntsville; see Patricia Johnson, "Leftovers Good Enough to Live In," *Houston Chronicle Magazine*, 23 May 2004, pages 8–11, 15.

37. Dan Phillips, "Do It Again, Leon," unpublished manuscript.

38. Phillips has, however, managed to win over code inspectors in Hunstville. "I don't always pass my inspections, but whenever I don't they have a ready suggestion. . . . I know I'm going to pass because they've suggested it." For more on this issue, see Phillips's Web site, www.phoenixcommotion.com.

39. See John Dewey, *Art as Experience* (New York: Perigree, 1980 [1934]).

40. Carl Sandburg, "Notes for a Preface," in Carl Sandburg, *The Complete Poems of Carl Sandburg* (New York: Harcourt Brace Jovanovich, 1969/1970), page xxxi; Vollis Simpson quoted on *Egg: The Arts Show* (PBS/WNET), 2001.

41. See Jeff Ferrell, *Crimes of Style: Urban Graffiti and the Politics of Criminality* (Boston: Northeastern University Press, 1996).

42. See Anonymous, *Evasion* (Atlanta: CrimethInc., 2003), pages 50–51, for a different take on scrounging as art; *Evasion*'s author also notes a "dump-umentary" shot with a scrounged 8 mm camera. During my months of scrounging I scavenged a working video camera, and several 35 mm cameras and disposable cameras, but didn't get around to shooting a scroungumentary. For more on the street politics of stencil art, see Ferrell, *Crimes of Style*, and Jeff Ferrell, "The World Politics of Wall Painting," in Jeff Ferrell and Clinton R. Sanders, editors, *Cultural Criminology* (Boston: Northeastern University Press, 1995), pages 277–294.

NOTES TO CHAPTER 6

1. Thorstein Veblen, *The Theory of the Leisure Class* (New York: New American Library, 1953 [1899]).

2. See Andrea Jares, "All Stored Up," *Fort Worth Star-Telegram*, 8 August 2004, pages 1F, 6F.

3. Thorstein Veblen, *The Portable Veblen*, ed. Max Lerner (New York: Viking, 1970 [1948]), pages 112, 116, 117.

4. Snoop Doggy Dogg, *DoggyStyle* (album/CD, reissue 2001), Death Row.

5. See Richard Peterson, *Creating Country Music: Fabricating Authenticity* (Chicago: University of Chicago Press, 1997). And this is not to mention that Indonesian laborers likely harbor no "magical memories" of the foreign cultural icon they are forced to manufacture.

6. William Greider, "Those Dark Satanic Mills," in David Newman and Jodi O'Brien, editors, *Sociology: Exploring the Architecture of Everyday Life* (Thousand Oaks, CA: Pine Forge, 2002), pages 320–331 (quotation page 327). See also David Redmon's documentary film, *Mardi Gras: Made in China* (2004, no distributor). And a footnote to this footnote: Out on a post-Christmas ride two years

later—31 December 2004—I find in a Dumpster big bags full of unopened Christmas gifts, almost all of them made in China, and one of them yet another faux *matryoshka* doll.

7. Lars Eighner, *Travels with Lizbeth* (New York: St. Martin's, 1993), page 119.

8. Jonathan Goldberg, "One Man's Trash," *American Prospect* (www.prospect.org), 30 January 2004.

9. In Anna Tinsley, "'Bottle Bounty' Funds Drying Up," *Fort Worth Star-Telegram*, 26 January 2004, page B10.

10. In Andrew Jacobs, "The Accidental Environmentalist," *New York Times*, 25 September 2004, page A24.

11. Dick Hebdige, *Subculture: The Meaning of Style* (London: Methuen, 1979), page 102. Albert Cohen's classic concept of subcultural status inversion might apply also to a world that I characterize as the *empire* of scrounge; see Albert K. Cohen, *Delinquent Boys* (New York: Free Press, 1955).

12. Leslie Hemstreet, "Out of the Dumpster," unpublished manuscript.

13. See Goldberg, "One Man's Trash."

14. Burkhard Bilger, "God Doesn't Need Ole Anthony," *New Yorker*, 6 December 2004, pages 70–81. My thanks to Mark Hamm for this.

15. At http://freegan.info/. This Web site also lists categories like "Trash Picking Tutorials" and "Pictures of Dumpstered Goodies." See also Jeff Ferrell, *Tearing Down the Streets: Adventures in Urban Anarchy* (New York: Palgrave/Macmillan, 2002), for more on the broader anarchist/antiauthoritarian/animal rights underground.

16. Anonymous, *Evasion* (Atlanta: CrimethInc., 2003), pages 79, 99–100, emphasis in original.

17. See Raoul Veneigem, *The Revolution of Everyday Life* (London: Rebel Press, 2001 [1967]).

18. Anonymous, *Evasion*, unnumbered back pages, emphasis in original.

19. Anonymous, *Evasion*, page 74. See similarly CrimethInc., *Recipes for Disaster* (Olympia, WA: CrimethInc. Workers' Collective, 2004); pages 219–228 explore the practice and politics of Dumpster diving.

20. See, for example, Clifford Shaw and Henry McKay, *Juvenile Delinquency in Urban Areas* (Chicago: University of Chicago Press, 1942); John Lea and Jock Young, "Relative Deprivation," in Eugene McLaughlin, John Muncie, and Gordon Hughes, editors, *Criminological Perspectives: Essential Readings*, 2nd ed. (London: Sage, 2003), pages 142–150.

21. The Worldwatch Institute, *State of the World 2004* (New York: W. W. Norton, 2004), pages 15–16, 19.

22. See Ferrell, *Tearing Down the Streets*. The term "symbolic economy" comes from Sharon Zukin, "Cultural Strategies of Economic Development and the Hegemony of Vision," in Andy Merrifield and Erik Swyngedouw, editors, *The Urbanization of Injustice* (New York: New York University Press, 1997), pages 223–243.

23. Whitehall police Chief J. William Schmidt, as quoted in Erik Siemers, "One Person's Trash, Another's Legal Treasure," *Pittsburgh Tribune-Review* (www.livesite.pittsburghlive.com), 7 September 2003.

24. As quoted in Anna Tinsley, "Garbage Bills Will Increase," *Fort Worth Star-Telegram*, 16 June 2002, pages 1B, 9B; and Anna Tinsley and April Marciszewski, "City Considers Increasing Rate to Fund Trash Cleanup," *Fort Worth Star-Telegram*, 24 June 2002, page 11B. On the concept of moral panic, see Stanley Cohen, *Folks Devils and Moral Panics*, 3rd ed. (London: Routledge, 2002).

25. As quoted in Michael Grabell, "Panhandling Fines Do Little to Deter Long-term Homeless," *Dallas Morning News*, 11 November 2003, pages 1A, 14A, 15A; and Kim Horner, "Losing Their Cart Blanche," *Dallas Morning News* (www.wfaa.com), 14 January 2004.

26. See Michael Grabell, "Homeless Find Ways to Roll with Shopping Cart Ban," *Dallas Morning News* (www.wfaa.com), 8 March 2004.

27. In "Newark Targets 'Poachers' of Curbside Recyclable Trash," *U.S. Water News* (www.uswaternews.com), October 1995.

28. Email, Jaime Lozano to Gary Liss (http://greenyes.grrn.org), 3 July 2003.

29. Ferrell, *Tearing Down the Streets*, page 4, and see *in toto*. See also Randall Amster, *Street People and the Contested Realms of Public Space* (New York: LFB, 2004). On British Anti-Social Behavior Orders, see Decca Aitkenhead, "When Home's a Prison," *The Guardian* (UK), 24 July 2004. Many of these strategies of urban legal constraint involve applications of the "broken windows" pseudotheory of crime causation; for a critique of this approach, see Jeff Ferrell, "The Aesthetics of Cultural Criminology," in Bruce Arrigo

and Chris Williams, editors, *Philosophy, Crime, and Criminology* (Champaign: University of Illinois Press, 2005), forthcoming.

30. Allan Turner, "'Civility' Push, Light Rail Tough on Panhandlers," *Houston Chronicle* (www.Houston Chronicle.com), 16 June 2002.

31. Anonymous, *Evasion*, page 61.

32. Miguel Machado quoted in Jon Jeter, "Scrap by Scrap, Argentines Scratch Out a Meager Living," *Washington Post* (www.mre.gov.br), 6 July 2003; Hector Tobar, "Scavengers Are Gauge of Rising Poverty," *Los Angeles Times* (www.latimes.com), 19 November 2002.

33. Michel de Certeau, *The Practice of Everyday Life* (Berkeley: University of California Press, 1984); Keith Hayward, *City Limits: Crime, Consumerism and the Urban Experience* (London: Glasshouse, 2004); see also Ferrell, *Tearing Down the Streets*, Chapter Six, pages 221–246.

34. Jock Young, "Merton with Energy, Katz with Structure: The Sociology of Vindictiveness and the Criminology of Transgression," *Theoretical Criminology* 7, no. 3 (2003), pages 389–414; quotation page 390.

NOTES TO CHAPTER 7

1. See Jeff Ferrell, "Degradation and Rehabilitation in Popular Culture," *Journal of Popular Culture* 24, no. 3 (1990), pages 89–100.

2. Anonymous, *Evasion* (Atlanta: CrimethInc., 2003), page 80.

3. See *Evasion*, page 78, emphasis in original: "But we were prepared, in true transient form, to *wait* by the Dumpster, for hours or forever, until they threw away a batch. I've always respected and enjoyed the company of the grumpy, old, scruffy homeless guys that hung out by the supermarket Dumpsters just drinking hairspray and spitting on people all day." And as Veneigem writes in *The Revolution of Everyday Life*, "Economic imperatives turn people into walking chronometers, with the mark of what they are around their wrists. This is the temporality of work, progress, productivity, production deadlines, consumption and planning"; Raoul Vaneigem, *The Revolution of Everyday Life* (London: Rebel Press, 2001 [1967]), page 226.

4. For a different metaphorical take on social bulimia see Jock Young, "Cannibalism and Bulimia: Patterns of Social Control in Late Modernity," *Theoretical Criminology* 3, no. 4 (1999), pages 387–407. And thus Vaneigem: "The world of reification is a world without a centre, like the new prefabricated cities that are its décor. The present fades away before the promise of an eternal future that is nothing but a mechanical extension of the past" (Raoul Vaneigem, "Totality for Kids," reprinted in Dark Star, editor, *Beneath the Paving Stones: Situationists and the Beach,* May 1968 (Edinburgh: AK Press Europe, 2001 [1962–1963]), pages 38–61; quotation page 59.

5. Chris Carlsson, "Cycling under the Radar: Assertive Desertion," in Chris Carlsson, editor, *Critical Mass: Bicycling's Defiant Celebration* (Oakland: AK Press, 2002), pages 75–82; quotation page 82.

6. See Jeff Ferrell, *Crimes of Style: Urban Graffiti and the Politics of Criminality* (Boston: Northeastern University Press, 1996). And as itinerant artist and activist Bob Waldmire writes on his hand-drawn postcards and posters, "Small is beautiful, old is beautiful, slow is beautiful, safe is beautiful."

7. See Robert Levine, *A Geography of Time* (New York: Basic Books, 1997); Carl Honore, *In Praise of Slowness* (San Francisco: HarperCollins, 2004); Jeff Ferrell, "Speed Kills," *Critical Criminology* 11, no. 3 (2003), pages 185–198.

8. And in contrast to the consumer class's "need to worry and betray time with urgencies false and otherwise, purely anxious and whiney," we might consider the beat-down temporal wanderings of Kerouac and Cassady, ". . . the point being that we know what *it* is and we know *time* and we know that everything is really *fine.*" See Jack Kerouac, *On the Road* (New York: New American Library, 1955), page 172.

9. As Gary Snyder says, "In the Buddhist view, what obstructs the effortless manifestation of this natural state is ignorance, fed by fear and craving. . . . Modern America has become economically dependent on a fantastic system of stimulation of greed which cannot be fulfilled, sexual desire which cannot be satiated, and hatred which has no outlet except against oneself or the person one is supposed to love" (Gary Snyder, "Buddhist Anarchism," in Max Blechman, editor, *Drunken Boat* (#2) (Brooklyn, NY: Autonomedia/Left Bank Books, 1994), pages 168–170;

quotation page 169. My thanks also to Trey Williams for his comments on scrounging, time, and social theory.

10. Once, while bicycling down a bumpy dirt road in the forest outside Flagstaff, Arizona, I found scattered over the course of three or four miles an almost complete set of wrench sockets, each a few hundred yards farther along.

11. Ferrell, *Crimes of Style.*

12. Harold Garfinkel, *Studies in Ethnomethodology* (Englewood Cliffs, NJ: Prentice Hall, 1967), page 37.

13. Hugh Mehan and Houston Wood, *The Reality of Ethnomethodology* (New York: John Wiley and Sons, 1975), page 117; as they point out, the phrase "elegant knowledge" originates with David Sudnow. And as Garfinkel says in introducing his *Studies in Ethnomethodology,* "The following studies seek to treat practical activities, practical circumstances, and practical sociological reasoning as topics of empirical study, and by paying to the most commonplace activities of everyday life the attention usually accorded extraordinary events, seek to learn about them as phenomena in their own right" (page 1).

14. Michael Keith, "Street Sensibility? Negotiating the Political by Articulating the Spatial," in Andy Merrifield and Erik Swyngedouw, editors, *The Urbanization of Injustice* (New York: New York University Press, 1997), pages 137–160; quotation pages 143, 144.

15. Michel de Certeau, *The Practice of Everyday Life* (Berkeley: University of California Press, 1984), pages 93, 95, 97. As de Certeau says, "In short, *space is a practiced place.* Thus the street geometrically defined by urban planning is transformed into a place by walkers" (page 117, emphasis in original). And as Stephanie Kane notes in relation to ethnographic research: "The linkage of map and text makes culture accessible as culture *area,* holistically rendered. . . . I wonder, though, if we are reifying such boundaries, as a matter of convenience, without establishing whether or not people render them significant in the course of what we catch ourselves describing as their everyday lives"; Stephanie Kane, "The Unconventional Methods of Cultural Criminology," *Theoretical Criminology* 8, no. 3 (2004), pages 303–321; quotation page 307. See Keith Hayward, *City Limits: Crime,*

Consumer Culture, and the Urban Experience (London: Glasshouse, 2004).

16. See, for example, Vaneigem, *The Revolution of Everyday Life*; Guy Debord, *Society of the Spectacle* (Detroit: Black and Red, 1983); Greil Marcus, *Lipstick Traces: A Secret History of the Twentieth Century* (Cambridge, MA: Harvard University Press, 1989); Jeff Ferrell, *Tearing Down the Streets: Adventures in Urban Anarchy* (New York: Palgrave/Macmillan, 2002).

17. Ivan Chtcheglov, "Formulary for a New Urbanism," 1953. Reproduced at www.bopsecrets.org, emphasis in original.

18. Guy Debord, "Theory of the *Dérive*," 1958. Reproduced at www.bopsecrets.org. Interestingly, Debord also references the work of the Chicago School of sociology/criminology on concentric urban zones.

19. Quoted in Ferrell, *Tearing Down the Streets,* page 114; see also Carlsson, *Critical Mass.*

20. Quotations from http://socialfiction.org/psychogeography; and Joseph Hart, "A New Way of Walking," *Utne Reader* (July–August 2004), pages 40–43; quotation page 41. The vegan author of *Evasion* also mentions "reverse shoplifting," though in a somewhat different context: realizing that he had shoplifted a watch with a leather band, he tossed it back into the store (page 97). See also Sadie Plant, *The Most Radical Gesture* (London: Routledge, 1992); http://glowlab.blogs.com; *Year Zero One Forum Issue #12—Summer 2003: Psychogeography— Space, Place, Perception* (www.year01.com/issue12.htm).

21. Kane, "Unconventional Methods," page 317; Stephanie Kane, "Reversing the Ethnographic Gaze: Experiments in Cultural Criminology," in Jeff Ferrell and Mark S. Hamm, editors, *Ethnography at the Edge* (Boston: North-eastern University Press, 1998), pages 132–145; quotation page 143.

22. Anonymous, *Evasion,* page 12.

23. These days that little bowl sits safely in my kitchen cabinet, when I'm not filling it with soy milk and cereal.

24. Vaneigem, *The Revolution of Everyday Life,* page 264: "One evening, just as night fell, my friends and I wandered into the Palais de Justice in Brussels. The building is a monstrosity, crushing the poor quarters beneath it and standing guard over the fashionable Avenue Louis—out of which, some day, we will make a breathtakingly beautiful wasteland." See Anonymous, *Evasion,* page 120, for a similar experience. See also Jeff

Ferrell, "Boredom, Crime, and Criminology," *Theoretical Criminology* 8, no. 3 (2004), pages 287–302.

25. See Jack Katz, *Seductions of Crime* (New York: Basic Books, 1988).

26. Edward Soja, *Postmodern Geographies* (London: Verso, 1989), page 11; see Ferrell, *Tearing Down the Streets*, on transformations in spatial meaning and experience spawned by skateboarding and other illicit urban activities. See also Hayward, *City Limits*.

27. After all, aren't city spaces and their meanings constructed out of the perceptions and desires of those who use them, as much as by the stern efforts of legal and economic authorities? Don't we as urban dwellers invest the city with meaning as we map and remap it, deciding safety and risk, creating efficient routes and little isolated pleasures, denoting favorite buildings or special pathways? If so, then simplistic notions of "broken windows" and the policing of everyday life will reflect not so much the intricacies of the urban environment as some sad mix of intellectual arrogance and experiential vacancy.

28. See Jeff Ferrell, "Criminological Verstehen: Inside the Immediacy of Crime," *Justice Quarterly* 14, no. 1 (1997), pages 3–23.

1. See Jock Young, "Searching for a New Criminology of Everyday Life: A Review of 'The Culture of Control,'" *British Journal of Criminology* 42 (2002), pages 228–261; Mike Presdee, *Cultural Criminology and the Carnival of Crime* (London: Routledge, 2000); Sex Pistols, "God Save the Queen," *Never Mind the Bollocks Here's the Sex Pistols* (album, 1977), Warner Bros.

2. My thanks also to Dan Phillips and Jeff Ross for ideas in this regard.

3. For more on cultural criminology, jazz, and improvisation, see Jeff Ferrell, "Boredom, Crime, and Criminology," *Theoretical Criminology* 8, no. 3 (2004), pages 287–302; and Jeff Ferrell, "The Aesthetics of Cultural Criminology," in Bruce Arrigo and Chris Williams, editors, *Philosophy, Crime, and Criminology* (Champaign: University of Illinois Press, 2005), forthcoming. See also Howard Becker's classic sociology of jazz in Howard S. Becker, *Outsiders: Studies in the Sociology of Deviance* (New York: Free Press, 1963).

4. Raoul Vaneigem, *The Revolution of Everyday Life* (London: Rebel Press, 2001 [1967]), page 195.

Index

About the Author

Jeff Ferrell is Professor in the Department of Sociology, Criminal Justice, and Anthropology at Texas Christian University. He is the author of the books *Crimes of Style* and *Tearing Down the Streets* and the lead coeditor of four books: *Cultural Criminology, Ethnography at the Edge, Making Trouble,* and *Cultural Criminology Unleashed.* He is the founding and current editor of the New York University Press book series Alternative Criminology and one of the founding and current editors of the journal *Crime, Media, Culture: An International Journal.* In 1998 he received the Critical Criminologist of the Year Award from the American Society of Criminology.